WEB DESIGN and ASP.NET

WEB DESIGN and ASP.NET

Shashikant S. Sutar
Sr. Application & Database Programmer
Health Quist (India) Pvt. Ltd.,Pune

PUBLISHING FOR ONE WORLD

NEW AGE INTERNATIONAL (P) LIMITED, PUBLISHERS
(formerly Wiley Eastern Limited)
New Delhi • Bangalore • Chennai • Cochin • Guwahati • Hyderabad
• Jalandhar • Kolkata • Lucknow • Mumbai • Ranchi
Visit us at **www.newagepublishers.com**

Published by New Age International (P) Ltd., Publishers
First Editions: 2008

ISBN 13: 978-81-224-2088-3

ISBN 10: 81-224-2088-5

Rs. 195.00

C-07-09-1985

Printed in India at Sarasgraphics, Rai.
Typeset at Bharti Composers, Delhi.

PUBLISHING FOR ONE WORLD
NEW AGE INTERNATIONAL (P) LIMITED, PUBLISHERS
(formerly Wiley Eastern Limited)
4835/24, Ansari Road, Daryaganj, New Delhi - 110002
Visit us at **www.newagepublishers.com**

Dedicated to

My Parents
and
Late Grandfather

Preface

This book is designed for college students taking the courses in Computer Engineering, Bachelor in Computer Application, and Master in Computer Application etc.

During my 5 years of teaching "Web Design" at both undergraduate and graduate levels, I have realized the need for solved examples and for a guide to help students with these techniques. This book is intended to use in conjunction with a textbook or lecture notes on Web Design. I wish to acknowledge the following:

Vinayak Jangam, my wonderful friend. Without his help, this book would not have been done. Mrs. M.S. Ranade, (*HOD, Computer Dept. LES Polytechnic, Sangli*). She has given great support for the completion of this book. My students, who provided the original inspiration for writing this material. My parents, due to them I became a Software Engineer, Lecturer, and Author.

I would like to thank to the executive of New Age Publishers, who suggested this book and the New Age Publishers editorial staff for their help and suggestions.

Shashikant Sukumar Sutar

Contents

1

Introduction to Web Design

1.1 WEB PAGE

Web page is a HTML document present on the web server. It is accessible on the World Wide Web. It has its own web address or URL.

1.2 WEB SITE

The collection of web pages is called as web site. It can be accessed with a web browser. When visitors tell the server what to get, then the server displays the requested pages or web site. There are two types of web sites: Static and Dynamic web sites.

Static web site contains HTML web pages that do not change frequently or they do not very according to user request. While dynamic web site's contents change frequently. In this user can send data to server and server stores it in the database or gives response to the user.

1.3 WEB PUBLISHING

To publish your web site, put the copy of its document on the server. The server then stores these documents and makes them available to web site visitors that request them.

For publishing you need the following things:

1. The address of HTTP server, so that files from folder in that server will be accessed.
2. The address of FTP server, to access the files stored in that server.
3. Password and userid to upload files to the server.

To transfer your web page to web server, your system should have File Transfer Protocol (FTP) which is standard file transfer software used to send files to the web server. This is called as file uploading. So to upload file on web server, you need to do following things:

1. User ID i.e., account name.
2. Password.
3. The FTP address for your site.
4. The folder name where page is placed.

The web pages that may be called interactive or online pages are created by using system of codes that is written in the most common language i.e., HTML, Hyper Text Markup Language. The World Wide Web Consortium was founded in 1994 at Massachusetts Institute of Technology develops web standard – including HTML standards. This consortium defines the tags and the attributes within the HTML document.

1.4 PROCESS OF WEB PUBLISHING

Planning

Before you start producing an web site, you need to do some planning: What your visitors except at your site? and what you want to provide? For example, they might general information about your company, about your product, prices, order forms, services and contact information. Accordingly you should planned provide information like product specification, costs, employees and their skills and marketing materials etc.

Organization

After planning what information to include in your site, you need to decide how to arrange the individual web pages. You can use following types of organization.

1. Hierarchical Organization

In hierarchical organization, you can present first group of equally important topics, followed by another group of equally important topics and so on. For example, multiple main points in one web page, followed by more sub-points in separate web pages, which are again followed by multiple sub-points in another web pages and so on.

2. Linear Organization

In linear organization, you can link the information presented in separate web pages in a particular order. For example, the microsoft-type wizard is linear organized in action. In linear organization, you can proceed in linear faction from one screen to another screen i.e., visitor can move forward and backward within a sequence of pages but can't jump to other pages.

3. Webbed Organization

In webbed organization, visitor is provided with multiple and unorganized paths between web pages. A visitor can link from one web page to many other pages at the same web site or at another web site.

These organizations are shown in following figures – 1.1, 1.2 & 1.3

Implementation

After planning and deciding how to organize the web pages, implement them by using which software to choose to design web pages, which tags to be used, which images (icons, logos, background images), links and other effects like video, sound, frames, scripts to be included, which database files to be included in the web site.

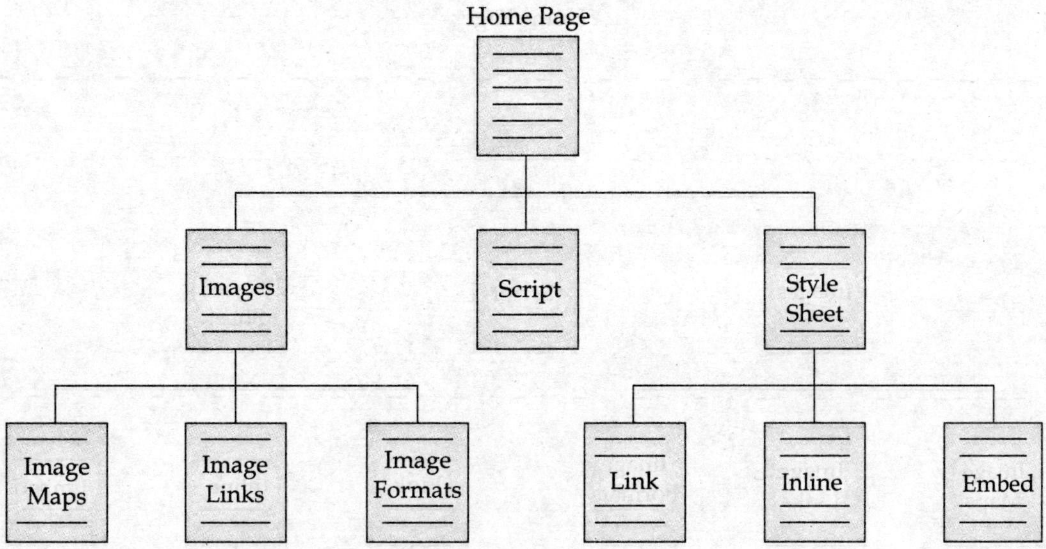

Fig. 1.1 *Hierarchical organisation.*

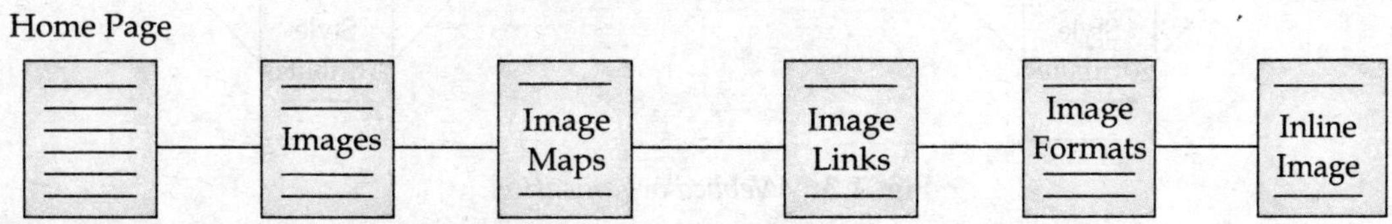

Fig. 1.2 *Linear organisation.*

Testing

Test the web pages by seeing how it will appear to the visitors- Is all contents (Text, Images) visible?, are all provided colors displayed?, are pages contains navigation tools?, are all scripts and style sheets working properly, etc.

Maintenance

Maintaining the web pages is the process of updating and revising the web pages – adding new pages and deleting the existing pages. Regularly maintaining web pages is essential if you want visitors to keep returning to your site.

HTML are plain text files, containing code and content you provide. The code generally contains the *tags* and *attributes* (which are discussed in the next chapter) that work together to identify document parts. The browser interpret the code to determine how display the HTML document.

1.5 HTML EDITORS

1. Notepad Editor.

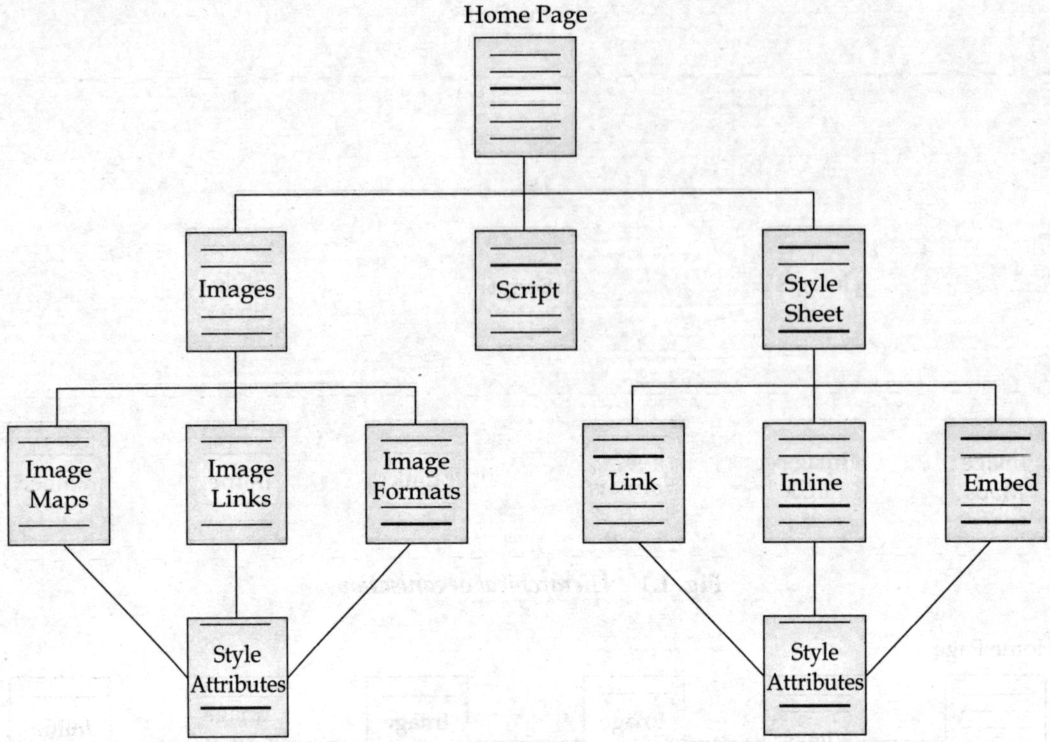

Fig. 1.3 *Webbed organisation.*

2. EditPlus Editor.
3. Microsoft Front Page.
4. Dream Viewer.

1.6 WEB BROWSERS

1. Microsoft Internet Explorer.
2. Netscape Navigator.
3. NCSA Mosaic.
4. Opera Browser.

QUESTIONS

1. What is Web Page and Web Site? Explain.
2. How to publish web site?
3. List processes of publishing. Explain them.

□□□

2

Introduction to HTML

2.1 COMPONENTS OF HTML

(a) Elements

The most important component of HTML is an element. An element is the markup that instructs the web browser or processor how to use particular chunks of the document. An element defines selected parts of a document and marks the boundaries for formatting or future processing. For example, you can use an element to identify and format a heading, body text or a note or a warning. Or you can use an element as a placeholder for document's future content, such as graphics.

In HTML documents, individual elements are part of an ordered system of elements. The top element is known as the root element or the document element; all other elements are children or descendent elements of root. In HTML, the HTML is the top of the hierarchy and the HEAD and the BODY are the child elements of HTML which are discussed in next point like as follows.

```
element1
      element2
      element3
            element4
            element5
```

(b) Tags

In HTML document, an element starts with a start tag (for example, <element>) and ends with an end tag (for example, </element>). The less-than (<) character marks beginning of both start and end tags, and the greater-than (>) character marks end of the both tags. Both the < and > characters are known as delimiters, as they marks the limits of the tags. The only difference between start tag and end tag is the slash (/), which identifies the end tag and is placed between the less-than character and the first character in the element name. Then the content resides between the start tag and end tag. For example:

```
<P> The content resides between the start tag and end tag. </P>
```

<P> is the start tag and </P> is the end tag.

(c) Attributes

Many elements have associated attributes, which specify characteristics (such as size, color, or dimension), limitations (such as whether elements use is required or optional) or initial values or list of possible values. In HTML, all attributes are predefined in the HTML 4.0 DTD.

In HTML, whenever you add the attributes and the values, they are located within the start tag. The start tag for an HTML element with an added attribute and an attribute value looks like this:

```
<P ALIGN= "LEFT">
```

The ALIGN attribute aligns the text within the paragraph left. Two or more attributes in the start tag are separated by space.

(d) Open and Closed Tags

The start tags are called as open tags which is represented as <element> and the end tags are called as the closed tags which is represented as </element>. This means that opening tag and closing tag must come in the matching sets; for every start tag there must be an end tag. In HTML, there are some tags which are used as single opening tags; they have or they require no closing tag.

For example, <H1>...</H1> tags representing opening and closing heading tags; but <HR> tag representing horizontal rule, used as single opening tag. The attributes are always written in the opening tags to specify characteristics (such as size, color, or dimension), limitations (such as whether elements use is required or optional) or initial values or list of possible values.

2.2 STRUCTURED TAGS

(a) The <!DOCTYPE...> Tag

The <!DOCTYPE...> tag tells browsers the HTML version with which the document compiles. The HTML 3.2 and 4 specifications require this non-paired tag and therefore you should use in all documents and enter it at the top of the HTML document, like this:

```
<!DOCTYPE HTML PUBLIC "-//W3C//DTD HTML 3.2 Final//EN"> ....(1)
or
<!DOCTYPE HTML PUBLIC "-//W3C//DTD HTML 4.0 Traditional//EN"> ....(2)
```

The key part of the <!DOCTYPE...> tag is the DTD element (Document Type Definition), which tells browsers that the document compiles with a particular HTML version – the above (1) statement compiles with HTML 3.2, and the (2) statement compiles with HTML 4.0 traditional specification.

(b) The <HTML> Tag

The <HTML> tag identifies that the document as an HTML document. This is paired tag. This tag appears after the <!DOCTYPE...> tag. To use the <HTML> tag, enter it in your document below the <!DOCTYPE...> tag, like this:

```
<!DOCTYPE HTML PUBLIC "-//W3C//DTD HTML 4.0 Traditional//EN">
<HTML>
</HTML>
```

(c) The <HEAD> Tag

The <HEAD> tag contains the information about the document, including the title, scripts used, style definitions, and the document description. This is also paired tag. To use the <HEAD> tag, enter it between the <HTML> tags, like this:

```
<!DOCTYPE HTML PUBLIC "-//W3C//DTD HTML 4.0 Traditional//EN">
<HTML>
  <HEAD>
  </HEAD>
</HTML>
```

(d) The <TITLE> Tag

The <TITLE> tag contains the document title. The title does not appear within the browser window, but it is usually visible in the browser's title bar. The title briefly summarizes the document content. It represents the document. To use the <TITLE> tag, enter it between the opening and closing <HEAD> tags, like this:

```
<!DOCTYPE HTML PUBLIC "-//W3C//DTD HTML 4.0 Traditional//EN">
<HTML>
  <HEAD>
    <TITLE> Title represents the document </TITLE>
  </HEAD>
</HTML>
```

(e) The <BODY> Tag

The <BODY> tag encloses all the tags, attributes, and the information that you want a visitor's browser to display. To use the <BODY> tag, enter it below the closing </HEAD> tag and the above the closing </HTML> tag, like this:

```
<!DOCTYPE HTML PUBLIC "-//W3C//DTD HTML 4.0 Traditional//EN">
<HTML>
  <HEAD>
    <TITLE> Title represents the document </TITLE>
  </HEAD>
  <BODY>
  The information here is displayed due to the tags and attributes used in the
  <BODY> tag.
  </BODY>
</HTML>
```

Figure 2.1 following shows the HTML document including all structured tags. The title appears in the title bar and information appears in the document window.

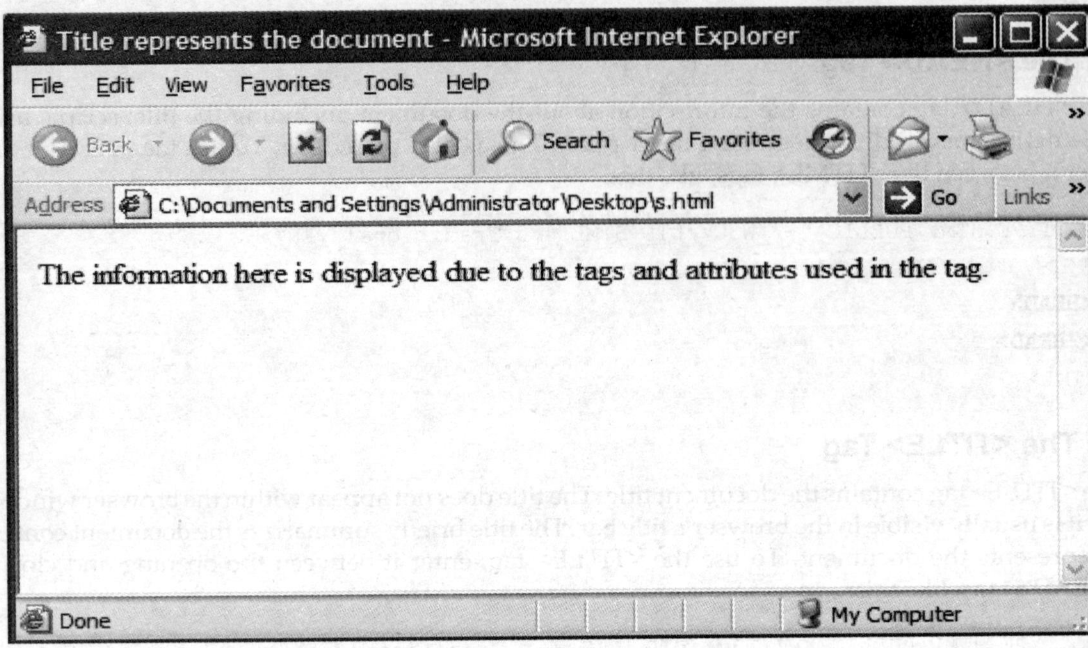

Fig. 2.1 *HTML document including all structured tags.*

2.3 BLOCK LEVEL TAGS

(a) Center

The center element specifies that all enclosed lines of text are centered between the current left and right margins. This element is written as <CENTER> ... </CENTER>.

For example,

```
<CENTER>
Introduction to HTML.<BR>
1. Components of HTML<BR>
2. Structure tags.
 </CENTER>
```

would appear as follows:

Introduction to HTML.

1. Components of HTML
2. Structure tags.

(b) Comment

The comment element is used when the author adds statements that will not appear in the output but are put in the document to make it more understandable for others. It is written as <COMMENT>...</COMMENT>. Any text placed between <COMMENT>...</COMMENT> will not be displayed on the screen, but will be placed in the HTML document.
For example,

```
<COMMENT> This statement is not displayed on the browser. </COMMENT>
```

The comment element is also written as <!– .... – >
For example,

```
< !– This statement is not displayed on the browser. – >
```

(c) Font Size

The font element is used for specifying various font styles, colors as well as sizes. The size attribute of this element is represented as <FONT SIZE= value>. The valid value ranges from 1 to 7 and the default size is 3. The value given to the size can optionally have a plus (+) or minus (–) sign in front of it to specify the relative size of the font to the base font of the document. If the font size is above 7 or below 1, then values 7 and 1 are used.

For example,

```
<FONT SIZE=5>Introduction to HTML</FONT>
```

Would appear as:

Introduction to HTML

(d) Paragraph

The paragraph element is one of the most commonly used elements, which formats the text as a paragraph by leaving extra line space. It is written with either opening <P> or both opening and closing paragraph tags like <P>…</P>.
For example,

```
<P> The paragraph element is one of the most commonly used elements. </P>
<P> The font element is used for specifying various font styles, colors as well as sizes.</P>
```

Would appear as:

The paragraph element is one of the most commonly used elements.

The font element is used for specifying various font styles, colors as well as sizes.

(e) Block Quote

This is also paragraph formatting tag used for formatting a quotation. The formatted text usually appears intended from both side with less space between lines than does a regular paragraph. It is written as opening and closing <BOCKQUOTE>…</BOCKQUOTE> tags.

For example,

```
<BOCKQUOTE>The paragraph element is one of the most commonly used elements.
</BOCKQUOTE>
```

Would appear as:

The paragraph element is one of the most commonly used elements.

(f) PRE

This is another paragraph formatting tag used for formatting a program code or similar information. The formatted text usually appears in fixed width font with ample space between words and lines. It is written as opening and closing <PRE>…</PRE> tags.

For example,

```
<PRE>The paragraph element is one of the most commonly used elements. </PRE>
```

Would appear as:

```
The paragraph element is one of the most commonly used elements.
```

(g) ADDRESS

This is another paragraph formatting tag used for formatting address and contact information. The formatted text usually appears in italic styles. It is written as opening and closing <ADDRESS>…</ADDRESS> tags.

For example,

```
<ADDRESS>The paragraph element is one of the most commonly used elements. </ADDRESS>
```

Would appear as:

The paragraph element is one of the most commonly used elements.

(h) Break

The Break element is used to break the line in a specific place, but it will not start the paragraph by leaving extra line space. It is written as only single opening <BR>. For example,

```
<P> The paragraph element is one of the most commonly used elements,<BR> which
formats the text as a paragraph.
```

Would appear as:

The paragraph element is one of the most commonly used elements,

which formats the text as a paragraph.

For example, following HTML document contains use of the text level tags.

```
<HTML>
  <HEAD>
    <TITLE> The Block Level Tags. </TITLE>
  </HEAD>
  <BODY>
    <CENTER> Introduction to HTML. </CENTER>
    < !– This statement is not displayed on the browser. – >
    <BR>
    <FONT SIZE=5>Introduction to HTML</FONT>
    <P>The center element specifies that all enclosed lines of text are centered
    between the current left and right margins. </P>
    <BOCKQUOTE>The paragraph element is one of the most commonly used elements.
    </BOCKQUOTE>
    <ADDRESS>The paragraph element is one of the most commonly used elements.
    </ADDRESS>
    <PRE>The paragraph element is one of the most commonly used elements. </PRE>
  </BODY>
</HTML>
```

The output is displayed in the browser as shown in following Fig. 2.2 containing the use of above block level tags.

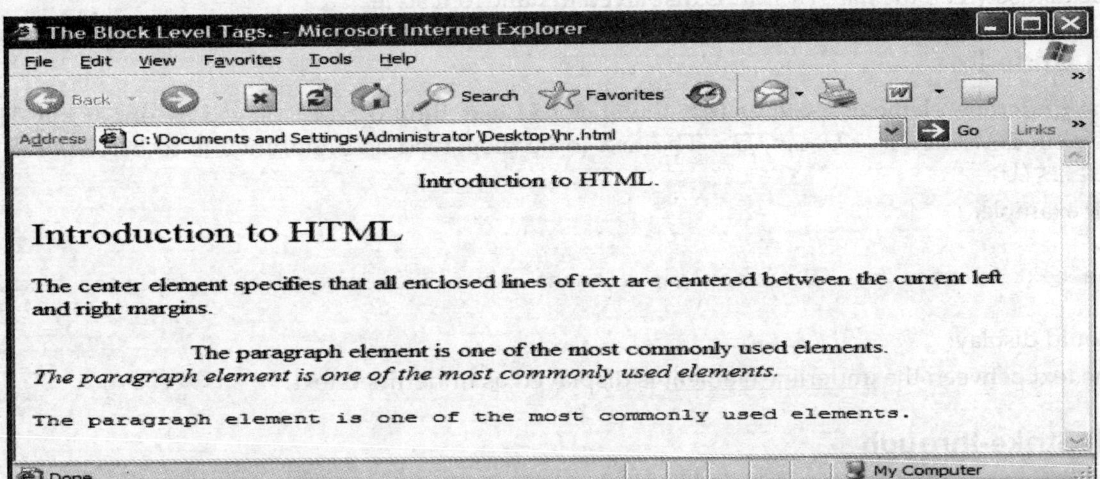

Fig. 2.2 *HTML document including block level tags.*

2.4 TEXT LEVEL TAGS

The text level tags are used for formatting text or characters. Using these tags, we can format overall document and put it efficiently on the user's screen. Some of the text level tags are discussed below:

(a) Bold

The bold element specifies that the enclosed text should be displayed in boldface. This element is written as <B>...</B>. The text to be displayed in boldface is to be enclosed in <B>...</B>.
For example,

```
The text between the <B> bold element </B> is displayed in boldface.
```

Would display:
The text between the **bold element** is displayed in boldface.

(b) Italic

The italic element specifies that the enclosed text should be displayed in italic font style. This element is written as <I>...</I>. The text to be displayed in italic font style is to be enclosed in <I>...</I>.
For example,

```
The text between the <I> italic element </I> is displayed in italic font style.
```

Would display:
The text between the *italic element* is displayed in italic font style.

(c) Underline

The underline element specifies that the enclosed text should be displayed as underline. This element is written as <U>...</U>. The text to be displayed as underlined is to be enclosed in <U>...</U>.
For example,

```
The text between the <U> underline element </U> is displayed as underlined text.
```

Would display:
The text between the <u>underline element</u> is displayed as underlined text.

(d) Strike-through

The strike element specifies that the enclosed text should be displayed with horizontal line striking through the text. This element is written as <STRIKE>...</STRIKE>. The text to be displayed with horizontal line striking through it, is to be enclosed in <STRIKE>...</STRIKE>.

For example,

```
The text between the <STRIKE> strike element </STRIKE> is displayed with horizontal
line striking through it.
```

Would display:

The text between the strike element is displayed with horizontal line striking through it.

(e) Superscript

The superscript element specifies that the enclosed text should be displayed as superscript, using smaller font. This element is written as ^{...}. The text to be displayed as superscript is to be enclosed in ^{...}.

For example,

```
The text between the <SUP> superscript element </SUP> is displayed as superscript.
```

Would display:

The text between the $^{\text{superscript element}}$ is displayed as superscript.

(f) Subscript

The subscript element specifies that the enclosed text should be displayed as subscript, using smaller font. This element is written as _{...}. The text to be displayed as subscript is to be enclosed in _{...}.

For example,

```
The text between the <SUB> subscript element </SUB> is displayed as subscript.
```

Would display:

The text between the $_{\text{subscript element}}$ is displayed as subscript.

(g) Moonscape

The moonscape element specifies that the enclosed text should be displayed as moonscape. This element is written as <MOONSCAPE>...</MOONSCAPE>. The text to be displayed as moonscape is to be enclosed in <MOONSCAPE>...</MOONSCAPE>.

For example,

The text between the <MOONSCAPE> moonscape element </MOONSCAPE> is displayed as moonscape.

For example, following HTML document contains use of the text level tags.

```
<HTML>
  <HEAD>
    <TITLE> The Text Level Tags. </TITLE>
  </HEAD>
```

```
  <BODY>
    <P>The text between the <B> bold element </B> is displayed in boldface.</P>
    <P>The text between the <I> italic element </I> is displayed in italic font
    style.</P>
    <P>The text between the <U> underline element </U> is displayed as underlined
    text.</P>
    <P>The text between the <STRIKE> strike element </STRIKE> is displayed with
    horizontal line striking through it.</P>
    <P>The text between the <SUP> superscript element </SUP> is displayed as
    superscript.</P>
    <P>The text between the <SUB> subscript element </SUB> is displayed as
    subscript.</P>
  </BODY>
</HTML>
```

The output is displayed in the browser as shown in following Fig. 2.3 containing the use of above text level tags.

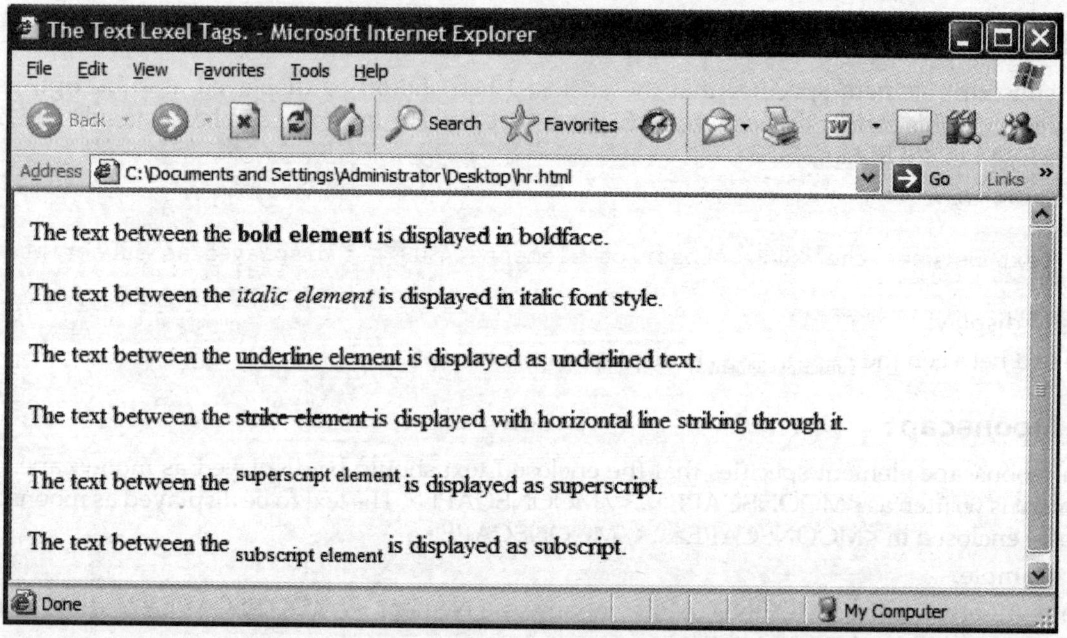

Fig. 2.3 *HTML document including text level tags.*

2.5 HORIZONTAL RULES

Horizontal rules are lines that break up long sections of text i.e., typically used to separate the sections within the document. It improves the overall document design. To use a horizontal rule, include the <HR> tag where you want the rule to appear, like this:

```
<P>Horizontal rules are lines that break up long sections of text i.e., typically used to separate the sections within the document.</P>
<HR>
<P>You can change a rule's shading, width, height, and alignment by including the appropriate attributes.</P>
```

By default, horizontal rules appear shaded, aligns center, spans the width of browser window, and are few pixels high. You can change a rule's shading, width, height, and alignment by including the appropriate attributes.

Table following shows the horizontal rule's tag and attributes used to insert the horizontal rules in the web pages.

Tags/Attributes	*Use*
<HR>	Places the shaded horizontal line in the web page.
SIZE= n	Specifies the rule height; measured in pixels.
WIDTH= n	Specifies the rule width or length; measured in pixels.
WIDTH= "n%"	Specifies the rule width or length; measured in percentage of the document width.
ALIGN = "..."	Specifies the alignment of the rule (LEFT, RIGHT, and CENTER). The default alignment is CENTER.
NOSHADE	Specifies that the rule has no shading.

For example, to use any of these attributes, include them in <HR> tag, like this:

```
<HTML>
  <HEAD>
    <TITLE> Horizontal rules </TITLE>
  </HEAD>
  <BODY>
    <HR>
    <HR WIDTH="50%" SIZE=10>
    <HR WIDTH="50%" SIZE=10 ALIGN="RIGHT">
    <HR NOSHADE>
  </BODY>
</HTML>
```

The output is displayed in the browser as shown in following Fig. 2.4 contains four horizontal rules with shades, centered aligned, right aligned and last with no shade respectively.

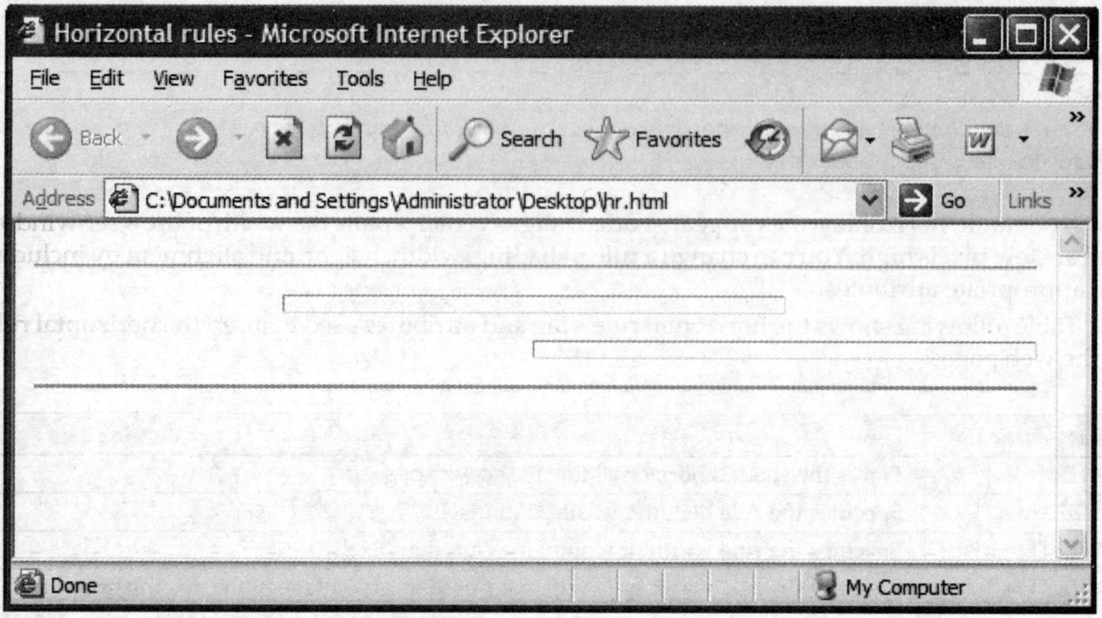

Fig. 2.4 *HTML document including horizontal rules.*

2.6 COLORS IN WEB PAGES

Background Color

Background color fills the color in the entire browser window. By default, browsers display a white or gray background color. To specify the background color for the document, simply include the attribute described in following table to the opening <BODY> tag.

Tags/Attributes	*Use*
<BODY>	Specifies the document's body.
BGCOLOR= "#... "	Sets the background color for the document with a color name or a #RRGGBB value..

For example, to fill the background color green in the document, use the following statement,

```
<BODY BGCOLOR= "#00FF00"> or <BODY BGCOLOR= "GREEN">
```

Any of the predefined colors or a #rrggbb hexadecimal triplet can be specified for the background color.

Text Color

Like background colors, you can give color to the text that appears throughout the body. By default, browsers display text color as black. To specify the text color throughout the body, simply add the attribute described in following table to the opening <BODY> tag.

Tags/Attributes	*Use*
<BODY>	Specifies the document's body.
TEXT= "#... "	Sets the text color within the document with a color name or a #RRGGBB value.

For example, to set text color 'red' in the document, use the following statement,

```
<BODY TEXT= "#FF0000"> or <BODY TEXT= "RED">
```

Any of the predefined colors or a #rrggbb hexadecimal triplet can be specified for the background color.

Link Color

Link colors set the visited and unvisited links to different colors to help visitor to know which likes they have followed and which one they have not. To specify the link colors, simply include the attributes described in following table to the opening <BODY> tag.

Tags/Attributes	*Use*
<BODY>	Specifies the document's body.
ALINK= "#... "	Sets the color for active links, which are the links at the time the visitors clicks on them, with a color name or a #RRGGBB value.
VLINK= "#... "	Sets the color for links, the visitors has recently followed, with a color name or a #RRGGBB value.
LINK= "#... "	Sets the color for unvisited links, with a color name or a #RRGGBB value.

For example, to set unvisited link color 'blue', visited link color 'red' in the document, use the following statement,

```
<BODY LINK="#0000FF"  VLINK="#FF0000">
```

Any of the predefined colors or a #rrggbb hexadecimal triplet can be specified for the background color.

2.7 LISTS

Lists are block level elements. Lists are used to organize text or information in a structured and easy to read format. They help visitor easily spot information and they draw attention to important information.

There are three types of lists: Unordered Lists, Ordered Lists, and Defined Lists.

Unordered Lists

These are also known as Bulleted Lists. Each item in the unordered list is preceded by a bullet. To create unordered list, you first specify the text or the information you want to format as a list and then you identify each line item in the list. Table following shows the unordered list and line item tags along with their attributes.

Tags/Attributes	*Use*
<UL>	Specifies that the information appears as an unordered (bulleted) list.
<LI>	Specifies a line item in either ordered or unordered list.
TYPE= "..."	Specifies the appearance of the bullets in unordered lists. Values are DISC, SQUARE, and CIRCLE. By default, unordered list use round bullets.

For example, to create an unordered list (bulleted list), use the following steps:

1. Start with text you want to format as a list.
   Banana.
   Apple.
   Orange.
2. Insert the <UL> tags around the list texts.
```
<UL>
Banana.
Apple.
Orange.
</UL>
```
3. Type the <LI> tag for each line item.
```
<UL>
<LI>Banana. </LI>
<LI>Apple. </LI>
<LI>Orange. </LI>
</UL>
```

The above steps are implemented in the HTML document as follows:

```
<HTML>
  <HEAD>
  <TITLE> An Unordered List </TITLE>
  </HEAD>
  <BODY>
  <UL>
    <LI>Banana. </LI>
    <LI>Apple. </LI>
    <LI>Orange. </LI>
  </UL>
  </BODY>
</HTML>
```

The output is displayed in the browser as shown in following Fig. 2.5 containing the unordered list.

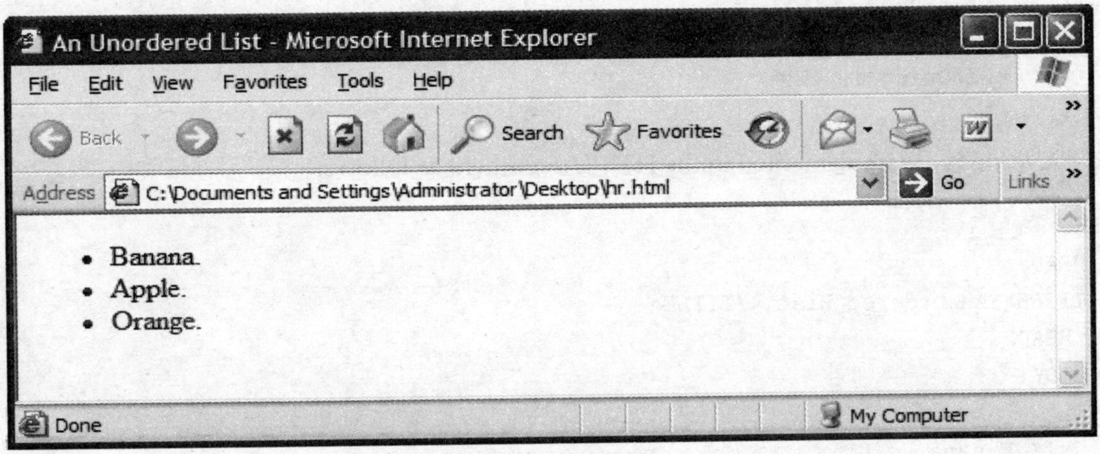

Fig. 2.5 *HTML document including unordered list.*

Ordered Lists

These are also known as Numbered Lists. Each item in the ordered list is preceded by a number or letter. To create ordered list, you first specify the text or the information you want to format as a list and then you identify each line item in the list. Table following shows the ordered list and line item tags along with their attributes.

Tags/Attributes	*Use*
<OL>	Specifies that the information appears as an ordered (numbered) list.
<LI>	Specifies a line item in either ordered or unordered list.
TYPE= "..."	Specifies the appearance of the numbers or letters in ordered lists. Values are A, a, I, i, or 1 (default). By default, ordered list use Arabic numerals like 1, 2, 3...

For example, to create a ordered list (numbered list), use the following steps:

1. Start with text you want to format as a list.
   Banana.
   Apple.
   Orange.
2. Insert the <OL> tags around the list texts.

```
<OL>
  Banana.
  Apple.
  Orange.
</OL>
```

3. Type the <LI> tag for each line item.

```
<OL>
   <LI>Banana. </LI>
   <LI>Apple. </LI>
   <LI>Orange. </LI>
</OL>
```

The above steps are implemented in the HTML document as follows:

```
<HTML>
  <HEAD>
  <TITLE> An Ordered List </TITLE>
  </HEAD>
  <BODY>
  <OL>
     <LI>Banana. </LI>
     <LI>Apple. </LI>
     <LI>Orange. </LI>
  </OL>
  </BODY>
</HTML>
```

The output is displayed in the browser as shown in following Fig. 2.6 containing the ordered list.

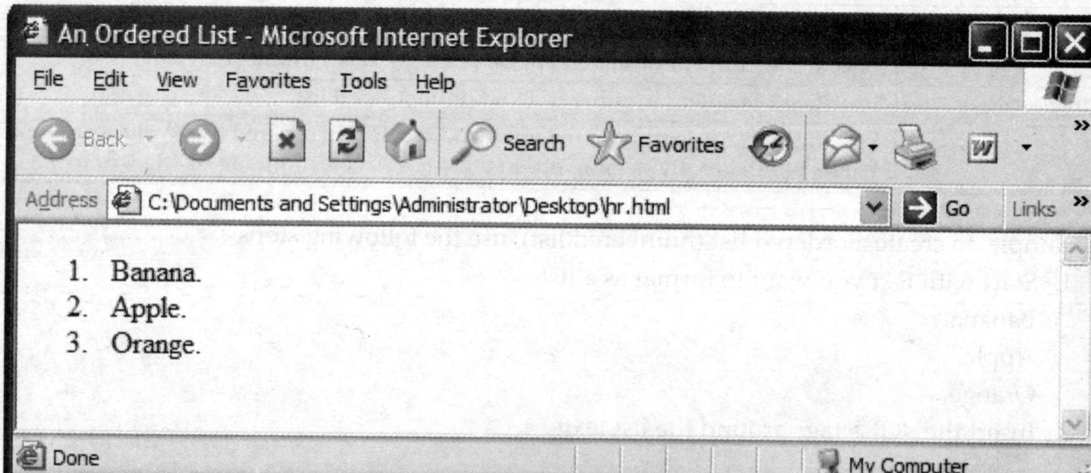

Fig. 2.6 *HTML document including ordered list.*

Definition Lists

Definition lists are as dictionary entries. Using definition lists you can present the information in two levels – definition name and followed by definition. To create ordered list, you first specify the text or the information you want to format as a list and then you identify definition terms i.e., the name of definition and definition in the list. Table following shows the definition list, definition term and definition tags.

Tags/Attributes	*Use*
<DL>	Specifies that the information appears as a definition list.
<DT>	Identifies definition terms.
<DD>	Identifies definitions.

For example, to create a definition lists, use the following steps:

1. Start with text you want to format as a list.

   Unordered Lists:

   These are also known as bulleted lists. Each item in the unordered list is preceded by a bullet.

   Ordered Lists:

   These are also known as numbered lists. Each item in the ordered list is preceded by a number or letter.

   Definition Lists:

   Definition lists are as dictionary entries. Using definition lists you can present the information in two levels – definition name and followed by definition.

2. Insert the <DL> tags around the list texts.

   <DL>

   Unordered Lists:

   These are also known as bulleted lists. Each item in the unordered list is preceded by a bullet.

   Ordered Lists:

   These are also known as numbered lists. Each item in the ordered list is preceded by a number or letter.

   Definition Lists:

   Definition Lists are as dictionary entries. Using definition lists you can present the information in two levels – definition name and followed by definition.

   </DL>

3. Type the <DT> tag for each definition term.

   <DL>

   <DT> Unordered Lists: </DT>

   These are also known as Bulleted Lists. Each item in the unordered list is preceded by a bullet.

<DT> Ordered Lists: </DT>

These are also known as numbered lists. Each item in the ordered list is preceded by a number or letter.

<DT> Definition Lists: </DT>

Definition lists are as dictionary entries. Using definition lists you can present the information in two levels – definition name and followed by definition.

</DL>

4. Type the <DD> tag for each definition.

<DL>

<DT> Unordered Lists: </DT>

<DD> These are also known as bulleted lists. Each item in the unordered list is preceded by a bullet. </DD>

<DT> Ordered Lists: </DT>

<DD> These are also known as numbered lists. Each item in the ordered list is preceded by a number or letter. </DD>

<DT> Definition Lists: </DT>

<DD>Definition Lists are as dictionary entries. Using definition lists you can present the information in two levels – definition name and followed by definition. </DD>

</DL>

The above steps are implemented in the HTML document as follows:

```
<HTML>
  <HEAD>
  <TITLE> The Definition List  </TITLE>
  </HEAD>
  <BODY>
    <DL>
      <DT> Unordered Lists: </DT>
        <DD> These are also known as Bulleted Lists. Each item in the unordered
        list is preceded by a bullet. </DD>
      <DT> Ordered Lists: </DT>
        <DD> These are also known as Numbered Lists. Each item in the ordered list
        is preceded by a number or letter. </DD>
      <DT> Definition Lists:</DT>
        <DD>Definition Lists are as dictionary entries. Using Definition Lists you
        can present the information in two levels-definition name and followed by
        definition.</DD>
    </DL>
  </BODY>
</HTML>
```

The output is displayed in the browser as shown in following Fig. 2.7 containing the definition list.

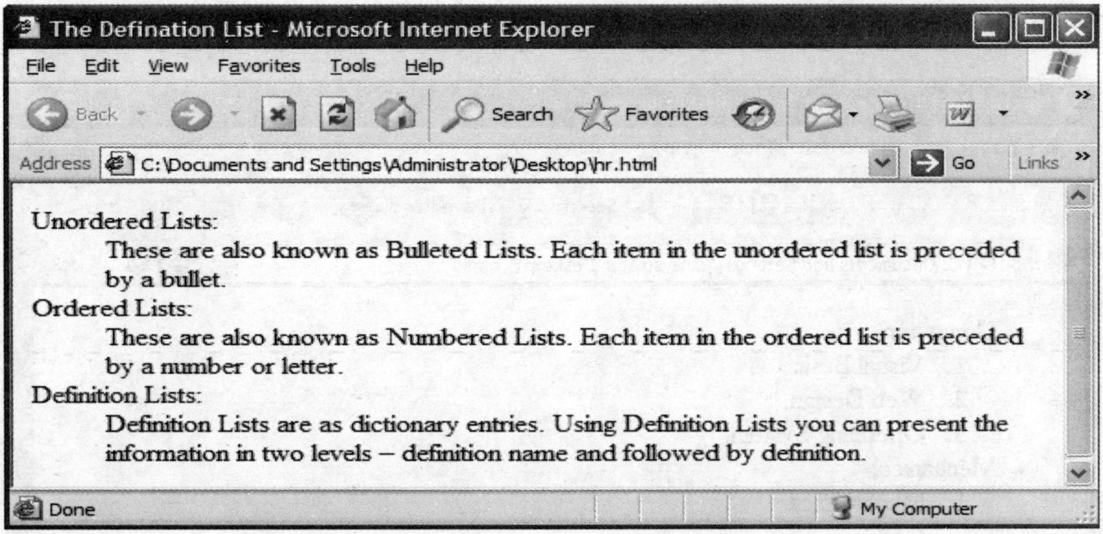

Fig. 2.7 *HTML document including definition list.*

Nested Lists

The list within the list is called nested lists. You can nest ordered list within unordered list, unordered list within ordered list, ordered list within definition list, or definition list within unordered list. For example, following document shows the nesting of the ordered list within the unordered list.

```
<UL>
  <LI>Computer. </LI>
    <OL>
      <LI>Visual Basic. </LI>
      <LI>Web Design. </LI>
      <LI>Operating System. </LI>
    </OL>
  <LI>Mechanical. </LI>
    <OL>
      <LI>Mechtronics. </LI>
      <LI>CNC. </LI>
      <LI>Engg. Drawing. </LI>
    </OL>
  <LI>Electronics. </LI>
    <OL>
      <LI>Image Processing. </LI>
      <LI>Applied Electronics. </LI>
      <LI>Amplitude Modulation. </LI>
    </OL>
</UL>
```

The output is displayed in the browser as shown in following Fig. 2.8 containing the nested list.

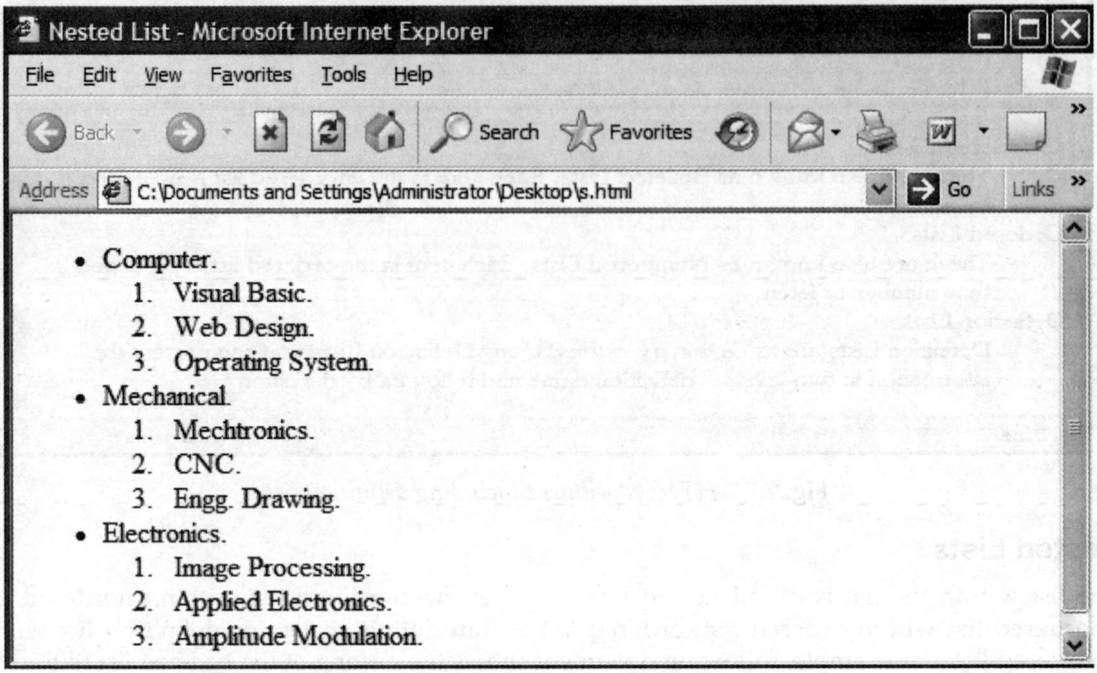

Fig. 2.8 *HTML document including nested list.*

2.8 HEADING

Headings are normally used to organize the document in sections, announce topics to follow, and arrange information according to logical hierarchy. HTML defines six levels of heading from <H1> to <H6>. The level <H1> is the highest level and the level <H6> is the smallest level. Heading level text is always formatted in bold. They require the end tags, like this:

```
<H1>...</H1>
<H2>...</H2>
<H3>...</H3>
<H4>...</H4>
<H5>...</H5>
<H6>...</H6>
```

By default, browsers align heading on the left. You can change the alignment by using alignment attribute. Table following shows the alignment attributes.

Heading Attribute	*Use*
ALIGN=LEFT	Aligns the heading on the left (default).
ALIGN=CENTER	Aligns the heading in the center.
ALIGN=RIGHT	Aligns the heading on the right.

For example, to use the heading tags, enter them around the heading text, like this:

```
<HTML>
  <HEAD>
    <TITLE> Heading Tags Example. </TITLE>
  </HEAD>
  <BODY>
    <H1>By Default First Level Heading.</H1>
    <H2 Align=CENTER>Center aligned Second Level Heading.</H2>
    <H3 Align=RIGHT>Right aligned Third Level Heading.</H3>
  </BODY>
</HTML>
```

The output is displayed in the browser as shown in following Fig. 2.9 containing three headings- by default First Level Heading, Center aligned Second Level Heading and Right aligned Third Level Heading.

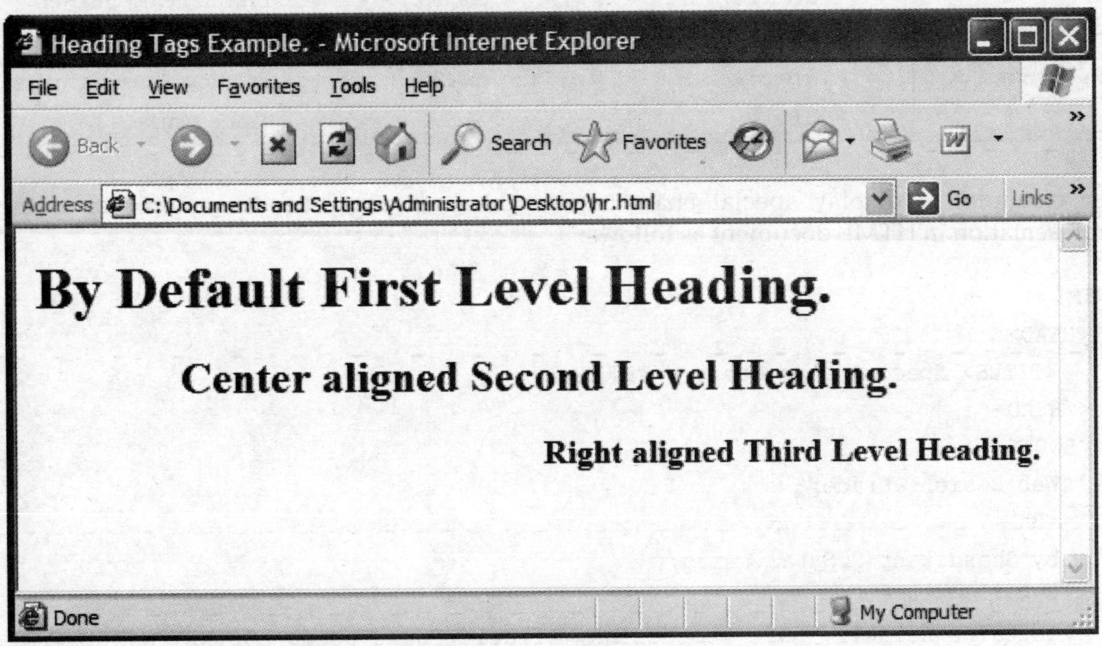

Fig. 2.9 *HTML document including Headings.*

2.9 SPECIAL CHARACTERS

Special characters are nothing but symbols that you display on the web page. Most browsers display these symbols by using mnemonic or numeric representation.

Table following lists some of the most frequently used special characters.

Special character/ Symbol	*Mnemonic Representation*	*Numeric Representation*	*Description*
			Blank space.
¡	¡	¡	Inverted Exclamation Mark.
¢	¢	¡	Cent.
£	£	£	Pound sterling.
¥	¥	¡	Yen.
§	§	§	Section.
©	©	©	Copyright Sign.
¬	¬	¬	Not.
®	®	®	Registered.
±	±	±	Plus-or-Minus.
µ	µ	µ	Micro.
¶	¶	¶	Paragraph.
¼	¼	¼	Fraction One-Quarter.
½	½	½	Fraction One-Half.
¾	¾	¾	Fraction Three-Quarters.
™	™	—	Trade Mark

For example, to display special characters in the web page, use mnemonic or numeric representation in HTML document as follows:

```
<HTML>
  <HEAD>
    <TITLE> Special Characters </TITLE>
  </HEAD>
  <BODY>
    Web Design &trade;
    <BR>
    by Shashikant S.Sutar. &reg;
    <BR>
    contains &frac12; part web design, &frac14; part using ASP.NET and remaining
    part database.
```

```
    <BR>
    the price of this book is 80 &cent;
  </BODY>
</HTML>
```

The output is displayed in the browser as shown in following Fig. 2.10 containing Registered, Fraction One-Half, Fraction One-Quarter, Cent, Trademark special characters.

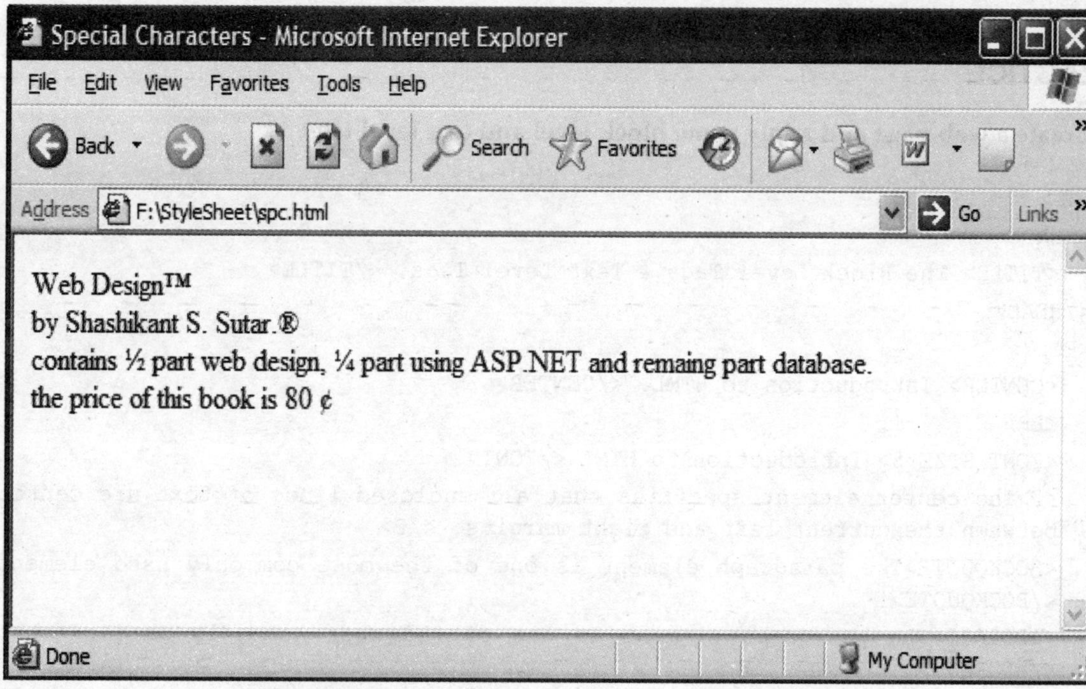

Fig. 2.10 *HTML document including Special Characters.*

2.10 META TAG/ELEMENT

This tag specifies information about the current document to browsers, applications, and search engines. To use this element, place the <META> tag within the document head. For example, the meta tag instructs the browser to load new document, or specifies the keywords, author name and other description for search engine to associate with your document, like this:

```
<HTML>
  <HEAD>
    <TITLE> New Document </TITLE>
    <META NAME="Generator" CONTENT="EditPlus">
    <META NAME="Author" CONTENT="Shashikant S.Sutar.">
```

```
    <META NAME="Keywords" CONTENT="colors, background colors, cell colors, row
    colors">
    <META NAME="Description" CONTENT="">
  </HEAD>
  <BODY>
  …
  </BODY>
</HTML>
```

PRACTICE

1. Create a web page and apply some block level and text level tags.

```
<HTML>
  <HEAD>
    <TITLE> The Block Level Tags & Text Level Tags. </TITLE>
  </HEAD>
  <BODY>
    <CENTER> Introduction to HTML. </CENTER>
    <BR>
    <FONT SIZE=5> Introduction to HTML </FONT>
    <P>The center element specifies that all enclosed lines of text are centered
    between the current left and right margins. </P>
    <BOCKQUOTE>The paragraph element is one of the most commonly used elements.
    </BOCKQUOTE>
    <ADDRESS>The paragraph element is one of the most commonly used elements.
    </ADDRESS>
    <PRE>The paragraph element is one of the most commonly used elements. </PRE>
    <P>The text between the <B> bold element </B> is displayed in boldface.</P>
    <P>The text between the <I> italic element </I> is displayed in italic font
    style.</P>
    <P>The text between the <U> underline element </U> is displayed as underlined
    text.</P>
    <P>The text between the <STRIKE> strike element </STRIKE> is displayed with
    horizontal line striking through it.</P>
    <P>The text between the <SUP> superscript element </SUP> is displayed as
    superscript.</P>
    <P>The text between the <SUB> subscript element </SUB> is displayed as
    subscript.</P>
  </BODY>
</HTML>
```

The output is displayed in the browser as shown in following figure showing the use of the Block Level Tags & Text Level Tags.

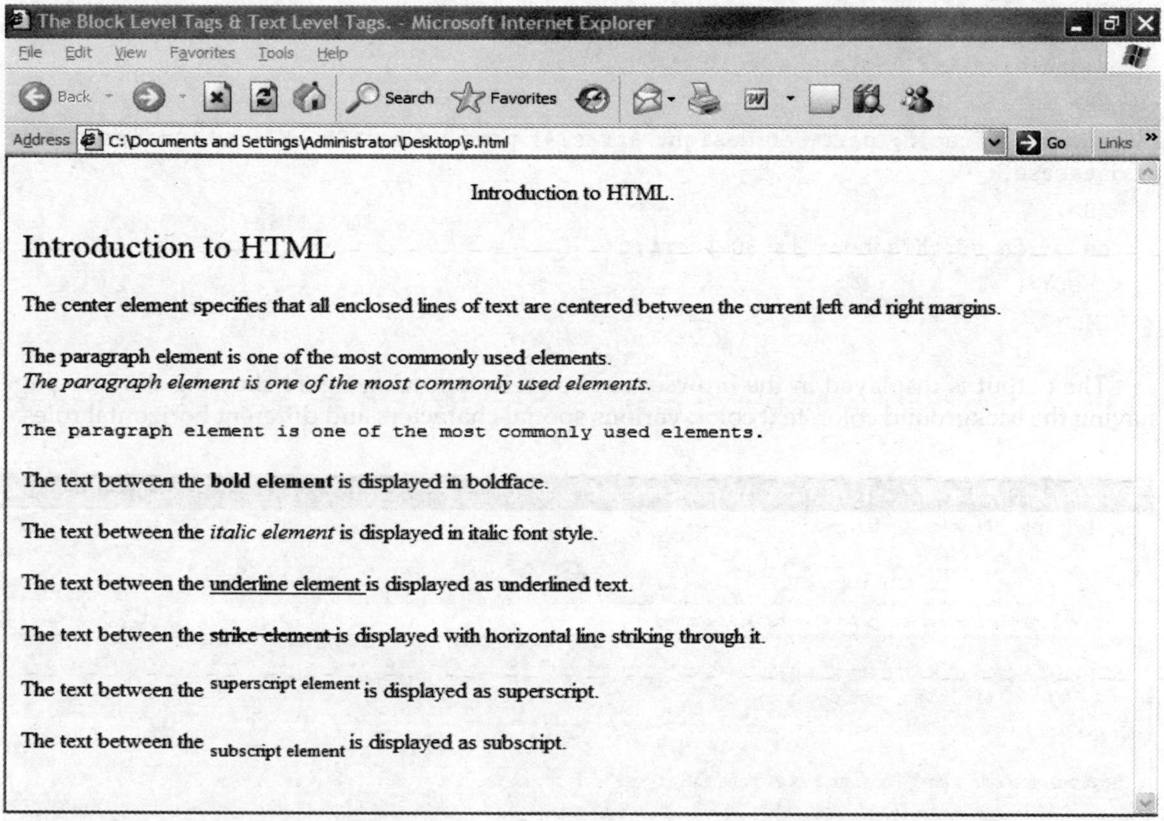

2. Create a web page and apply the background color, text color, horizontal rules and special characters.

```
<HTML>
  <HEAD>
  <TITLE> The Block Level Tags & Text Level Tags. </TITLE>
  </HEAD>
  <BODY BGCOLOR=#FFCCCC TEXT= "#FF0000">
  <P>The Horizontal rule with full width and shade. </P>
  <HR>
  <P>The Horizontal rule with 50% width and 10% height. </P>
  <HR WIDTH="50%" SIZE=10>
  <P>The Horizontal rule with 50% width and 10% height and right aligned. </P>
  <HR WIDTH="50%" SIZE=10 ALIGN="RIGHT">
```

```
  <P>The Horizontal rule with no shade. </P>
  <HR NOSHADE>
  Web Design &trade;
  <BR>
  by Shashikant S. Sutar. &reg;
  <BR>
  contains &frac12; part web design, &frac14; part using ASP.NET and remaining part
  database.
  <BR>
  the price of this book is 80 &cent;
  </BODY>
</HTML>
```

The output is displayed in the browser as shown in following figure showing the web page having the background color, text color, various special characters and different horizontal rules.

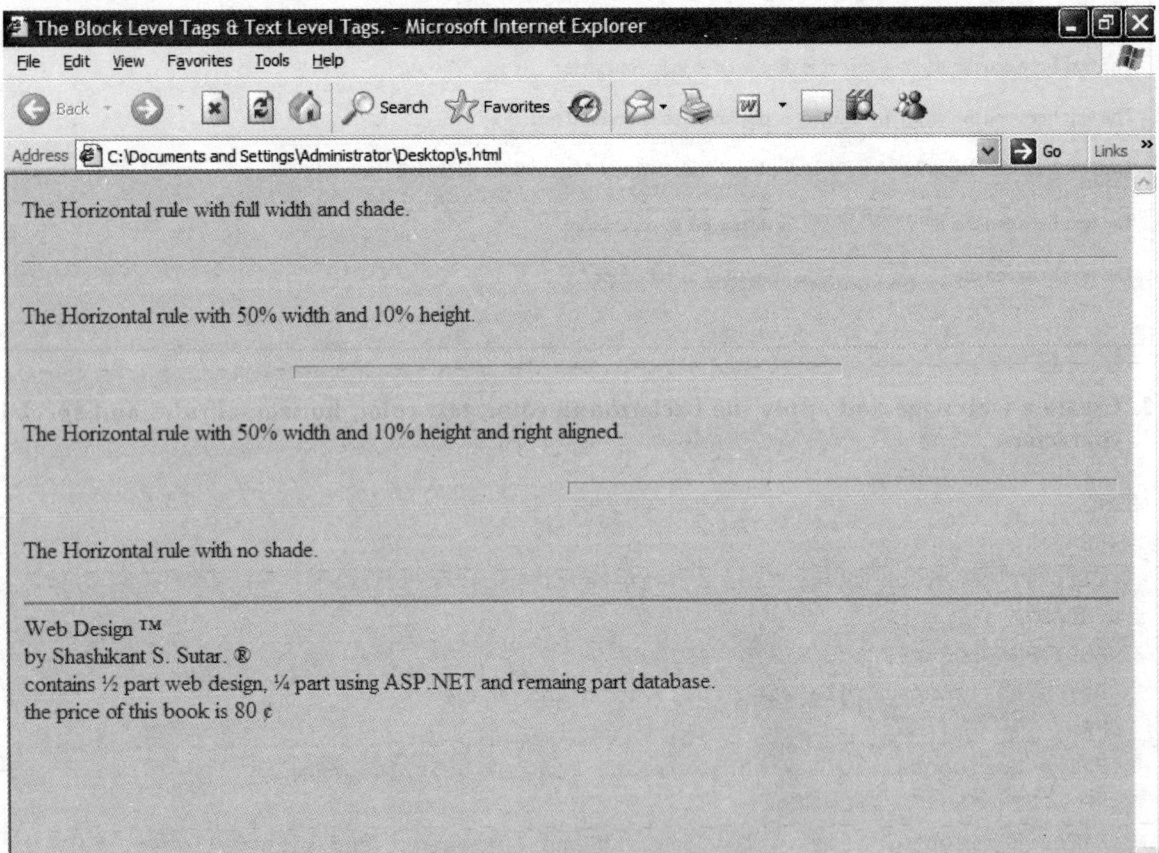

3. Create a web page and include ordered list, unordered list, definition list and nested list.

```
<HTML>
<HEAD>
<TITLE> An Unordered List, Definition List, Nested List  </TITLE>
</HEAD>
<BODY>
<UL>
  <LI>Banana. </LI>
  <LI>Apple. </LI>
  <LI>Orange. </LI>
</UL>
<DL>
  <DT> Unordered Lists: </DT>
    <DD> These are also known as Bulleted Lists. Each item in the unordered list is
    preceded by a bullet. </DD>
  <DT> Ordered Lists: </DT>
    <DD> These are also known as Numbered Lists. Each item in the ordered list is
    preceded by a number or letter. </DD>
  <DT> Definition Lists:</DT>
    <DD>Definition Lists are as dictionary entries. Using definition lists you can
    present the information in two levels-definition name and followed by
    definition.</DD>
</DL>
<UL>
  <LI>Computer. </LI>
      <OL>
      <LI>Visual Basic. </LI>
      <LI>Web Design. </LI>
      <LI>Operating System. </LI>
      </OL>
  <LI>Mechanical. </LI>
      <OL>
      <LI>Mechtronics. </LI>
      <LI>CNC. </LI>
      <LI>Engg. Drawing. </LI>
      </OL>
  <LI>Electronics. </LI>
    <OL>
      <LI>Image Processing. </LI>
```

```
        <LI>Applied Electronics. </LI>
        <LI>Amplitude Modulation. </LI>
        </OL>
</UL>
</BODY>
```

The output is displayed in the browser as shown in following figure containing ordered list, unordered list, definition list and nested list.

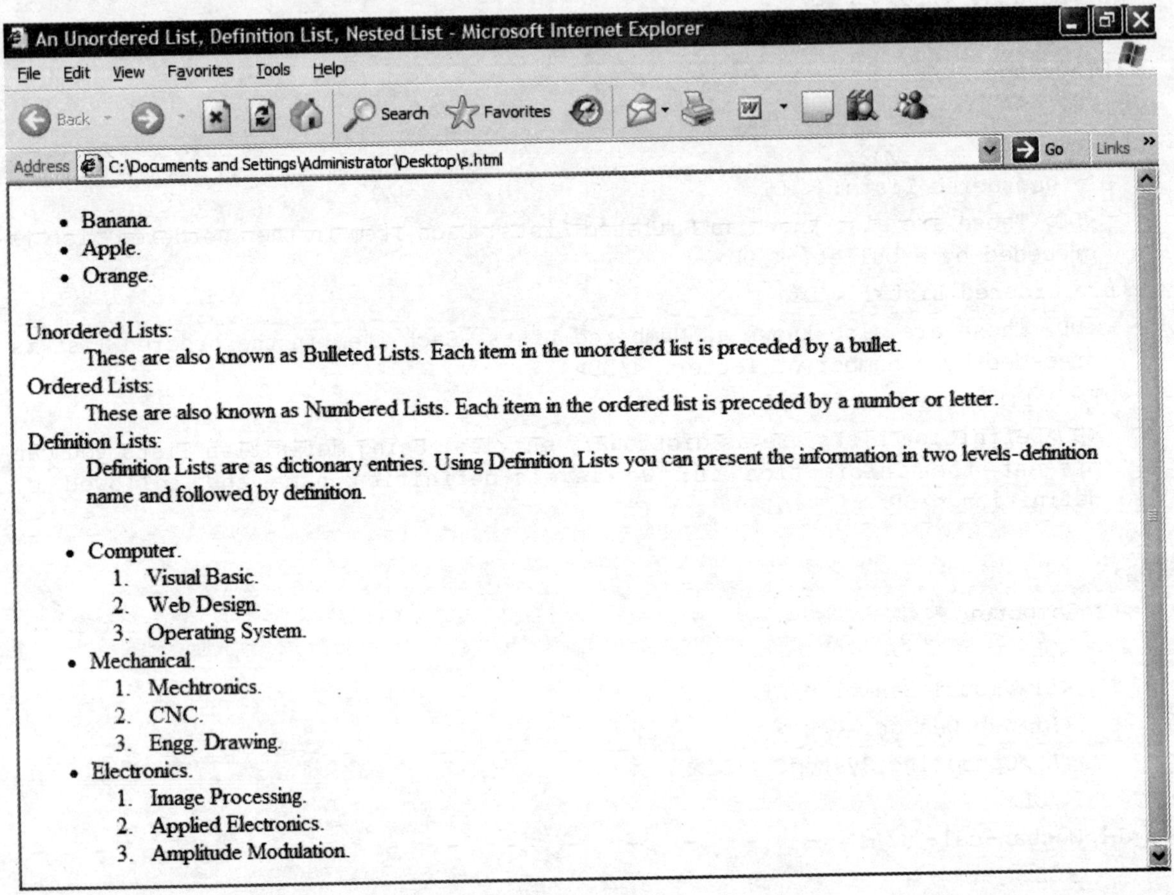

Questions

1. Which are the components of HTML? Explain.
2. Explain structure tags of HTML.
3. List and explain any five Block-Level tags used in HTML Document.
4. List and explain any five Block-Level tags used in HTML Document.

5. Write short note on – Horizontal Rules and Meta tag.
6. Explain Lists used HTML document.
7. Write a short note on – Special Characters.
8. How to give text color to the HTML document?
9. How to give background color to the HTML document?
10. Explain Meta tag in details.

□□□

3

Linking to HTML Documents

3.1 URL

URL stands for Uniform Resource Locator, which is the address of the document on the web or more accurately, on the internet. URL looks complex and long. It contains four basic parts-protocols, hostname, folder name and filename – each of which has specific function.

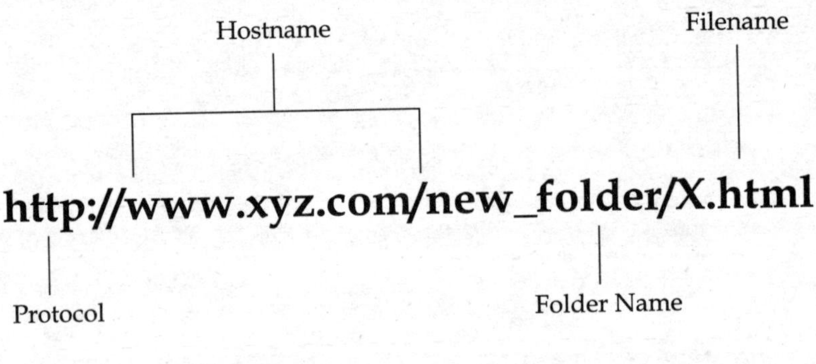

Protocol

Protocol specifies the computer language used to transfer the information. Specifically, a protocol tells the browser where the.information is located (for example, on a local terminal, an FTP server, on web server and so on.) and tells the browser what to except from document retrieval process (for example, what information will be provided by the browser).

Hostname

The hostname is the name of the server that holds the HTML documents and related files. Each server has specific address and all documents stored on the server share the same hostname. For example, your server name is XYZ, then your hostname would be something like *www.XYZ.com.*

Folder Name

Folder names are the next chunk of information in the URL, indicating the folder in which the files or documents are located. Folders are nothing but containers for the HTML documents you create.

Filename

Filenames are names of specific HTML documents having file name and its extention.

3.2 TYPES OF URL

Absolute URL

An absolute URL contains all information including the protocol, hostname, folder name and the filename, which are all essential for linking to the website. If any piece of information is missing, then linking will not made to the document on the web site. To linking to another web site, you have to provide all these information so that right server, folder, and document can be found.
Some sample absolute URLs.

```
http://www.xyz.com/XYZ/DocumentX.html

http://www.abc.com/ABC/DocumentA.html
```

Relative URL

A relative URL usually contains only folder name and filename or even just a filename. This type of URL is a partial URL- not all information is essential. You can use this partial URL when you are pointing to a file that is located in the same folder or on the same server as the originating file. In this case, browser do not need the server name or protocol indicator because it assumes that the files are in a folder or on a server that is relative to the originating document.
Relative URL are of two types:

1. Document Relative URL

You use this URL to refer to the document in relation to the originating document. In this URL, you use the folder name and the filename or in the most cases you include only the filename. For example, from following Fig. 3.1 for linking from A.html to the Z.html, use the document relative URL, which is as follows:

XYZ/Z.html

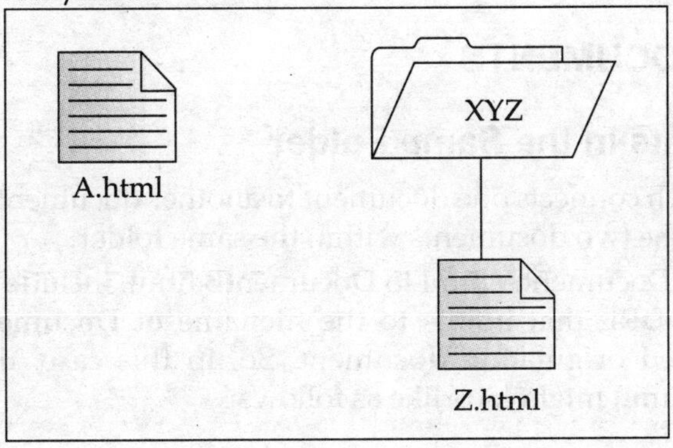

Fig. 3.1 *Document relative URL.*

2. Server Relative URL

You use this URL to the server on which the originating document resides. A server relative URL is relative to the server root- that is relative to the hostname part of URL.

Server relative URLs have a forward slash (/) at the beginning of the filename, which indicates that you interpret the path of the document from the top of the current server i.e., server root, rather than from current document location. So, from anywhere in our site, we could use server relative URL. For example, from following Fig. 3.2 for linking from A.html to the Z.html, use the server relative URL, which is as follows:

/XYZ/Z.html

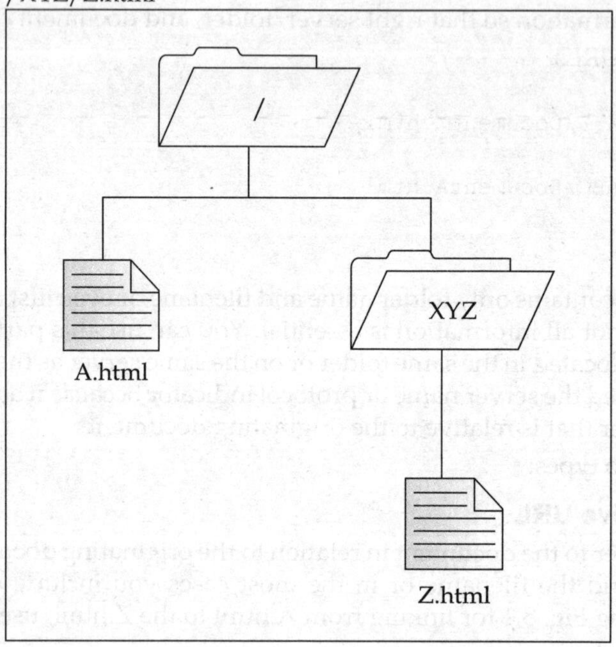

Fig. 3.2 *Server relative URL.*

3.3 LINKING TO DOCUMENTS

Linking to Documents in the Same Folder

This is the basic link, which connects one document to another document or file in the same folder. Fig. 3.3 following shows the two documents within the same folder.

To create a link from DocumentA.html to DocumentB.html, include the anchor tag (<A>), the HREF= attribute, and a URL that points to the filename of DocumentB.html. The link from DocumentA.html is called originating document. So, in this case, the link from originating document (DocumentA.html) might look like as follows:

```
<A HREF= "DocumentB.html">Click Here </A>
```

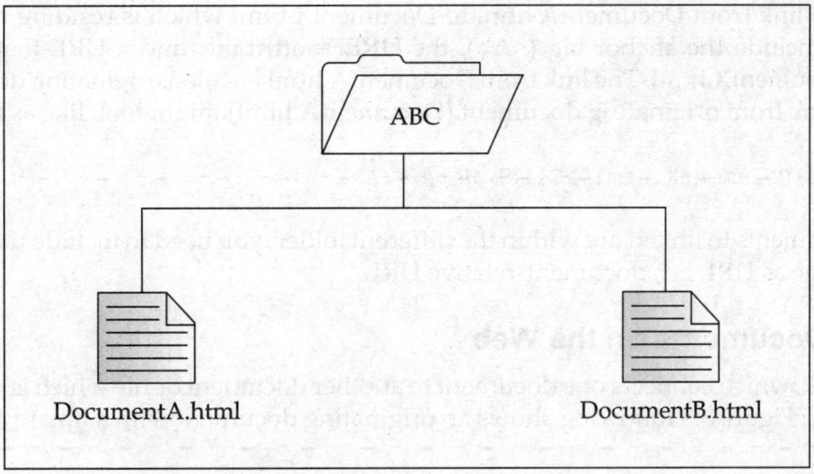

Fig. 3.3 *Linking to Documents in the same folder.*

When documents to linked are within the same folder, you need to include only the filename as URL i.e., relative URL. Without additional information, browser will look in the same folder as originating document. In this case, both locations of DocumentA and DocumentB are relative to the folder in which they reside.

Linking to Documents in a Different Folder

This is another type of link, which connects one document to another document or file which is residing in the different folder. Figure 3.4 following shows the two documents in which one residing in the different folder.

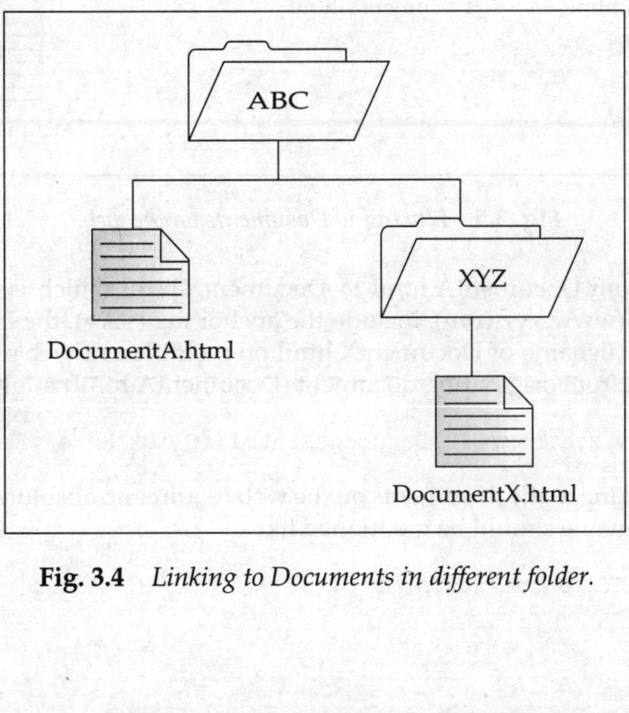

Fig. 3.4 *Linking to Documents in different folder.*

To create a link from DocumentA.html to DocumentX.html which is residing in the different folder (XYZ). include the anchor tag (<A>), the HREF= attribute, and a URL that points to the filename of DocumentX.html. The link from DocumentA.html is called originating document. So, in this case, the link from originating document (DocumentA.html) might look like as follows:

```
<A HREF= "XYZ/DocumentX.html">Click Here </A>
```

When documents to linked are within the different folder, you need to include the folder names and the filename as URL i.e., document-relative URL.

Linking to Documents on the Web

This type of link, which connects one document to another document or file which is residing on the different server. Figure 3.5 following shows an originating document with a link to a document on the web.

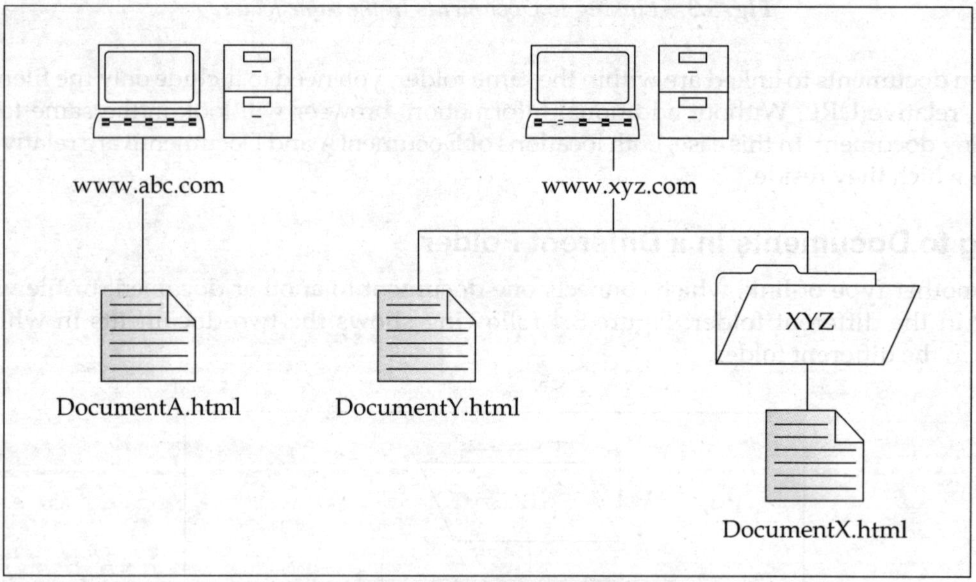

Fig. 3.5 *Linking to Documents on the web.*

To create a link from DocumentA.html to DocumentX.html which is residing in the folder (XYZ) on the Web Site (www.xyz.com). include the anchor tag (<A>), the HREF= attribute, and a URL that points to the filename of DocumentX.html on the different web server (www.xyz.com). So, in this case, the link from originating document (DocumentA.html) might look like as follows:

```
<A HREF= "http://www.xyz.com/XYZ/DocumentX.html">Click Here </A>
```

Remember that linking to the documents on the web requires an absolute URL, so that the right host, folder and the filename should be mentioned like:

```
http://www.xyz.com/XYZ/DocumentX.html
```

Linking to a Specific Location in a Document

This is a different type of like, in addition to link from one document to another document; you can link one document to a specific location within another document. This allows visitors to move directly to the information they search, rather than having them a document and scroll to that information. The specific location may be paragraph, lists or heading element in the document.

To create a link from one document to specific location within another document, use named anchor tag, which gives name to the location to be linked (targeted linked location) and then link directly to that named location from another document.

For example, to create a link from DocumentA.html to the head location (<H1>) within DocumentB.html, use named anchor <A NAME= "Specific"> tag, which gives the name, "Specific", to the head location (<H1>) within DocumentB.html and then link directly to that location from DocumentA.html.

The named anchor tag for marking head location (<H1>) in DocumentB.html is as follows:

```
<A NAME= "Specific"> <H1>Linking to a Specific Location in a Document </H1></A>
```

Then create a link to this location in DocumentB.html from DocumentA.html, by using anchor tag (<A>) and HREF= attribute in DocumentA.html as follows:

```
<A HREF= "DocumentB.html #Specific"> Link </A>
```

#Specific is the targeted link that tells the browsers to link to that heading.

Figure 3.6 following shows an originating document with (Document A) with link to specific location in document B.

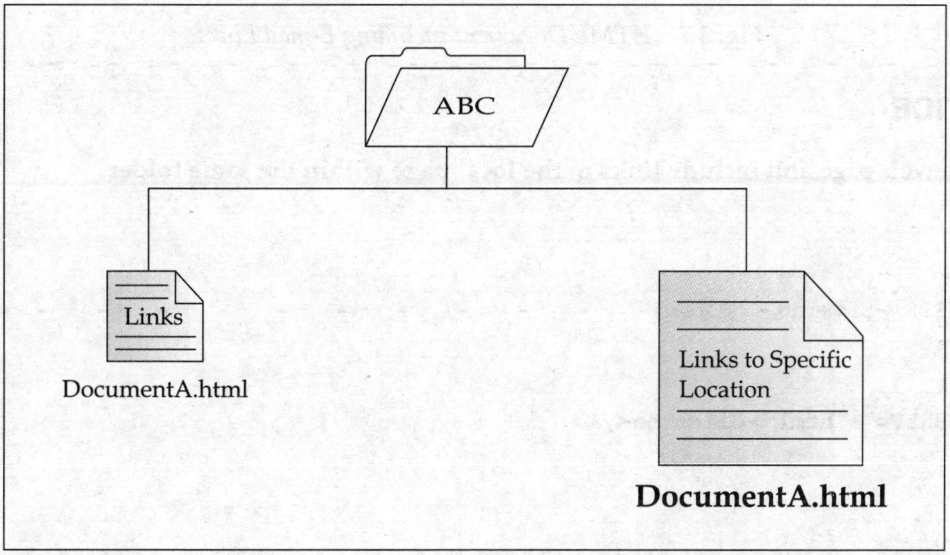

Fig. 3.6 *Linking to specific location in a Document.*

3.4 INSERTING E-MAIL LINKS

Email links are the links which takes visitors from the web page to already addressed blank e-mail message in their e-mail program. By including e-mail links you can lets visitors easily contact you.

To create an e-mail link, simply add mailto: protocol indicator with e-mail address in anchor tag. For example, you might include a link to send the feedback of this book, with a link like this:

```
<A HREF="mailto:lbsmkg2oct@indiatimes.com"> Send me!!! </A>
```

Figure 3.7 following shows the E-mail link in the web page linking to *lbsmkg2oct@indiatimes.com* address.

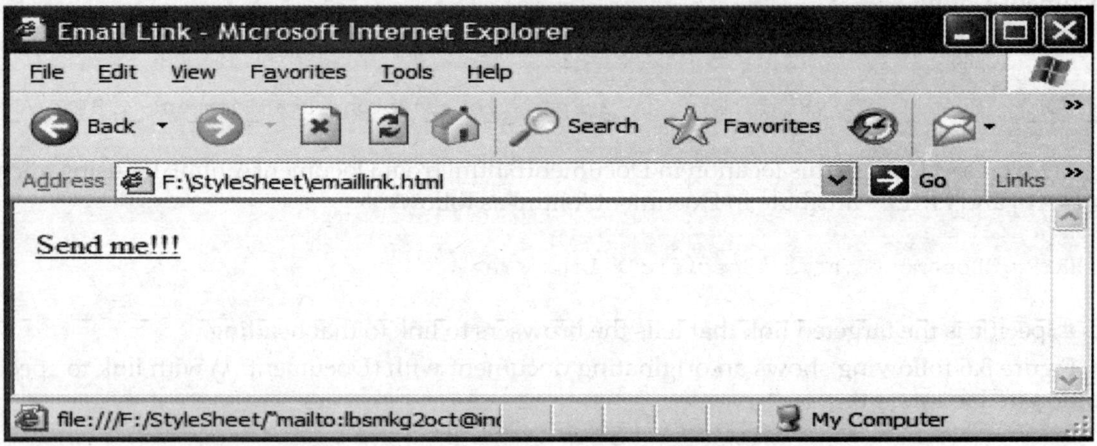

Fig. 3.7 *HTML Document including E-mail Links.*

PRACTICE

1. Create web page and include links to the local page within the same folder.

```
<HTML>
  <HEAD>
    <TITLE> Linking </TITLE>
  </HEAD>
  <BODY>
    <A HREF="s.html">Click Me</A>
  </BODY>
</HTML>
```

Here there is a link from link.html to s.html. Both documents reside in a same folder (sss folder). So link.html uses the relative URL as in above HTML statements.

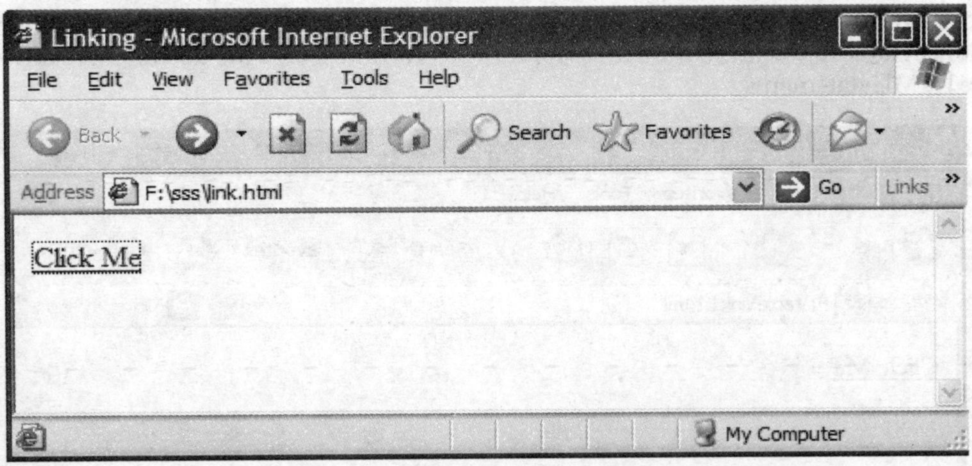

When you click on the "Click Me" text in link.html, you switched on to the s.html document which is in the same folder (sss folder) as follows.

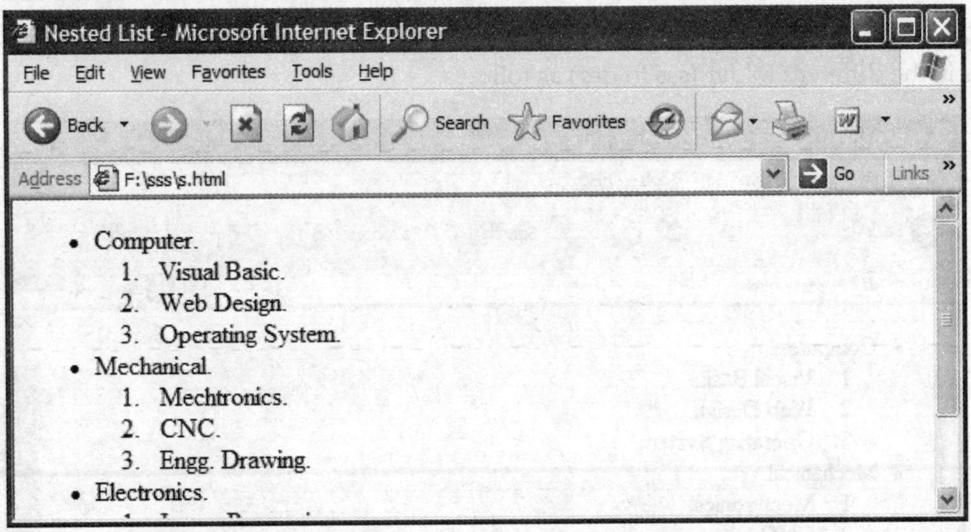

2. Create web page and include links to the page within the different folder.

```
<HTML>
  <HEAD>
    <TITLE> Linking </TITLE>
  </HEAD>
  <BODY>
    <A HREF="\sss\s.html">Click Me</A>
  </BODY>
</HTML>
```

Here there is a link from link1.html to s.html. Both documents reside in the different folder (link1.html in table folder and s.html in sss folder). So link1.html uses the document relative URL as in above HTML statements.

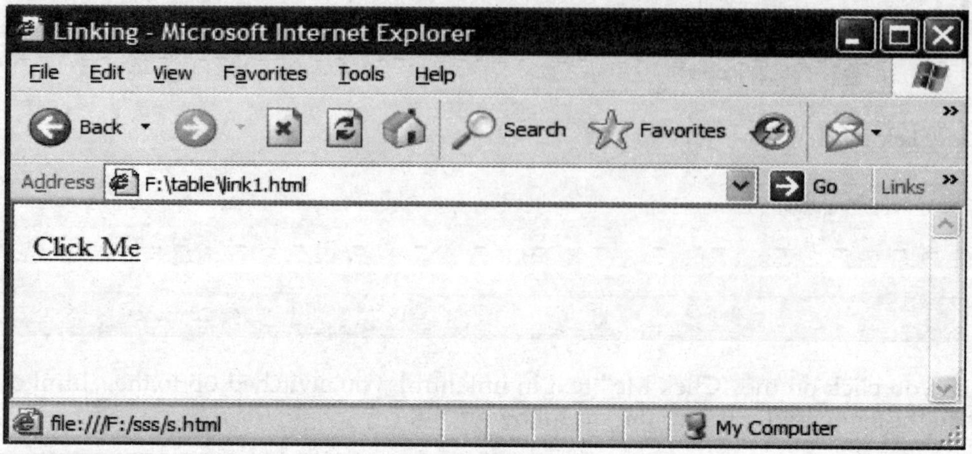

When you click on the "Click Me" text in link1.html, you switched on to the s.html document which is in the different folder (sss folder) as follows.

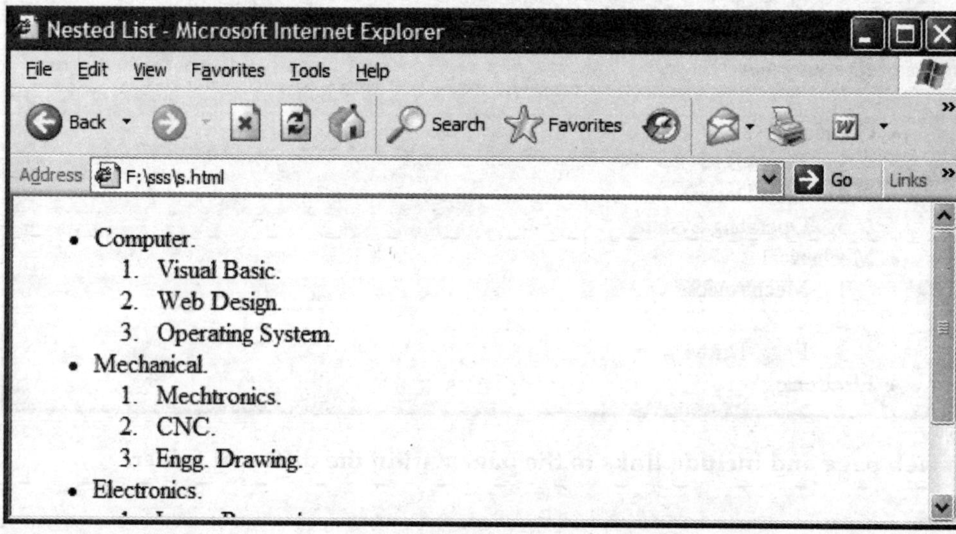

3. Create web page and include links to the page within the web server.

```
<HTML>
   <HEAD>
      <TITLE> Linking </TITLE>
   </HEAD>
```

```
   <BODY>
      <A HREF="http://localhost/postinfo.html">Click Me</A>
   </BODY>
</HTML>
```

Here there is a link from link1.html to postinfo.html. The document link1.html is in table folder and the postinfo.html is on the localhost server. So link1.html uses the absolute URL as in above HTML statements.

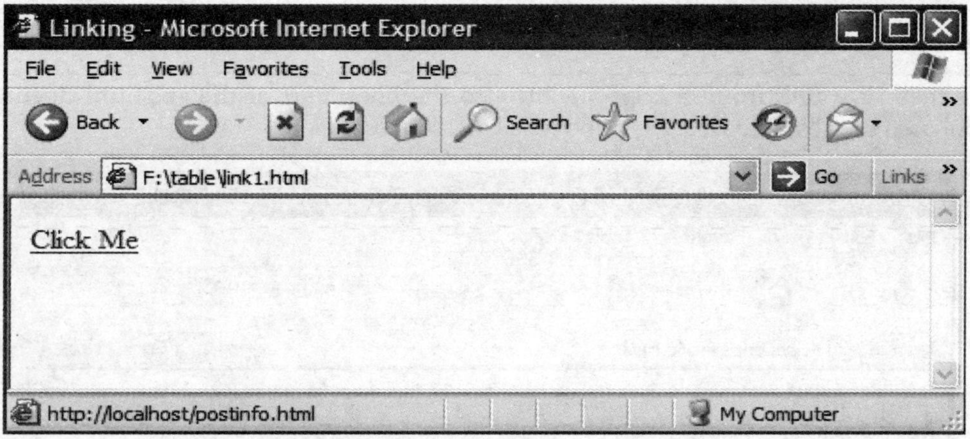

When you click on the "Click Me" text in link1.html, you switched on to the postinfo.html document which is on the server named localhost server as follows.

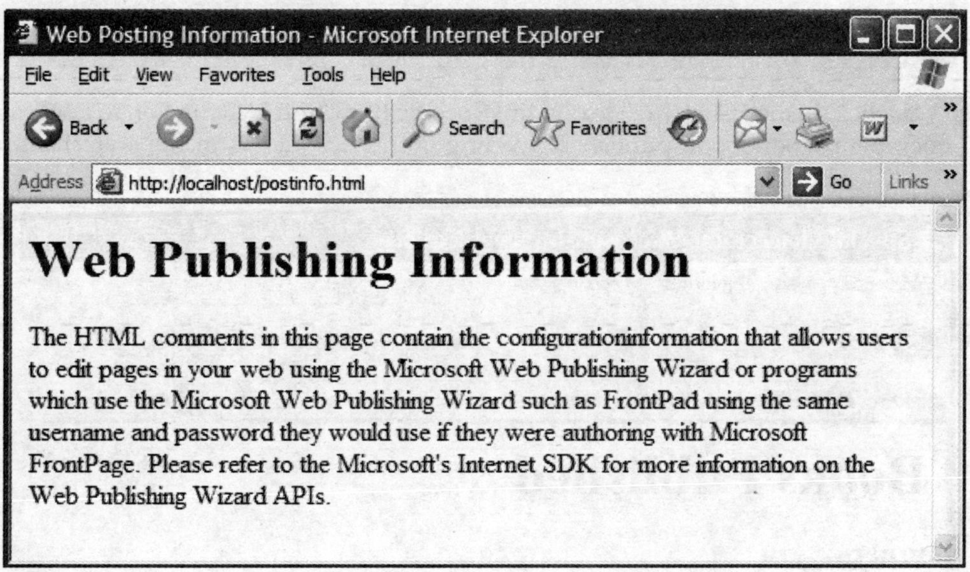

4. Create web page and include links to the specific location within the page.

```
<HTML>
  <HEAD>
    <TITLE> Linking </TITLE>
  </HEAD>
  <BODY>
    <A HREF="F:\StyleSheet\spc.html#Book">Click Me</A>
  </BODY>
</HTML>
```

Here there is a link from linkSpecific.html to the book part of the spc.html document. So link1.html uses the absolute URL as in above HTML statements.

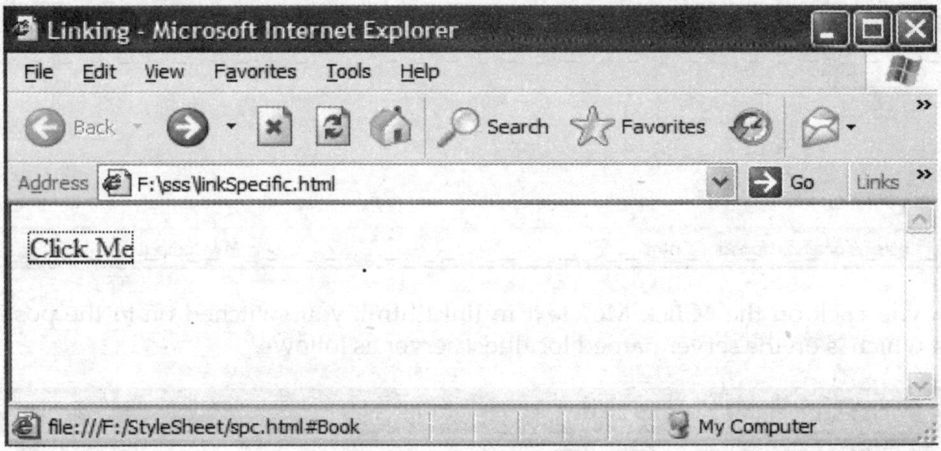

When you click on the "Click Me" text in linkSpecific.html, you switched on to book part of the spc.html document where book published heading is there, which is in the stylesheet folder as follows.

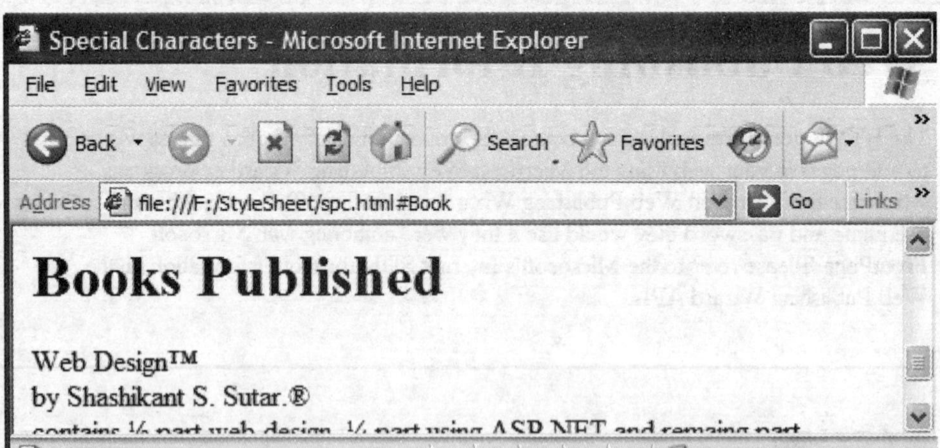

QUESTIONS

1. What is URL? Which are types of URL? Explain.
2. How to link documents in the same folder? Explain.
3. How to link documents in a different folder?
4. How to link a specific location in a document?
5. Write a note on – Insert E-mail links in the web page.

4

Creating Frames

4.1 CREATING BASIC FRAMES

Introduction to Frames

The layout of the web pages can be made flexible by using frames which allows visible client area, that is, the browser to be divided into more than one sub regions. So these sub regions on the web page are called frames. Each frame or sub region has the following properties:

1. It can load using its own URL, independent of the other frames.
2. It can be given a name, so that it can be targeted by other URLs.
3. It can change its size dynamically according to the change in size of the visible client area.

Frames allow the user to create the web pages in a different manner from the usual way. Information such as messages, title graphics and tables that the page designer wants to keep constant and always visible can be stored on separate frame. As the user moves through the site in one frame, the other frames are always remains visible and unchanged.

For example, one frame could contain a set of links, each of which when clicked, targets its result into another frame.

Frame documents are made from following two tags:

(a) FRAMESET tags.
(b) FRAME tags.

FRAMESET Tags: Creating a Frameset

The basic structure of a frame document is same as HTML document, except that the <BODY> container is replaced by a <FRAMESET> container that contains frames and in it you can specify the general frame layout- either vertical (using columns) or horizontal (using rows).

The table following describes the use of frameset tag and attributes.

Tags/Attributes	*Use*
<FRAMESET>	Create a layout (frameset) document that determines the location and characteristics of the frames. It is a fundamental or container tag, which contains other tags like frame tag.
COLS= "n1, n2, ..."	Sets the size for rows- horizontal frames- in pixels, percentage, or as a proportion of the remaining space with "*".
ROWS= "n1, n2, ..."	Sets the size for columns- vertical frames- in pixels, percentage, or as a proportion of the remaining space with "*".

Following example sets up a basic frameset document within two columns.

1. Add opening and closing <FRAMESET> tags to establish frameset document, instead of using <BODY> tags in HTML document.

```
<HTML>
  <HEAD>
    <TITLE> FRAME </TITLE>
  </HEAD>
  <FRAMESET>

  </FRAMESET>
</HTML>
```

2. Add a COLS= or ROWS= attribute, depending on whether you want vertical or horizontal frames. In this example, use COLS= attribute with values 30% and * to get two vertical frames (columns), one filling the 30% and one filling the remaining space.

```
<HTML>
  <HEAD>
    <TITLE> FRAME </TITLE>
  </HEAD>
  <FRAMESET COLS="30%,*">

  </FRAMESET>
</HTML>
```

The frames will be displayed in the browser as shown in following Fig. 4.1.

To divide browser window into columns and then subdivide each column into rows, use nesting of <FRAMESET> tags, as follows:

```
<FRAMESET COLS="30%,*">
  <FRAMESET ROWS= 50%,*>
```

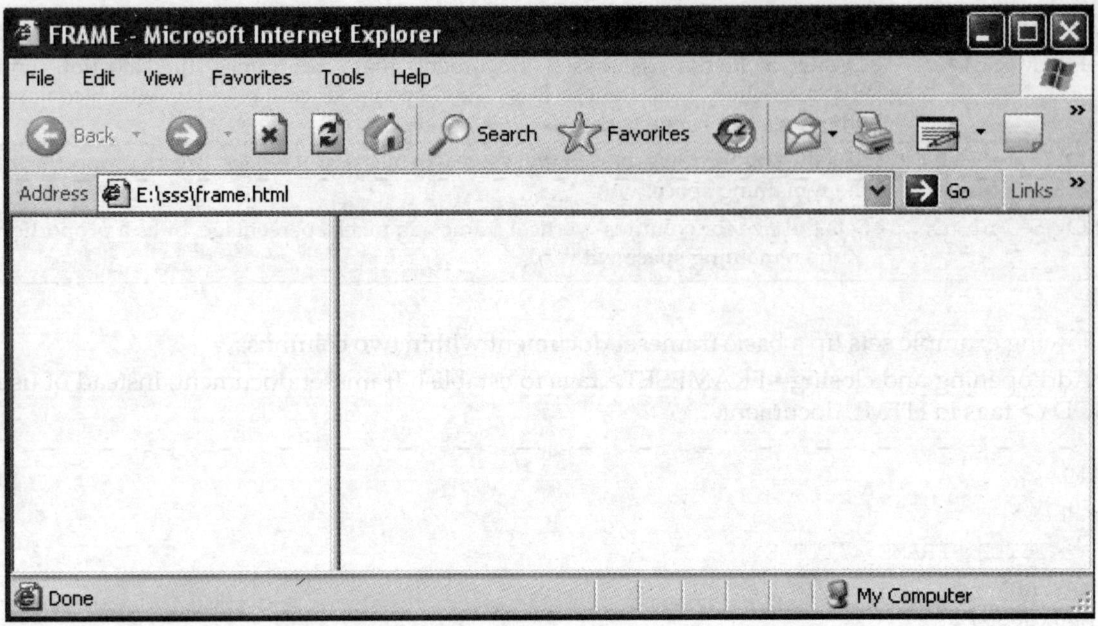

Fig. 4.1 *HTML document including two vertical frames.*

```
   </FRAMESET>
   <FRAMESET ROWS= 30%,*,*>

   </FRAMESET>
</FRAMESET>
```

The frames will be displayed in the browser as shown in following Fig. 4.2.

The first nested <FRAMESET> tag will divide the left column of width 30% of the frameset document and the second nested <FRAMESET> tag will divide the right column of remaining space of the frameset document.

You can specify the frame size in percentage (*e.g.* 50%) of entire browser window, in pixel values (*e.g.* 100px), or by using asterisk (*) sign to fill the remaining space. You can use asterisk (*) sign to set up proportional columns and rows. For example, to divide the frameset document into three equally vertical frames use three asterisks (*) signs as values of COLS= attribute which is as follows:

```
<FRAMESET COLS="*,*,*">
```

and to make middle frame twice as large as the other two, add 2 to the * as follows:

```
<FRAMESET COLS="*,2*,*">
```

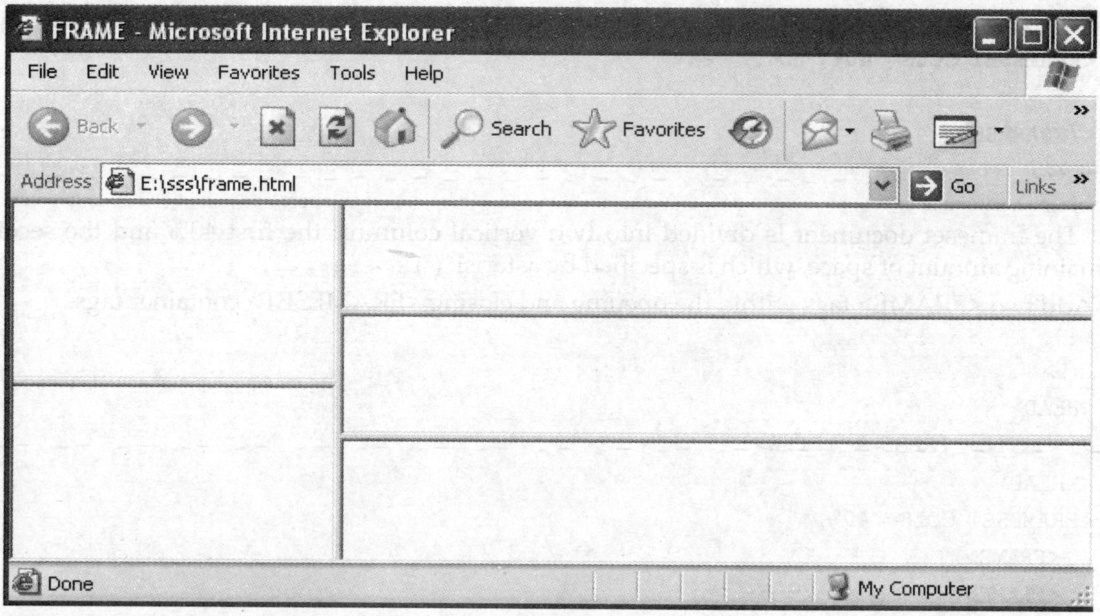

Fig. 4.2 *HTML document including two vertical frames, each containing horizontal frames.*

Frame Tags: Adding Frames

To include the frames in the frameset document, simply add the <FRAME> tag for each row or column in the frameset document which is specified by <FRAMESET> tag, specify the content for each frame by using SRC= attribute and finally assign name to each frame by using NAME= attribute.

The table following describes the use of frame tag and attributes.

Tags/Attributes	*Use*
<FRAME>	Create a frame in frameset document. It identifies frame characteristics and initial content.
SRC= "…"	Identifies the source for the frame content as a standard URL.
NAME= "…"	Labels a frame so that it can be targeted or referred to from other frames or windows.
<NOFRAME>	Sets a section of an HTML document to be visible to nonframed browsers.

For example, to add two vertical frames in frameset document, write document as follows:

1. Add opening and closing <FRAMESET> tags to establish frameset document, instead of using <BODY> tags in HTML document, with COLS= attribute with 40% and * values to add two vertical frames.

```
<HTML>
  <HEAD>
    <TITLE> FRAME </TITLE>
```

```
   </HEAD>
   <FRAMESET COLS="40%,*">

   </FRAMESET>
</HTML>
```

The frameset document is divided into two vertical columns: the first 40% and the second remaining amount of space, which is specified by asterisk (*).

2. Add two <FRAME> tags within the opening and closing <FRAMESET> container tags.

```
<HTML>
   <HEAD>
      <TITLE> FRAME </TITLE>
   </HEAD>
   <FRAMESET COLS="40%,*">
      <FRAME>
      <FRAME>
   </FRAMESET>
</HTML>
```

3. Now to fill these two frames with HTML documents, use SRC= attribute in each <FRAME> tag.

```
<HTML>
   <HEAD>
      <TITLE> FRAME </TITLE>
   </HEAD>
   <FRAMESET COLS="40%,*">
      <FRAME SRC="E:\Web Project\TempKop\HomeBazar\Html\Home.htm">
      <FRAME SRC="E:\Web Project\TempKop\HomeBazar\Html\Purchase.htm">
   </FRAMESET>
</HTML>
```

4. And finally assign name to each frame by using NAME= attribute.

```
<HTML>
   <HEAD>
      <TITLE> FRAME </TITLE>
   </HEAD>
```

```
  <FRAMESET COLS="40%,*">
    <FRAME SRC="E:\Web Project\TempKop\HomeBazar\Html\Home.htm" NAME="A">
  <FRAME SRC="E:\Web Project\TempKop\HomeBazar\Html\Purchase.htm" NAME="B">
  </FRAMESET>
</HTML>
```

So the frame named 'A' will contained in the left part of the frameset having width of 40% and the second frame named 'B' will contained in the right part of the frameset as shown in following Fig. 4.3.

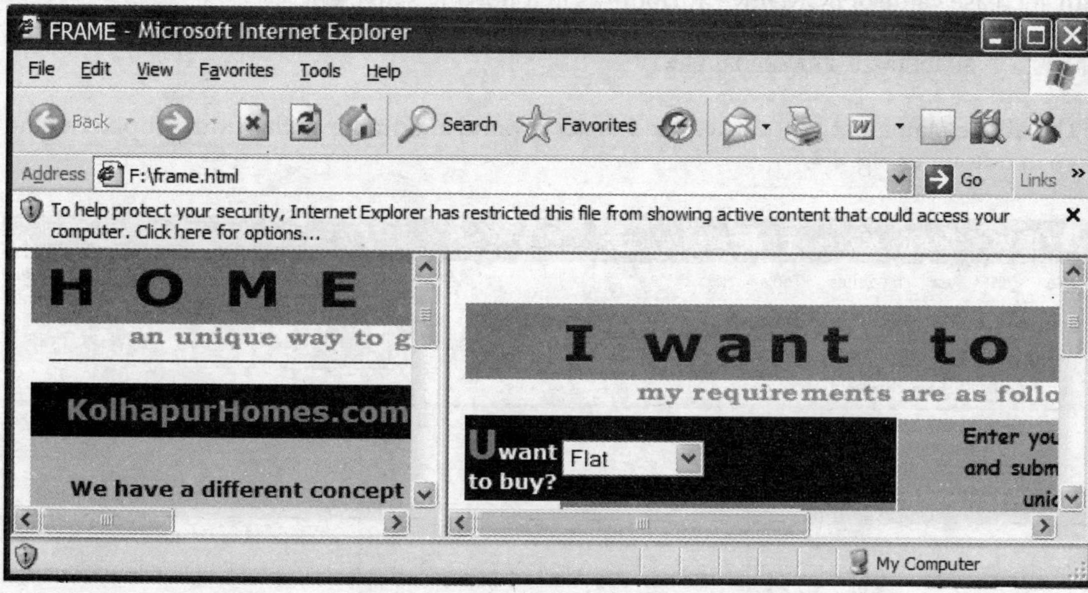

Fig. 4.3 *HTML document including two vertical frames.*

4.2 FORMATTING FRAMES

Formatting frames involves changing its borders and adjusting its margins by using attributes border, bordercolor, marginheight, marginwidth, scrolling etc. which are described as follows. These attributes generally either to <FRAMESET> tag or to <FRAME> tag.

(a) Border and Frameborder

The BORDER attribute draws the border around the frame. The width of the border can be specified by using BORDER= *n* and FRAMEBORDER = *n* where *n* should be a pixel value. Table following shows the use of the BORDER= and FRAMEBORDER= attributes in the <FRAMESET> tag.

Tags/Attributes	*Use*
<FRAMESET>	Create a frame in frameset document. It identifies frame characteristics and initial content.
BORDER= *n*	Specifies the width of the border. *n* should be a pixel value. For uniform result in all browsers, use it in conjunction with the FRAMEBORDER= attribute.
FRAMEBORDER= *n*	Sets or removes the border around the frame. For uniform result in all browsers, use it in conjunction with the BORDER= attribute.

For example, to draw the borders set FRAMEBORDER=1 and BORDER=1. And to set border width, increase value of BORDER= attribute as in following statement:

```
< FRAMESET BORDER=20 FRAMEBORDER=1>
```

The above statement will draws the border around the frame with width 20 pixel value as shown in following Fig. 4.4.

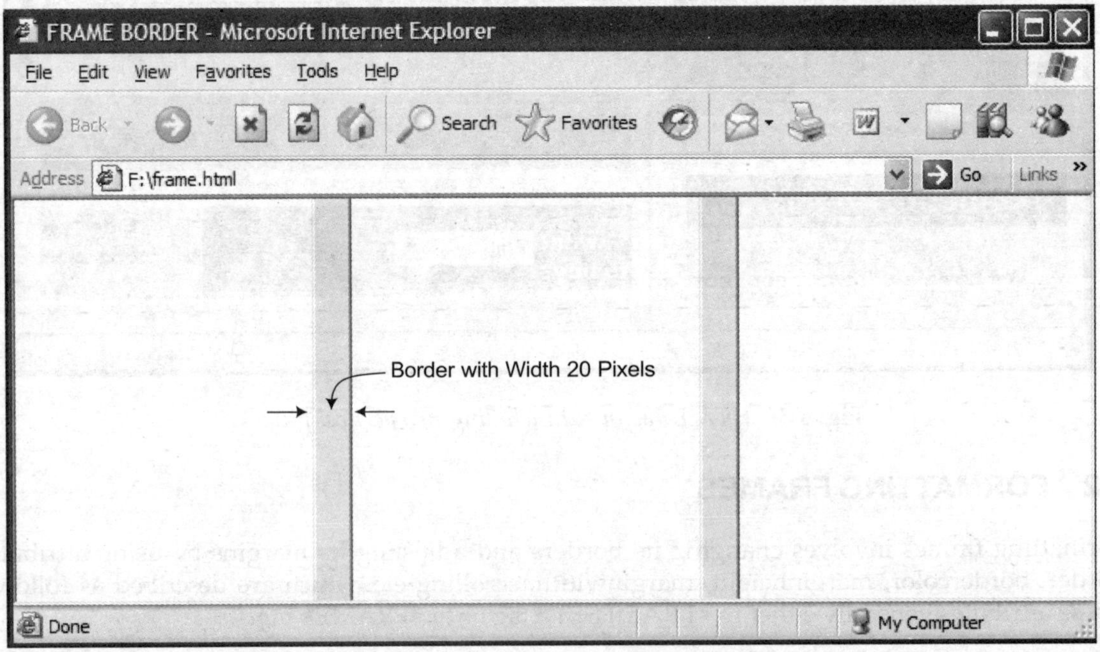

Fig. 4.4 *HTML document including frame borders.*

(b) Bordercolor

The BORDERCOLOR sets the color for the border of the frame. Any of the predefined colors or a #rrggbb hexadecimal triplet can be specified for the border color. Table following shows the use of the BORDERCOLOR= attribute in the < FRAME > tag. Table following shows the use of the BORDERCOLOR= attribute in the < FRAME > tag.

Tags/Attributes	*Use*
<FRAME>	Create a frame in frameset document. It identifies frame characteristics and initial content.
BORDERCOLOR = "..."	Sets the color for the border of the frame. Any of the predefined colors or a #rrggbb hexadecimal triplet can be specified for the border color.

For example, to set color for the border of the frame, use BORDERCOLOR= attribute in the < FRAME > tag as in following statement:

```
<FRAME BORDERCOLOR= #FF0000>
```

The above statement sets the color of the border of the frame to red as shown in following Fig. 4.5.

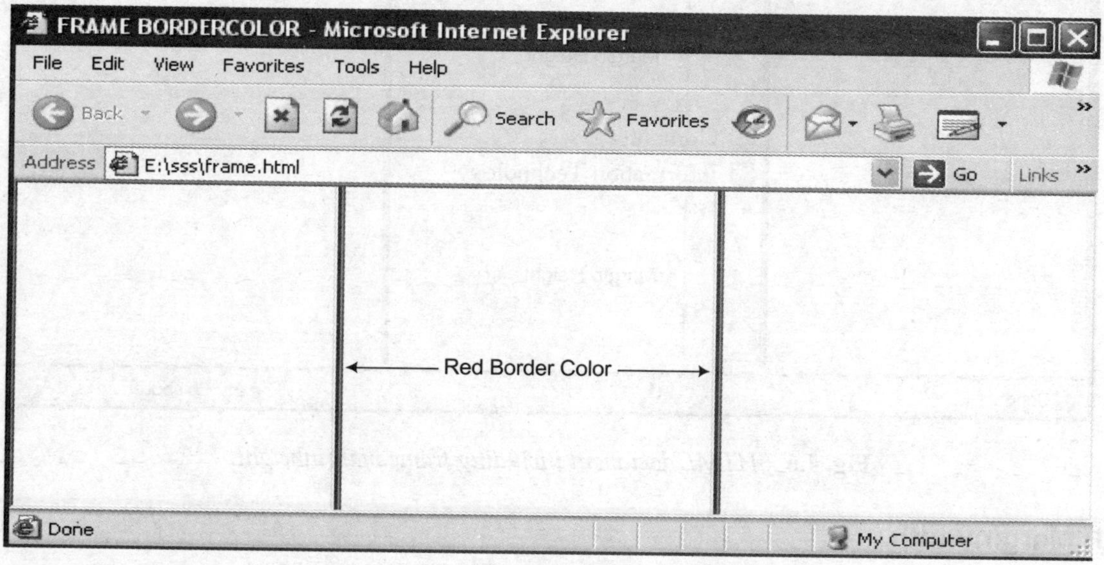

Fig. 4.5 *HTML document including frame bordercolor.*

(c) Marginheight

The MARGINHEIGHT leaves the space above and below the content of the frame. The space is specified by using MARGINHEIGHT= *n*, where *n* is number of pixels. Table following shows the use of the MARGINHEIGHT= attribute in the < FRAME > tag.

Tags/Attributes	*Use*
<FRAME>	Create a frame in frameset document. It identifies frame characteristics and initial content.
MARGINHEIGHT= *n*	Leaves the space above and below the content of the frame. Value is number of pixels.

For example, to leave the space above and below the content of the frame, use MARGINHEIGHT= attribute in the < FRAME > tag as in following statement:

```
<FRAME SRC="E:\sss\form.html" MARGINHEIGHT=70>
```

The above statement leaves the 70 pixels space above and below the content of the frame as shown in following Fig. 4.6.

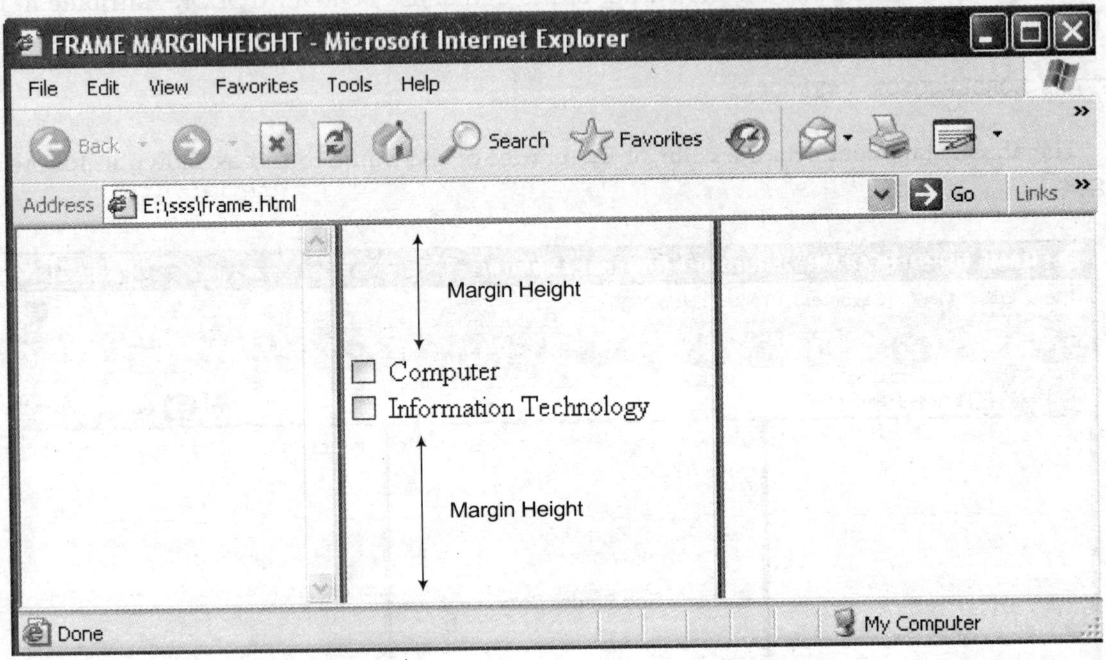

Fig. 4.6 *HTML document including frame marginheight.*

(d) Marginwidth

The MARGINWIDTH leaves the space to the left and right the content of the frame. The space is specified by using MARGINWIDTH= *n*, where *n* is number of pixels. Table following shows the use of the MARGINWIDTH= attribute in the < FRAME > tag.

Tags/Attributes	*Use*
<FRAME>	Create a frame in frameset document. It identifies frame characteristics and initial content.
MARGINWIDTH= *n*	Leaves the space to the left and right the content of the frame. Value is number of pixels.

For example, to leave the space left and right the content of the frame, use MARGINWIDTH= attribute in the < FRAME > tag as in following statement:

```
<FRAME SRC="E:\sss\form.html" MARGINWIDTH=40>
```

The above statement leaves the 40 pixels space to the left and right the content of the frame as shown in following Fig. 4.7.

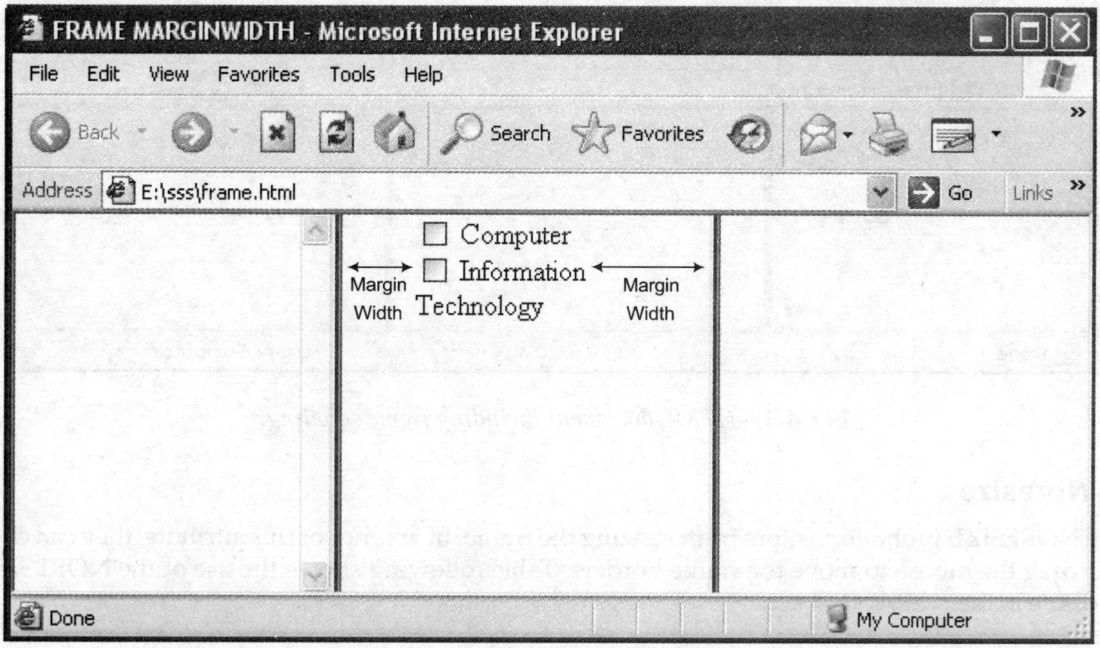

Fig. 4.7 *HTML document including frame marginwidth.*

(e) Scrolling

The SCROLLING lets the browser provide scrolling if required (by default). It is specified by using SCROLLING= "…", where quotation marks contains possible values- YES, NO, and AUTO. Table following shows the use of the SCROLLING= attribute in the < FRAME > tag.

Tags/Attributes	*Use*
<FRAME>	Create a frame in frameset document. It identifies frame characteristics and initial content.
SCROLLING= "…"	Provides scrolling if required (by default). Quotation marks contain possible values- YES, NO, and AUTO.

For example, to provide the scroll bar if required for the frame, use SCROLLING= attribute in the < FRAME > tag as in following statement:

```
<FRAME BORDERCOLOR=#ff0000 SCROLLING=YES>
```

The above statement provides scrolling to the frame as shown in following Fig. 4.8.

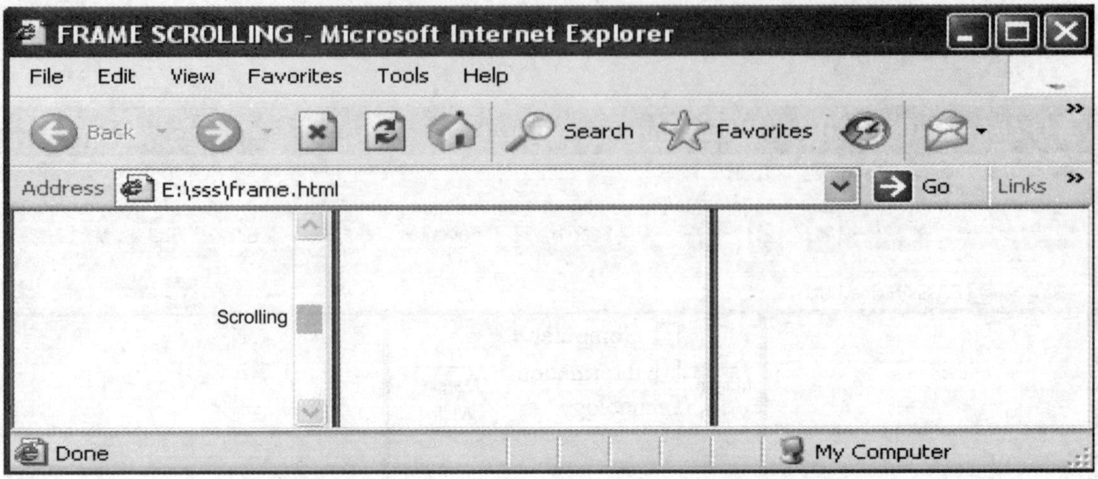

Fig. 4.8 *HTML document including frame scrolling.*

(f) Noresize

The NORESIZE prohibits visitors from resizing the frame. In absence of this attribute, they can click and drag the mouse to move the frame borders. Table following shows the use of the NORESIZE attribute in the < FRAME > tag.

Tags/Attributes	*Use*
<FRAME>	Create a frame in frameset document. It identifies frame characteristics and initial content.
NORESIZE	Prohibits visitors from resizing the frame.

For example, to prohibit visitors from resizing the frame, use NORESIZE attribute in the < FRAME > tag as in following statement:

```
<FRAME NORESIZE>
```

The above statement prohibits visitors from resizing the frame.

To format frames, use above attributes in the <FRAME> or <FRAMESET> tag in the HTML document, as follows:

```
<HTML>
  <HEAD>
    <TITLE> FRAME </TITLE>
  </HEAD>
```

```
  <FRAMESET COLS="30%,*,*" BORDER=20 FRAMEBORDER=1 BORDERCOLOR= #FF0000>
    <FRAME SRC="" NAME="A" SCROLLING=YES>
    <FRAME SRC="F:\image.html" NAME="B" MARGINWIDTH=40>
    <FRAME SRC="" NAME="C">
  </FRAMESET>
</HTML>
```

The output is displayed in the browser as shown in following Fig. 4.9 containing frames formatted using bordercolor, marginwidth, scrolling attributes.

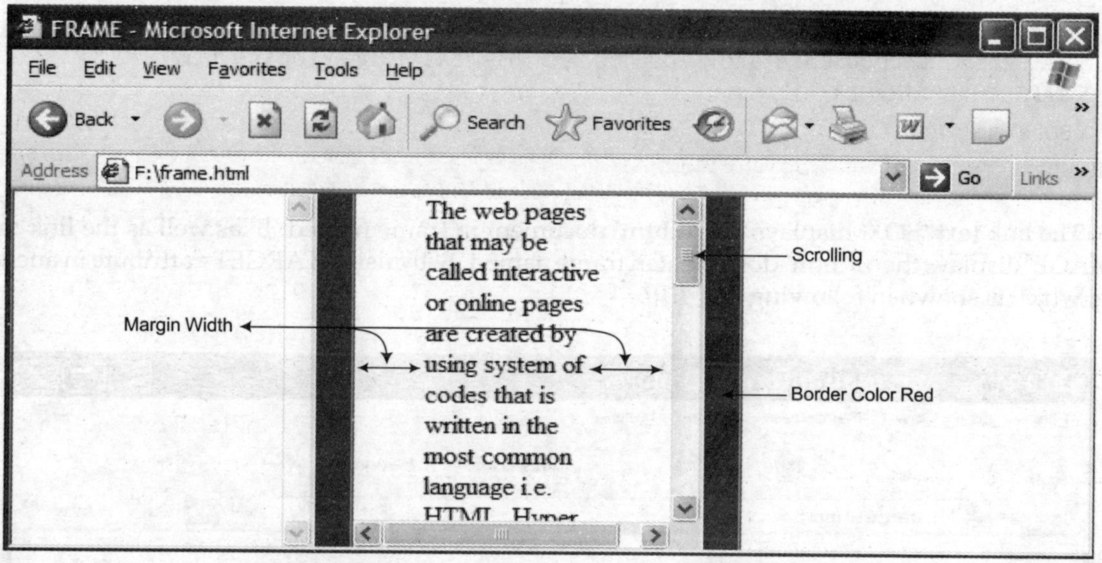

Fig. 4.9 *HTML document including all frame attributes.*

4.3 FRAME TARGETING

HTML enables you to place specific content in a particular window or place. Use NAME= attribute of <FRAME> tag to target the named frame.

Following example shows how to make frame targeting from frame A to frame B.

```
<HTML>
  <HEAD>
    <TITLE> FRAME TARGETING </TITLE>
  </HEAD>
  <FRAMESET COLS="30%,*">
    <FRAME SRC="F:\link.html" NAME="A">
    <FRAME SRC="" NAME="B">
  </FRAMESET>
</HTML>
```

Frame named 'A' is called as source frame and frame named 'B' is called as destination frame or target frame. Frame 'A' contains 'link.html' document containing following lines.

```
<HTML>
  <HEAD>
    <TITLE>FRAME</TITLE>
  </HEAD>
  <BODY>
    <A HREF="C:\Documents and Settings\Administrator\Desktop\d.htm"
    TARGET="B">BOX</A>
    <BR>
    <A HREF="C:\Documents and Settings\Administrator\Desktop\s1.htm"
    TARGET="B">IMAGE</A>
  </BODY>
</HTML>
```

The link text 'BOX' displays the 'd.htm' document in frame named 'B' as well as the link text 'IMAGE' displays the 's1.htm' document in frame named 'B' by using TARGET= attribute in anchor tag, which is shown in following Fig. 4.10.

Fig. 4.10 *HTML document containing frame targeting.*

Use of TARGET attribute in anchor tag is described in following table.

Target/Attributes	*Use*
TARGET= "..."	Sets the link to open in the frame named between the quotes.
TARGET="_self"	Sets the link to open in the current frame.
TARGET="_blank"	Sets the link to open in the new window.
TARGET="_parent"	Sets the link to open in the current frameset of the current document. If only one frameset is present, this removes the frameset.
TARGET="_top"	Sets the link to open in the browser window, breaking out all frames.

4.4 ADVANTAGES AND DISADVANTAGES OF FRAMES

Advantages

1. Frames can make your site easier to navigate because it divides the browser window into set of smaller windows each contains related documents.
2. Frames can make your site faster because it reduces downloading time. Visitors can download only the content pages and not static elements such as logos and navigation menus.
3. Use of frames can make easier to design and maintain your site because frames separate content from navigation element and structural element.
4. Frames can improve site usability. Navigation remains visible as content changes in a separate frame.
5. Frames can make your site more interesting and can also allow you to have permanently visible advertising banner.

Disadvantages

1. Frame navigation is mystery to many and the mystery is compounded because many frame sites have links that seem to appear randomly in different frames or windows.
2. Frames may take up more space than required. Because some site was designed for 800 by 600 or better resolution, but when this site is viewed at some 640 by 480 resolution, appearance degrades drastically.
3. Frames can make difficult for visitors to direct to particular page on your site.

PRACTICE

Create a frameset that divides the browser window into horizontal and vertical frames.

```
<HTML>
<HEAD>
<TITLE> FRAME </TITLE>
</HEAD>
<FRAMESET COLS="30%,*">
```

```
<FRAMESET ROWS= "50%,*">
   <FRAME SRC="" NAME="A">
   <FRAME SRC="" NAME="B">
</FRAMESET>
   <FRAME SRC="" NAME="C">
</FRAMESET>
</HTML>
```

Initially the browser is divided into two vertical frames each of is 30% width and * i.e. remaining width of the browser. The first vertical frame of width 30% has further divided horizontally into frames each of has 50% width and * i.e., remaining width of the first vertical frame. The result of the above HTML document is shown in following figure.

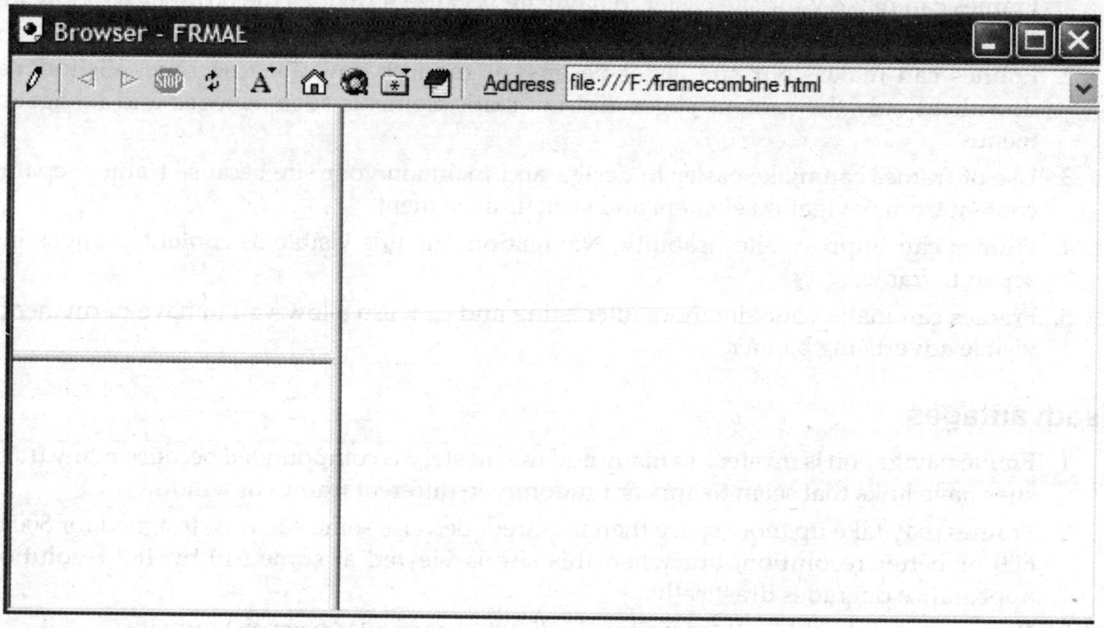

QUESTIONS

1. How to create frames in the HTML Document? Explain?
2. Explain the use of the Border, Bordercolor, Marginwidth, Marginheight and Scrolling attributes of the frame in HTML.
3. Write short note on – Frame Targeting.
4. Explain the advantages and disadvantages of the frame.
5. How to nest the frames?

5

Development of Tables

5.1 CREATING BASIC TABLE TAGS

A table is nothing but combination of rows and columns. The single combination of row and column is called cell, which contains actual data. The table usually contains four components- table heading, column labels, row labels, and actual data containing cell. These components are organized in following elements.

Table Element

Table which defines the entire table is the root table creation element i.e., it acts as the basic table element which contains all the other table elements. It is represented by <TABLE> element. To define table in the web page, include opening and closing <TABLE> tags containing all the other table elements, as follows:

```
<TABLE>
    ...
</TABLE>
```

So, all other table elements are children elements of TABLE element, which are discussed as follows:

TR Element: Table Row Element

The TR element is represented by <TR> tag. The TR element is used to introduce single row into the table. To include rows, use opening and closing <TR> tags in the basic opening and closing <TABLE> tags, as follows:

```
<TABLE>
   <TR> ...</TR>
   <TR> ...</TR>
</TABLE>
```

So, it follows that TR is a child element of TABLE.

TD Element: Table Data Element

The TD element is represented by <TD> tag. The TD element is used to introduce the data cell in the row of the table. To include the data cell, use opening and closing <TD> tags in the basic opening and closing <TR> tags of the <TABLE> tag, as follows:

```
<TABLE>
  <TR> <TD> …</TD> </TR>
  <TR> <TD> …</TD> </TR>
</TABLE>
```

So, it follows that TD is a child element of TR.

TH Element: Table Heading Element

The TH element is represented by <TH> tag. The TH element is used to introduce the single heading cell within a defined row of the table. To include the heading cell, use opening and closing <TH> tags in the basic opening and closing <TR> tags of the <TABLE> tag, as follows:

```
<TABLE>
  <TH> …</TH>
  <TH> …</TH>
</TABLE>
```

So, it follows that TH is a child element of TABLE. By default, a table heading is formatted in boldface.

5.2 FORMATTING TABLES USING ATTRIBUTES BORDERS, BORDER COLOR, BACKGROUND, ALIGN, WIDTH, NO WRAP, CELL SPACING, AND CELL HEIGHTING

The HTML 'TABLE' element is the basic table element which contains all the other table elements. If this table element is omitted, then rest of the elements will be ignored. All other table elements have to be included between < TABLE >…</TABLE> elements.

The TABLE element has following table attributes:

(a) Border

The BORDER attribute draws the border around the table. By default, tables are shown without border. The size of the border can be specified by using BORDER=Value, where Value should be a pixel value. Table following shows the use of the BORDER attribute in the <TABLE> tag.

Tags/Attributes	*Use*
<TABLE>	Defines the entire table in the web page.
BORDER= *n*	Specifies the width of the border. *n* should be a pixel value.

For example, to include border to the table, add the BORDER= attribute in the <TABLE> tag, like this:

```
<TABLE BORDER=5>...</TABLE>
```

The above statement will draws the border around the table with border size 5 pixel value as shown in following Figure 5.1.

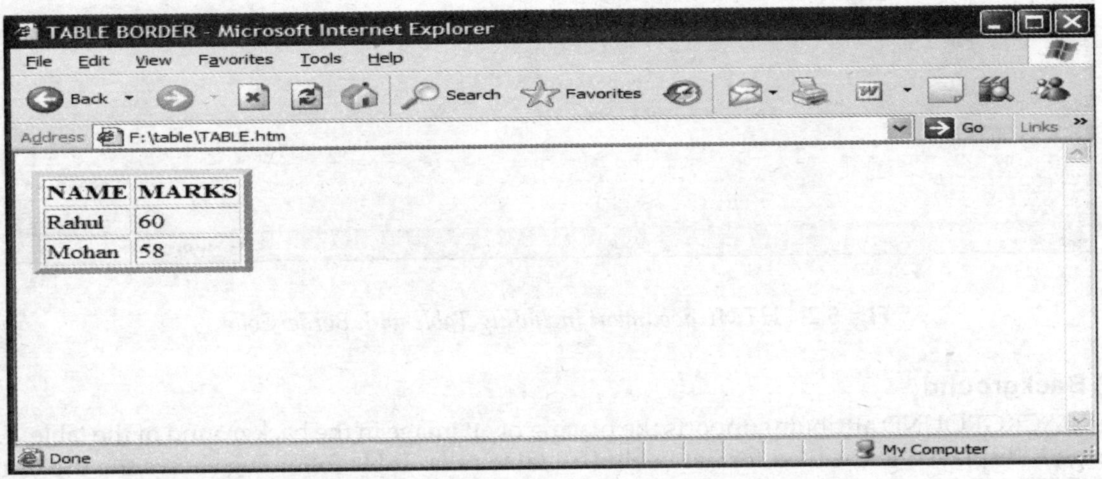

Fig. 5.1 *HTML document including Table with Border.*

(b) Bordercolor

The BORDERCOLOR sets the color of the border of the table. Any of the predefined colors or a #rrggbb hexadecimal triplet can be specified for the border color. Table following shows the use of the BORDERCOLOR= attribute in the <TABLE> tag.

Tags/Attributes	*Use*
<TABLE>	Defines the entire table in the web page.
BORDERCOLOR= "..."	Sets the color for the border of the table. Any of the predefined colors or a #rrggbb hexadecimal triplet can be specified for the bordercolor.

For example, to include bordercolor to the table, add the BORDERCOLOR= attribute in the <TABLE> tag, like this:

```
<TABLE BORDER=2 BORDERCOLOR=green>...</TABLE>
```

The above statement sets the color of the border of the table to green as shown in following Figure 5.2.

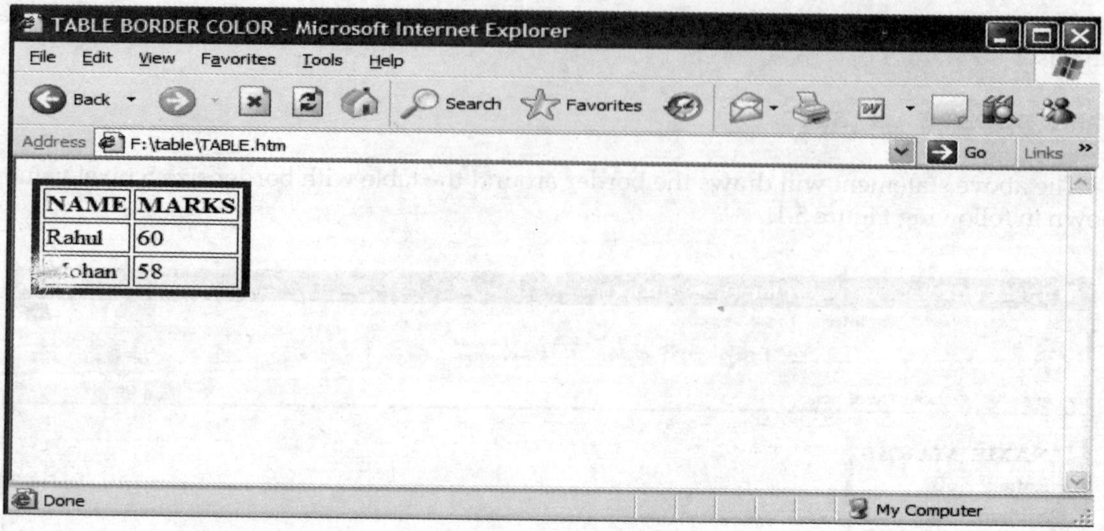

Fig. 5.2 *HTML document including Table with BorderColor.*

(c) Background

The BACKGROUND attribute supports the placing of an image in the background of the table. The image is displayed in the tiled format behind all table cells. Table following shows the use of the BACKGROUND attribute in the <TABLE> tag.

Tags/Attributes	*Use*
<TABLE>	Defines the entire table in the web page.
BACKGROUND = "URL"	Places an image in the background of the table. URL specifies the location of the image file on the internet or on the local machine.

The syntax of this attribute is as follows:

```
<TABLE BACKGROUND="URL">...</TABLE>
```

Where URL is the location of the image file on the internet or on the local machine.

For example, to include background image to the table, add the BACKGROUND= attribute in the <TABLE> tag, like this:

```
<TABLE BORDER=2 WIDTH=50% HEIGHT=50% BACKGROUND="E:/Web Project/TempKop/HomeBazar/
NewAds/DELTON.GIF">
```

The above statement places DELTON.GIF picture file in the background of the table as shown in following Figure 5.3.

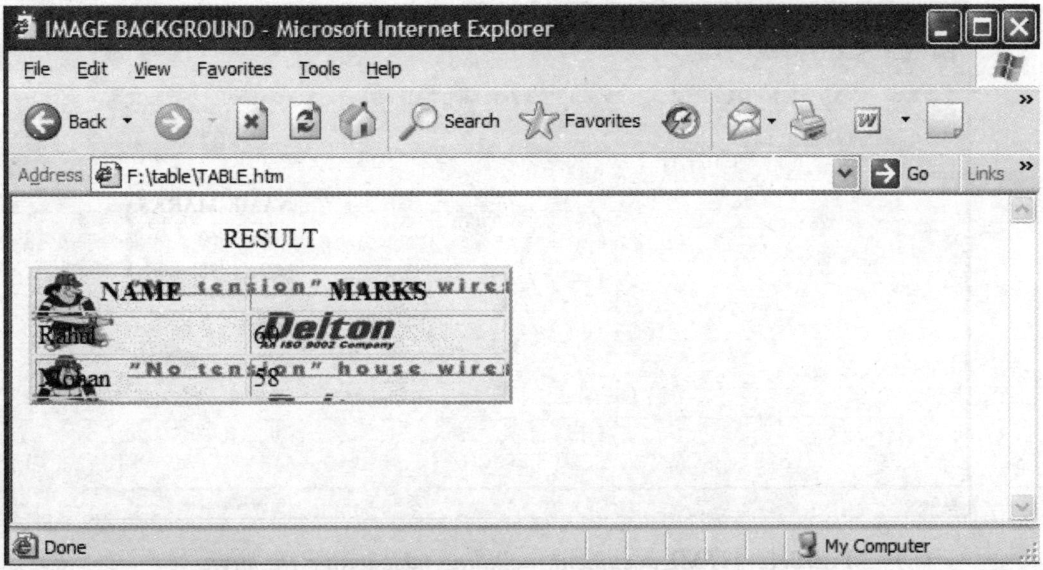

Fig. 5.3 *HTML document including table with background image.*

(d) Align

This attribute is used to align the table to either left or right of the page. By default, the table is aligned to the left of the page. Table following shows the use of the ALIGN attribute in the <TABLE> tag.

Tags/Attributes	*Use*
<TABLE>	Defines the entire table in the web page.
ALIGN= "..."	Specifies the table alignment as LEFT, CENTER, and RIGHT.

For example, to include table alignments, add the ALIGN= attribute in the <TABLE> tag, like this:

```
< TABLE ALIGN= "right">...</TABLE>
```

The above statement aligns the table to the right of the page as shown in following Figure 5.4.

(e) Width

This attribute is used to set the width of the table. The width is measured either as absolute width or a percentage of the document width. Table following shows the use of the WIDTH= attribute in the <TABLE> tag.

Tags/Attributes	*Use*
<TABLE>	Defines the entire table in the web page.
WIDTH= "*n or %* "	Specifies the table width in pixels or as a percentage of the window width.

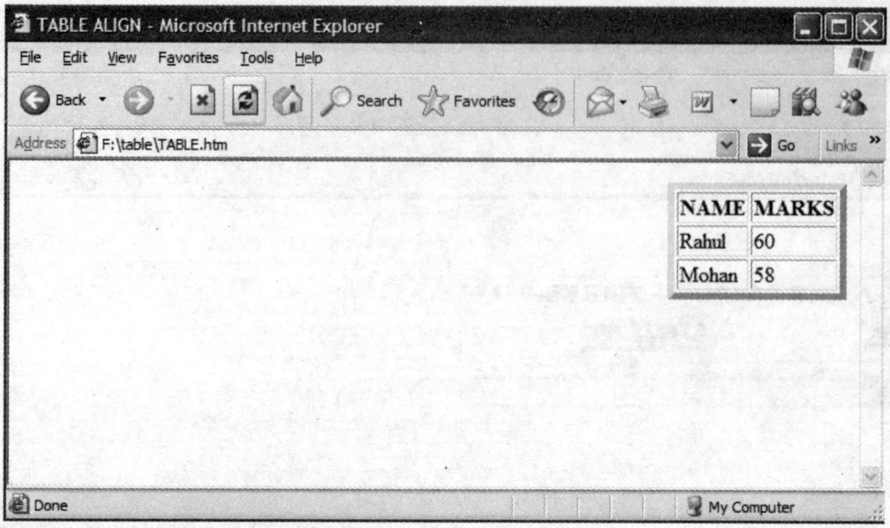

Fig. 5.4 *HTML document including table with right align.*

The syntax of this attribute is as follows:

```
<TABLE WIDTH= n or Percentage>…</TABLE>
```

For example, to change the width of the table, add the WIDTH= attribute in the <TABLE> tag, like this:

```
<TABLE WIDTH= 50%>…</TABLE>
```

The above statement specifies that the table occupies the half width of the total width of the web page as shown in following Figure 5.5.

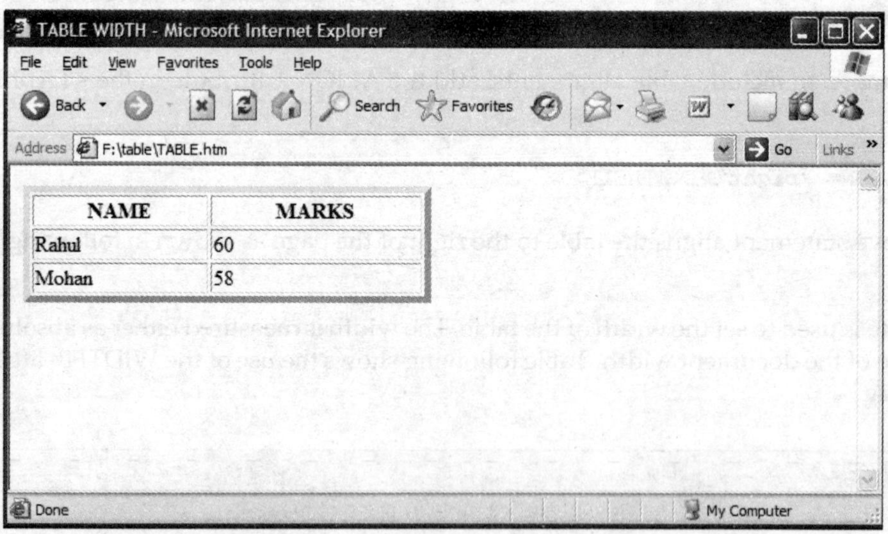

Fig. 5.5 *HTML document including table with table width.*

(f) Nowrap

If the NOWRAP attribute is used, the lines within the cell can not be broken to fit the width of the cell. This attribute should be used carefully because resulting width will be increased. Table following shows the use of the NOWRAP attribute in the <TABLE> tag.

Tags/Attributes	*Use*
<TABLE>	Defines the entire table in the web page.
NOWRAP	Prohibits text wrapping within the cell, thus all text appears on one line.

For example, to include nowrap to the table, add the NOWRAP attribute in the <TABLE> tag, like this:

```
<TABLE WIDTH= 50%  NOWRAP>…</TABLE>
```

The above statement specifies that the table as shown in following Figure 5.6.

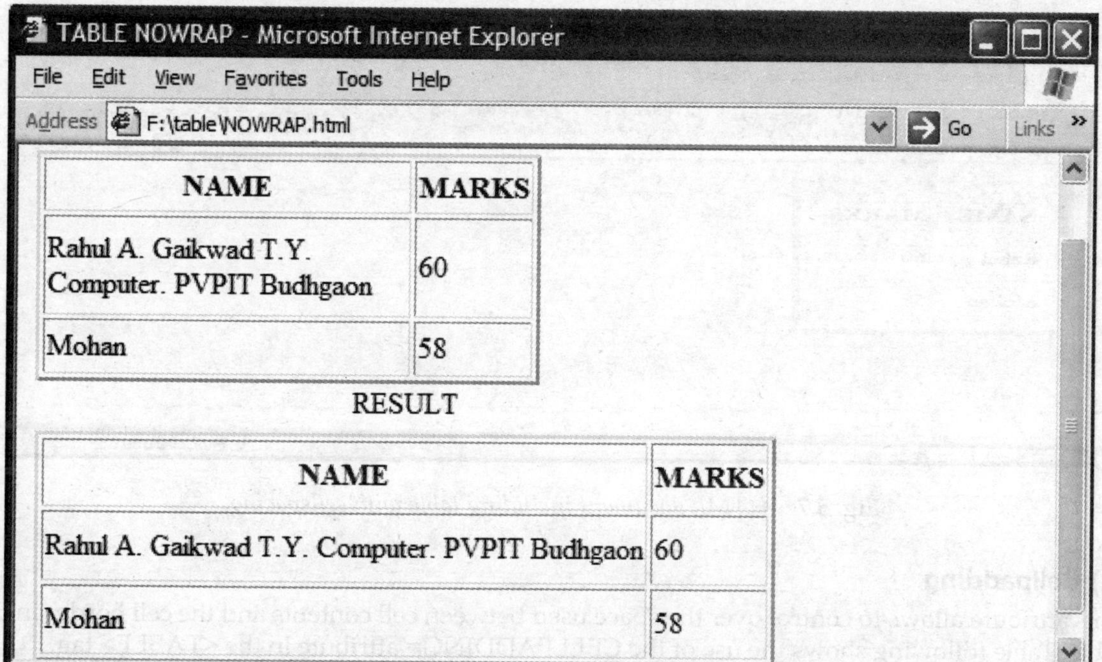

Fig. 5.6 *HTML document including table with nowrap.*

(g) Cellspacing

This attribute allows to control over the space used between cells in the table. Table following shows the use of the CELLSPACING= attribute in the <TABLE> tag.

Tags/Attributes	*Use*
<TABLE>	Defines the entire table in the web page.
CELLSPACING = "*n*"	Specifies in pixels the amount of space between cells.

The syntax of this attribute is as follows:

```
<TABLE CELLSPACING = n>...</TABLE>
```

Where *n* should be a pixel value.

For example, to include space between cells in the table, add the CELLSPACING = attribute in the <TABLE> tag, like this:

```
<TABLE CELLSPACING = 15>...</TABLE>
```

The above statement introduces 15 pixels space between cells in the table as shown in following Figure 5.7.

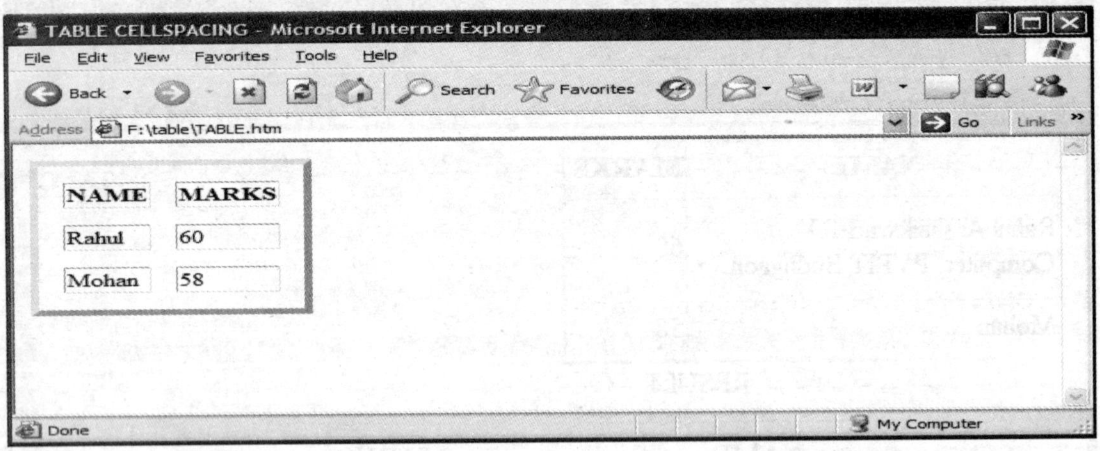

Fig. 5.7 *HTML document including table with cellspacing.*

(h) Cellpadding

This attribute allows to control over the space used between cell contents and the cell border in the table. Table following shows the use of the CELLPADDING= attribute in the <TABLE> tag.

Tags/Attributes	*Use*
<TABLE>	Defines the entire table in the web page.
CELLPADDING = "*n*"	Specifies in pixels the amount of space between cell contents and the cell border.

The syntax of this attribute is as follows:

```
<TABLE CELLPADDING = n>…</TABLE>
```

Where *n* should be a pixel value.

For example, to include space between cell contents and the cell border in the table, add the CELLSPADDING = attribute in the <TABLE> tag, like this:

```
<TABLE CELLPADDING = 15>…</TABLE>
```

The above statement introduces 15 pixels space between cell contents and the cell border in the table as shown in following Figure 5.8.

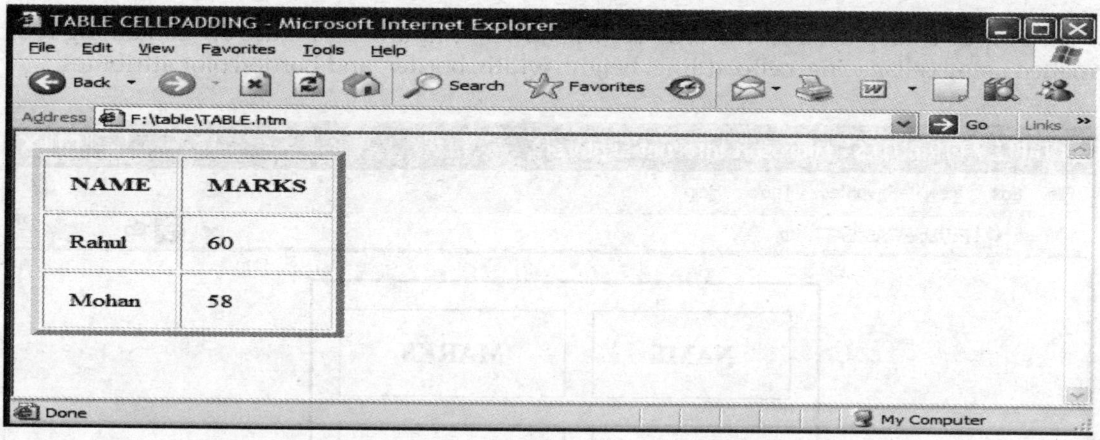

Fig. 5.8 *HTML document including table with cellpadding.*

For example, to edit table, use above attributes in the <TABLE> tag in the HTML document, as follows:

```
<HTML>
  <HEAD>
    <TITLE>TABLE ATTRIBUTES</TITLE>
  </HEAD>
  <BODY>
    <TABLE BORDER=2 BORDERCOLOR=#6600FF CELLSPACING=15 CELLPADDING=15 ALIGN=CENTER
    WIDTH=50% HEIGHT=50%>
    <CAPTION>RESULT</CAPTION>
      <TR>
        <TH>NAME </TH>
        <TH>MARKS </TH>
      </TR>
```

```
      <TR>
         <TD>Rahul</TD>
         <TD>60</TD>
      </TR>
      <TR>
         <TD>Mohan</TD>
         <TD>58</TD>
      </TR>
    </TABLE>
  </BODY>
</HTML>
```

The output is displayed in the browser as shown in following Figure 5.9 containing a table formatted using cellspacing, cellpadding, height, width, border, and bordercolor attributes.

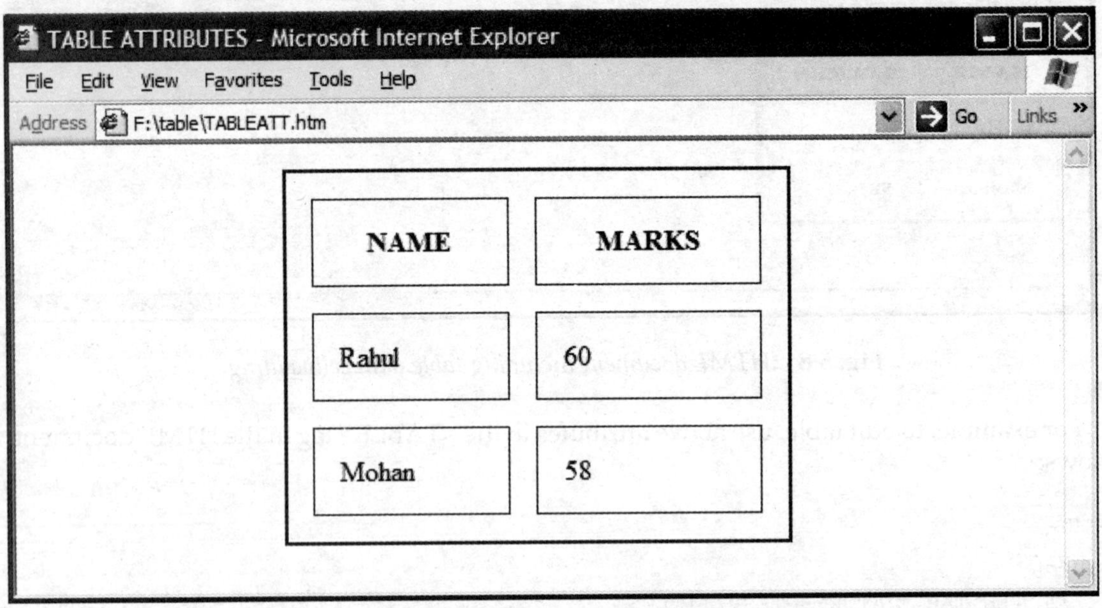

Fig. 5.9 *HTML document including Table with all table formatting attributes.*

5.3 ADDING CAPTION:- <CAPTION>…</CAPTION>

This element is used to specify the caption for the table. The CAPTION element should appear inside the TABLE element, but not inside table rows or cells. So, it follows that CAPTION is a child element of TABLE element. This element, by default, displays text center aligned at top of the table.

For example,

```
<TABLE>
<CAPTION>Table</CAPTION>
.
.
.
</TABLE>
```

Displays caption 'Table' center-aligned at the top of the table.

To include caption for the table, include above statements in the following HTML document as:

```
<HTML>
<HEAD>
<TITLE>EDITING COLUMNS</TITLE>
</HEAD>
<BODY>
<TABLE BORDER=2 WIDTH=50% HEIGHT=50%>
<CAPTION>RESULT</CAPTION>
  <TR>
    <TH>NAME </TH>
    <TH>MARKS </TH>
  </TR>
  <TR>
    <TD>Rahul</TD>
    <TD>60</TD>
  </TR>
  <TR>
    <TD>Mohan</TD>
    <TD>58</TD>
  </TR>
</TABLE>
</BODY>
</HTML>
```

The output is displayed in the browser as shown in following Figure 5.10 containing the caption "RESULT" for the table.

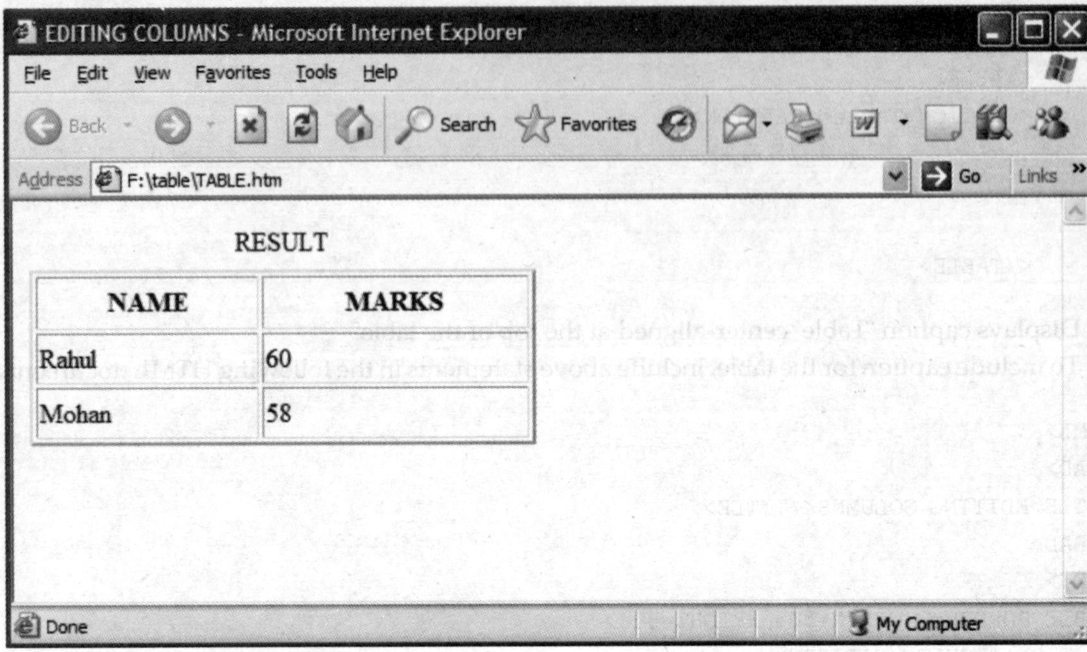

Fig. 5.10 *HTML document including Table with Caption.*

5.4 EDITING ROWS AND COLUMNS OF THE TABLE

In order to introduce a single row in the table, we use <TR>…</TR> element in the <TABLE>…</TABLE> element. It is container element which contains the <TD>…</TD> element. The number of rows in a table depends on how many <TR> elements are contained within the table, regardless of the cells that may attempt to use the ROWSPAN attribute, where one row can span the width of more than one row.

In order to edit the rows in the table, the TR element has following attributes:

(a) Align

This attribute controls the alignment of the text inside the table row cells to the left, right, or center by using values left, right, or middle. This attribute for example, can be set as follows:

```
<TR ALIGN=left>…</TR>
```

The above statement aligns the text of the cells contained in single row to the left.

(b) Valign

This attribute controls the alignment of the text inside the row cells to the top, bottom or center vertically. The values used are TOP, MIDDLE, BOTTOM and BASELINE. This attribute, for example can be set as follows:

```
<TR VALIGN=MIDDLE>...</TR>
```

The above statement aligns the text of the cells contained in single row to the middle.

(c) Bgcolor

This attribute of the TR element allows the background color to be set for the table row. Either the predefined color names or #rrggbb hexadecimal triplet can be used to specify the background color.

For example, the statement,

```
<TR BGCOLOR = #ff0000>...</TR>
```

Shows the color of the row as red.

(d) Bordercolor

The BORDERCOLOR attribute sets the bordercolor of the row. Either the predefined color names or #rrggbb hexadecimal triplet can be used to specify the bordercolor of the row.

For example, the statement,

```
<TR BORDERCOLOR = #00ff00>...</TR>
```

Shows the color of the border of the row as green.

(e) Bordercolorlight

This attribute is set independently with the lighter color to be displayed on a three dimensional table border. Any of the predefined color names or #rrggbb hexadecimal triplet can be used to specify the color.

For example, the statement,

```
<TR BORDERCOLORLIGHT = green>...</TR>
```

Shows a lighter green color of the row border.

(f) Bordercolordark

This attribute is set independently with the darker color to be displayed on a three dimensional table border. Any of the predefined color names or #rrggbb hexadecimal triplet can be used to specify the color.

For example, the statement,

```
<TR BORDERCOLORDARK = green>...</TR>
```

Shows a darker green color of the row border.

For example, to edit table rows, add above attributes in the <TR> tag in the HTML document, as follows:

```
<HTML>
<HEAD>
<TITLE>EDITING ROWS</TITLE>
</HEAD>
<BODY>
<TABLE BORDER=2 WIDTH=50% HEIGHT=50%>
  <TR BORDERCOLOR = green>
    <TH>NAME </TH>
    <TH>MARKS </TH>
  </TR>
  <TR BGCOLOR = #ff0000>
    <TD>Rahul</TD>
    <TD>60</TD>
  </TR>
  <TR ALIGN=RIGHT>
    <TD>Mohan</TD>
    <TD>58</TD>
  </TR>
</TABLE>
</BODY>
</HTML>
```

The output is displayed in the browser as shown in following Figure 5.11 containing the heading row with border color green, second row with background color red and third row containing alignment right.

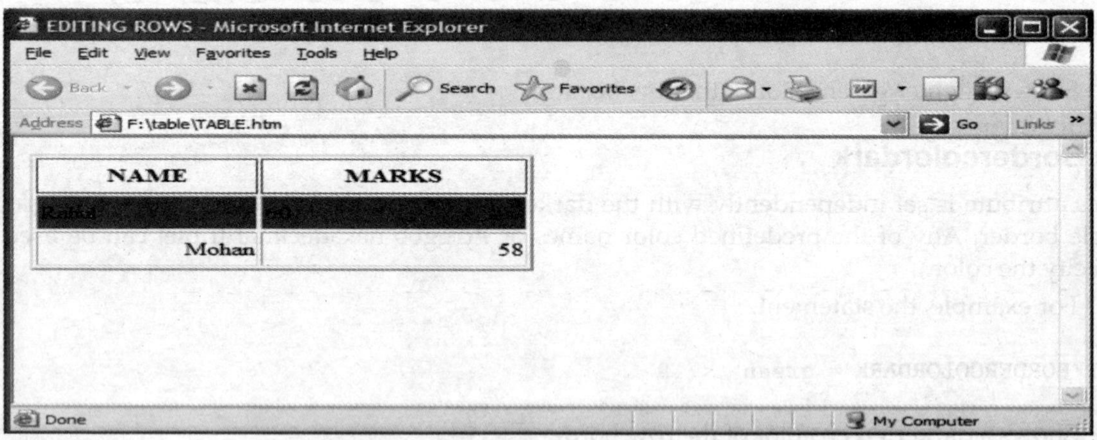

Fig. 5.11 *HTML document including Table with Row Editing.*

In order to introduce a columns in the table, use <TH>...</TH> elements to the top row and <TD>...</TD> elements to each of the other rows. In order to edit the columns in the table, the TH or TD element has following attributes:

(a) Align

This attribute controls the alignment of the text inside the table data or heading cell to the left, right, or center by using values Left, Right, or Middle. This attribute for example, can be set as follows:

```
<TH ALIGN=left>…</TH>
Or
<TD ALIGN=left>…</TD>
```

The above statement aligns the text of the data or heading cell to the left.

(b) Valign

This attribute controls the alignment of the text inside the table data or heading cell to the top, bottom or center vertically. The values used are TOP, MIDDLE, BOTTOM and BASELINE. This attribute for example, can be set as follows:

```
<TH VALIGN= BOTTOM >…</TH>
Or
<TD VALIGN= BOTTOM >…</TD>
```

The above statement aligns the text of the data or heading cell to the bottom.

(c) Bgcolor

This attribute of the TR or TD element allows the background color to be set for the table data cell or heading cell. Either the predefined color names or #rrggbb hexadecimal triplet can be used to specify the background color.

For example, the statement,

```
<TH BGCOLOR = #ff0000>…</TH>
Or
<TD BGCOLOR = #ff0000>…</TD>
```

Shows the color of the table data cell or heading cell as red.

(d) Bordercolor

The BORDERCOLOR attribute sets the bordercolor of the table data cell or heading cell. Either the predefined color names or #rrggbb hexadecimal triplet can be used to specify the bordercolor of the table data cell or heading cell.

For example, the statement,

```
<TH BGCOLOR = #ff0000>...</TH>
Or
<TD BGCOLOR = #ff0000>...</TD>
```

Shows the color of the border of the table data cell or heading cell as red.

(e) Bordercolorlight

This attribute is set independently with the lighter color to be displayed on a table data cell or heading cell border. Any of the predefined color names or #rrggbb hexadecimal triplet can be used to specify the color.

For example, the statement,

```
<TH BORDERCOLORLIGHT = #00ff00>...</TH>
Or
<TD BORDERCOLORLIGHT = #00ff00>...</TD>
```

Shows a lighter green color of the table data cell or heading cell border.

(f) Bordercolordark

This attribute is set independently with the darker color to be displayed on a table data cell or heading cell border. Any of the predefined color names or #rrggbb hexadecimal triplet can be used to specify the color.

For example, the statement,

```
<TH BORDERCOLORDARK = #00ff00>...</TH>
Or
<TD BORDERCOLORDARK = #00ff00>...</TD>
```

Shows a darker green color of the table data cell or heading cell border.

For example, to edit table columns, add above attributes in the <TH> or <TD> tag in the HTML document, as follows:

```
<HTML>
<HEAD>
<TITLE>EDITING COLUMNS</TITLE>
</HEAD>
<BODY>
<TABLE BORDER=2 WIDTH=50% HEIGHT=50%>
```

```
   <TR>
     <TH BORDERCOLOR = green>NAME </TH>
     <TH>MARKS </TH>
   </TR>
   <TR>
     <TD>Rahul</TD>
     <TD BGCOLOR = #00ff00>60</TD>
   </TR>
   <TR>
     <TD ALIGN=RIGHT>Mohan</TD>
     <TD>58</TD>
   </TR>
</TABLE>
</BODY>
</HTML>
```

The output is displayed in the browser as shown in following Figure 5.12 containing the one heading cell in first row with bordercolor green, second data cell in second row with background color green and first data cell in third row containing alignment right.

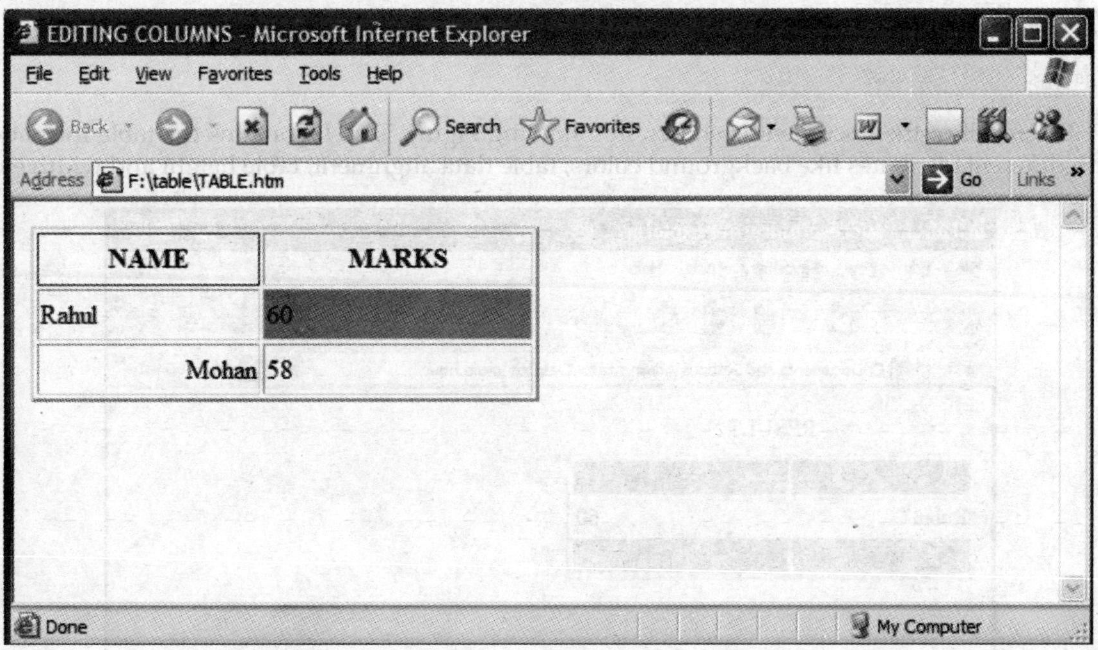

Fig. 5.12 *HTML document including table with cell editing.*

PRACTICE

Create table and format it using basic table tags and attributes.

```
<HTML>
<HEAD>
<TITLE>EDITING COLUMNS</TITLE>
</HEAD>
<BODY>
<TABLE BORDER=2 WIDTH=50% HEIGHT=50%>
  <CAPTION>RESULT</CAPTION>
  <TR BGCOLOR = #ff0000>
    <TH>NAME </TH>
    <TH>MARKS </TH>
  </TR>
  <TR>
    <TD>Rahul</TD>
    <TD ALIGN=RIGHT>60</TD>
  </TR>
  <TR BGCOLOR = #0000ff>
    <TD>Mohan</TD>
    <TD>58</TD>
  </TR>
</TABLE>
</BODY>
</HTML>
```

The result of the document is shown in following Figure 5.12. It contains the table formatted with different attributes like background colors, table data alignment, table height and width etc.

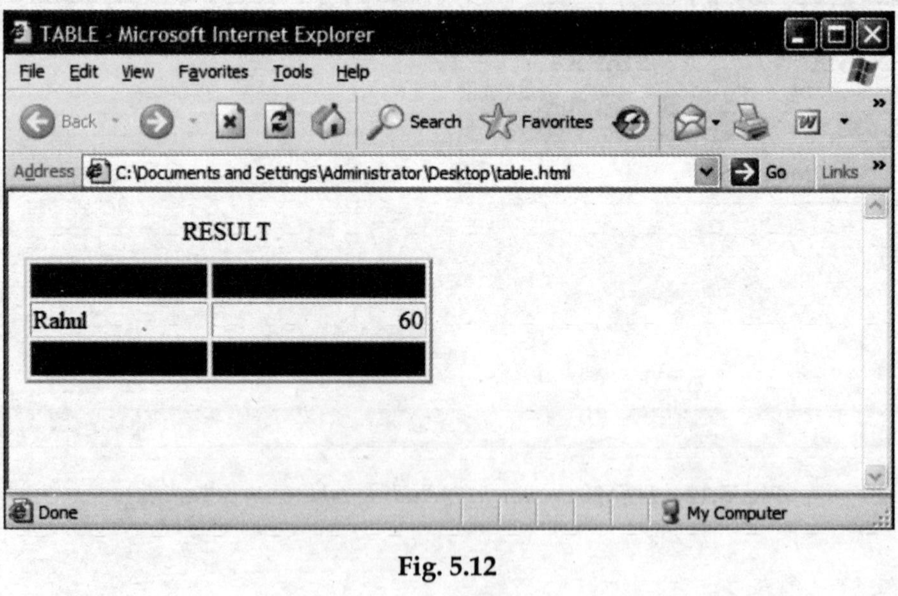

Fig. 5.12

QUESTIONS

1. Explain TABLE, TR, TD, and TH element in details.
2. Explain the use of the Border, BorderColor, CellSpacing, Scale Heightening, NoWrap and align attributes of the tables in HTML.
3. Write short note on Adding caption for the table.
4. How to edit the rows of the table?
5. How to edit the columns of the table?

□□□

6

Including Images

6.1 IMAGE FORMATS

Before understanding how to add inline images in our web page, it is important to look at a few of the different popular image formats found on the internet.

1. GIF (Graphical Interchange Format) Images

The GIF stands for Graphical Interchange Format. The GIF image format was introduced by CompuServe Inc. These images are most commonly found images on the web. Two common versions of the GIF formats are GIF87A and GIF89A.

The size of the GIF image format is smaller than that of other image formats. The GIF supports transparency, interlacing, and a tight and lossless compression technique.

2. JPG/JPEG (Joint Photographic Experts Group) Images

JPG/JPEG stands for Joint Photographic Experts Group. This is the second most popular image file format. This image file format is accepted on the most browsers. Like GIF, this format does not support rendering options. This has ability to accommodate millions of colors so this is good for photographs and for line art. This image format uses a more effective but lossy compression algorithm; they are much smaller and download faster. Lossy compression discards some details of the image to decrease the file size, even though this is best for photographs, because the compression ratio and resulting quality is much better for photographs.

3. PNG (Portable Network Graphics) Images

PNG stands for Portable Network Graphics. This new image file format is not accepted on the most browsers; but it is only supported by most recent browser versions like Microsoft Internet Explorer 4 or later versions and Netscape Navigator 4.04 or later versions. However, PNG images combine the most of the fractures of the GIF, including transparency and interlacing, plus ability to accommodate millions of colors (good for photographs and for line art) and a tight and lossless compression technique.

6.2 EFFECT OF PHYSICAL SIZE AND FILE SIZE OF IMAGE ON DOWNLOADING

File Size: Image is weighted element in the web, so it takes more time to download or to display on the web page. This is due to it is three dimensional file having height, width and color depth in terms of layers. You can reduce the file size and make images as efficient as possible.

There are three ways to reduce the file size:

1. Reduce the depth of the image means reduce the number of colors. Instead of using millions of colors, use 256 colors.
2. Reduce the physical size (height and width) of the image.
3. Use a format which can compress the file and can store more data in less space.

Physical Size: Physical size means the height and the width of image which affects the appearance on the page as well as time to download it. It is included according to it purpose, visitor's requirement, as well as for designing the page.

6.3 THE INLINE IMAGE

The image, which you insert within the web page is called inline image because it is inserted within the body element.

Adding Inline Image: Adding image is similar to adding the tags and attributes you have already used.

To add inline image, use the <IMG> tag, which specifies an image and SRC= attribute to specify the image filename or URL, like this:

```
<IMG SRC= "">
```

if image is located within the same folder as the document.

```
<IMG SRC= "http://www.">
```

if image is located on the web i.e. include absolute URL.

Table following shows the main image tag and attribute used to insert the images in the web pages.

Tags/Attributes	*Use*
<IMG>	Marks an image within an HTML document.
SRC= "..."	Points to an image file (URL).

For example, to add inline image, use the <IMG> tag, along with SRC= attribute to specify the image filename or URL in the HTML document, as follows:

```
<HTML>
  <HEAD>
    <TITLE> INLINE IMAGE </TITLE>
  </HEAD>
  <BODY>
    <IMG SRC= "E:\sss\weblog_r3_c1.jpg">
  </BODY>
</HTML>
```

The output is displayed in the browser as shown in following Fig. 6.1 containing the inline image.

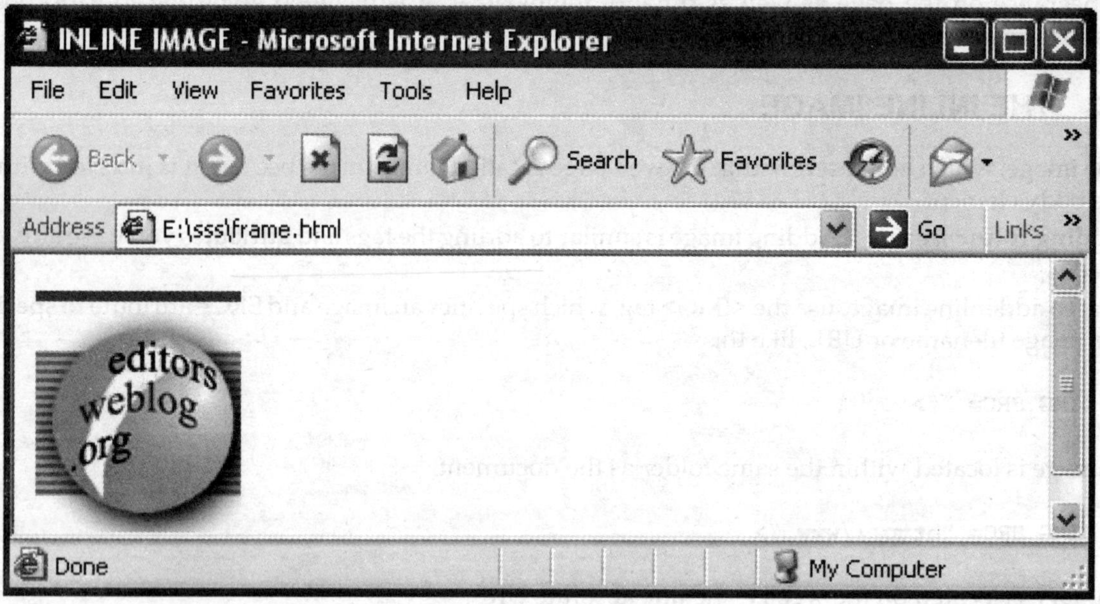

Fig. 6.1 *HTML document including Inline Image.*

Image Alternatives

Alternative text will be used as image alternatives. Alternative text describes an image that you have inserted. Include alternative text because sometimes browsers do not display image correctly, some browsers are text-only browsers, sometimes images are turned off, image links (URL) are not working properly etc.

Alternative text provides the enough information to the visitors, so that they can understand the image without viewing it. For example, it should be image name or its clear and concise specification.

To specify image alternative text, add the ALT= attribute in the <IMG> tag, like this:

```
<IMG SRC= "" ALT= "" >
```

Table following shows the use of the ALT= attribute in the <IMG> tag.

Tags/Attributes	*Use*
<IMG>	Marks an image within an HTML document.
ALT= "..."	Specifies the alternative text to display if an image is not displayed.

For example, to specify image alternative text, add the ALT= "..." attribute in the <IMG> tag in the HTML document, as follows:

```
<HTML>
  <HEAD>
    <TITLE> IMAGE ALTERNATIVE </TITLE>
  </HEAD>
  <BODY>
    <IMG SRC= "E:\sss\weblog_r3_c1.jpg" ALT="weblog Logo">
  </BODY>
</HTML>
```

The output is displayed in the browser as shown in following Fig. 6.2 containing the inline image with Image Alternative attribute.

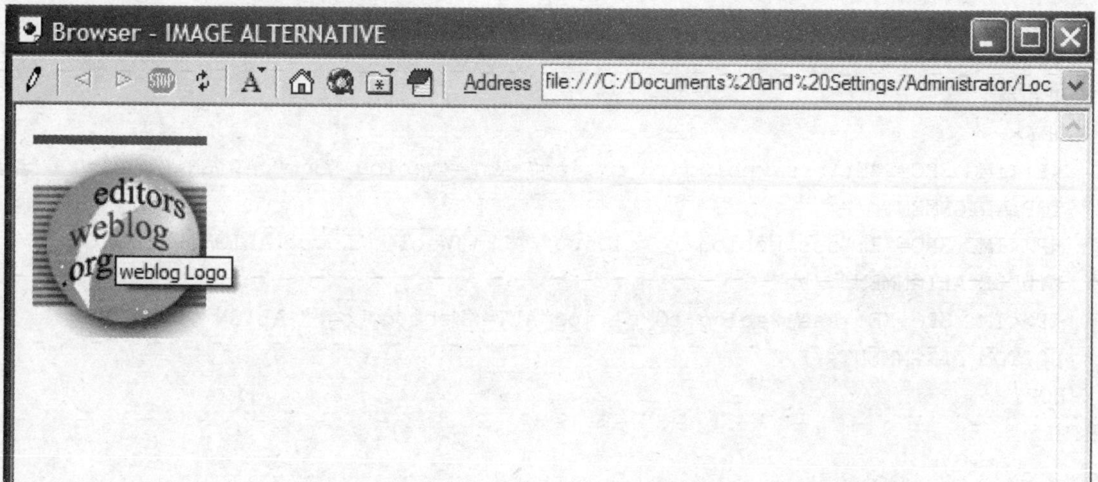

Fig. 6.2 *HTML document including Inline Image with Image Alternative.*

Image Alignment

HTML provides two ways of alignments:

1. Three vertical options align the image with respect to a line of text (top, middle and bottom).
2. Two horizontal options align the image to the left or to the right of the window (with corresponding text wrap).

By default, images align on the left, with a single line of text appearing on the same line; however long text wraps to the following line.

To specify image alignment, add the ALIGN= attribute in the <IMG> tag, like this:

```
<IMG SRC= "" ALT= "" ALIGN= "RIGHT">
```

Displays right aligned image.

Table following shows the use of the ALIGN= attribute in the <IMG> tag.

Tags/Attributes	*Use*
<IMG>	Marks an image within an HTML document.
ALIGN= "..."	Specifies the image alignment as TOP, MIDDLE, BOTTOM, LEFT or RIGHT.

For example, to specify image alignments, add the ALIGN= "..." attribute in the <IMG> tag in the HTML document, as follows:

```
<HTML>
  <HEAD>
    <TITLE> IMAGE ALIGNMENT </TITLE>
  </HEAD>
  <BODY>
    <P><IMG SRC= "E:\sss\weblog_r3_c1.jpg" ALT="Weblog Logo" ALIGN="TOP">
    TOP ALIGNMENT</P>
    <P><IMG SRC="E:\sss\weblog_r3_c1.jpg" ALT="Weblog Logo" ALIGN="MIDDLE">
    MIDDLE ALIGNMENT</P>
    <P><IMG SRC="E:\sss\weblog_r3_c1.jpg"ALT="Weblog Logo" ALIGN="BOTTOM">
    BOTTOM ALIGNMENT</P>
  </BODY>
</HTML>
```

The output is displayed in the browser as shown in following Fig. 6.3 containing the inline image with various Image Alignments with respect to text vertically.

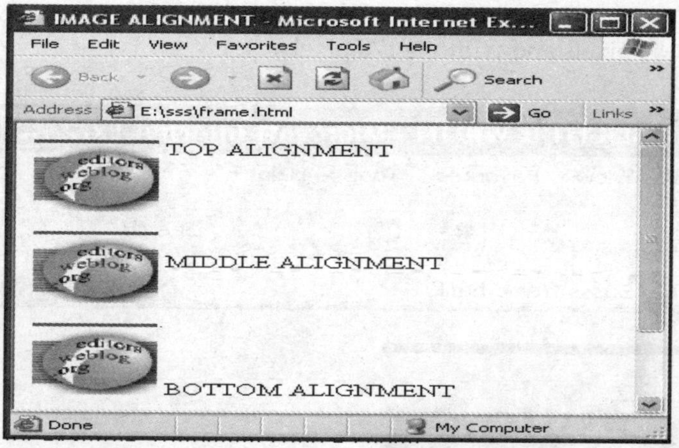

Fig. 6.3 *HTML document including Inline Image with Image Alignment .*

Height and Width

To speed up the loading time of images, specify the image height and width. As the browser loads the page, it notes the height and width attributes and leaves that much space for the image. Next, it lays out the remaining text and then it goes back and fills the image.

To specify image height and width, add the HEIGHT= and WIDTH= attributes in the <IMG> tag, like this:

```
<IMG SRC= "" HEIGHT= "" WIDTH= "" >
```

Table following shows the use of the HEIGHT= and WIDTH= attributes in the <IMG> tag.

Tags/Attributes	*Use*
<IMG>	Marks an image within an HTML document.
HEIGHT= n	Specifies the height of the image in pixels.
WIDTH= n	Specifies the width of the image in pixels.

For example, to specify image height and width, add the HEIGHT=n and WIDTH=n attributes in the <IMG> tag in the HTML document, as follows:

```
<HTML>
  <HEAD>
    <TITLE> IMAGE HEIGHT & WIDTH </TITLE>
  </HEAD>
  <BODY>
    <IMG SRC= "E:\sss\weblog_r3_c1.jpg" ALT="Weblog Logo" HEIGHT=150 WIDTH=170>
  </BODY>
</HTML>
```

The output is displayed in the browser as shown in following Fig. 6.4 containing the inline image with height is 150 pixels and width is 170 pixels.

Fig. 6.4 *HTML document including Inline Image with Image Height and Width.*

HSPACE AND VSPACE

To leave the space horizontally and vertically between the image and the text, specify the amount of horizontal and vertical space in pixels.

To specify horizontal space between the images and the text, add the HSPACE = attribute in the <IMG> tag, like this:

```
<IMG SRC= "" HSPACE= >
```

To specify vertical space between the image and the text, add the VSPACE = attribute in the <IMG> tag, like this:

```
<IMG SRC= "" VSPACE= >
```

Table following shows the use of the HSPACE= and VSPACE= attributes in the <IMG> tag.

Tags/Attributes	*Use*
<IMG>	Marks an image within an HTML document.
HSPACE= n	Specifies the horizontal space between the image and the text in pixels.
VSPACE= n	Specifies the vertical space between the image and the text in pixels.

For example, to specify image horizontal space and vertical space, add the HSPACE= n and the VSPACE= n attributes in the <IMG> tag in the HTML document, as follows:

```
<HTML>
  <HEAD>
    <TITLE> IMAGE HORIZONTAL & VERTICAL SPACE </TITLE>
  </HEAD>
  <BODY>
    <P>IMAGE HORIZONTAL SPACE
    <IMG SRC= "E:\sss\weblog_r3_c1.jpg" ALT="Weblog Logo" HSPACE=170 VSPACE=70>
    </P>
  </BODY>
</HTML>
```

The output is displayed in the browser as shown in following Fig. 6.5 containing the inline image with image horizontal space is 170 pixels from left side and vertical space 70 pixels from the top of the browser.

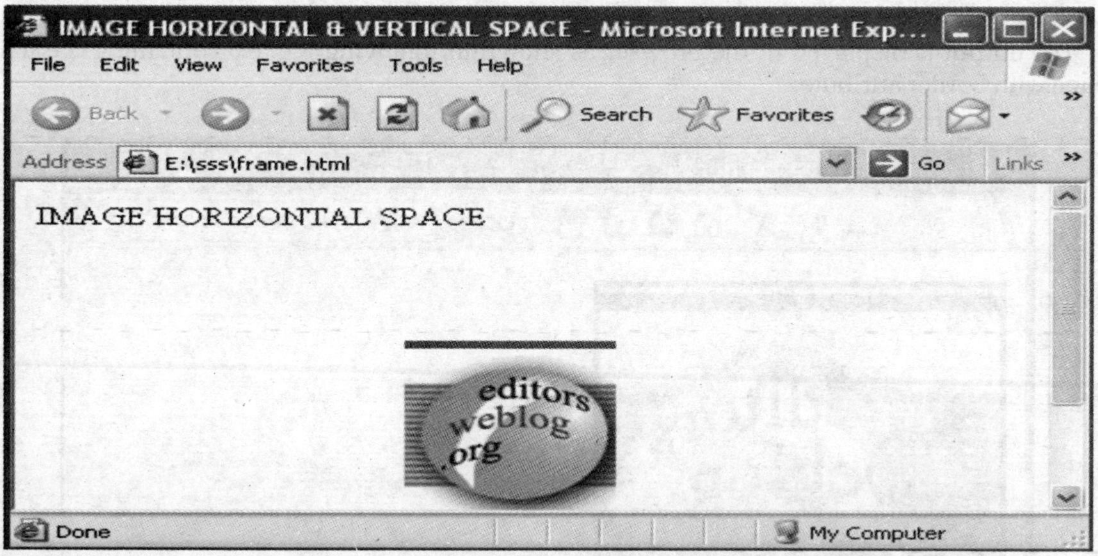

Fig. 6.5 *HTML document including Inline Image with Horizontal and Vertical Space from browser's border.*

Image Border

Image Border provides the border around the image. To specify image border, add the BORDER= attribute in the <IMG> tag, like this:

```
<IMG SRC= "" BORDER= n >
```

Table following shows the use of the BORDER= attribute in the <IMG> tag.

Tags/Attributes	*Use*
<IMG>	Marks an image within an HTML document.
BORDER= *n*	Specifies the border around the image.

For example, to specify image alternative text, add the BORDER= *n* attribute in the <IMG> tag in the HTML document, as follows:

```
<HTML>
  <HEAD>
    <TITLE> IMAGE BORDER </TITLE>
  </HEAD>
  <BODY>
    <IMG SRC= "F:\sss\weblog_r3_c1.jpg" BORDER=5>
  </BODY>
</HTML>
```

The output is displayed in the browser as shown in following Fig. 6.6 containing the inline image with border attribute.

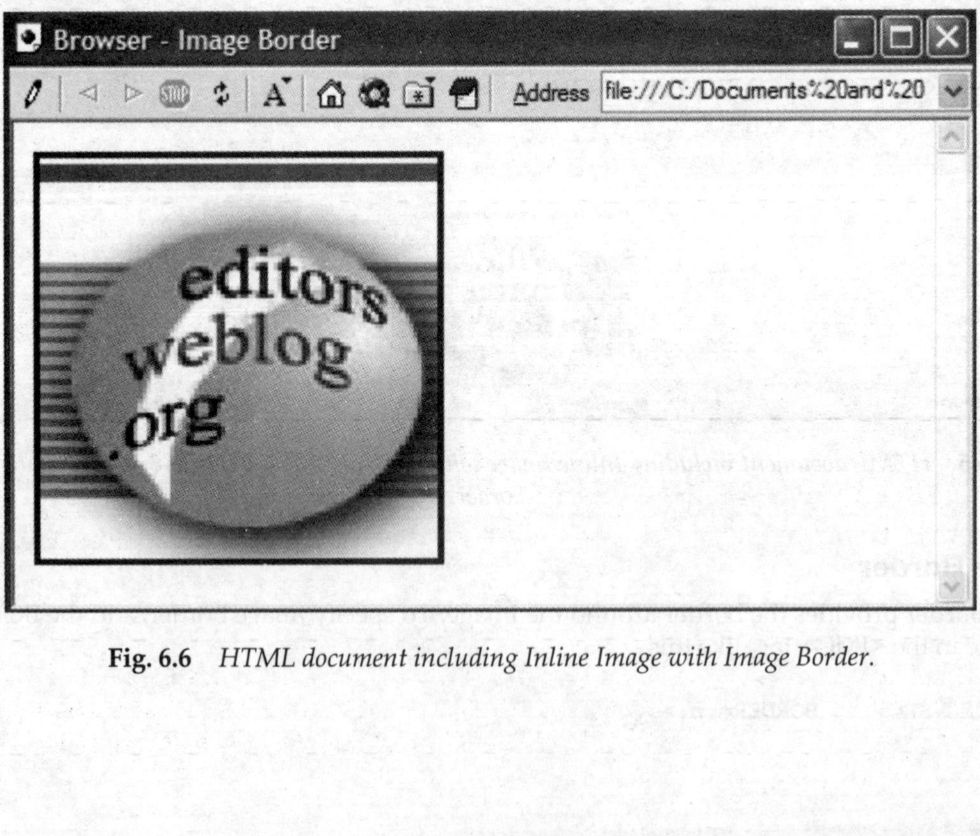

Fig. 6.6 *HTML document including Inline Image with Image Border.*

6.4 CREATING IMAGE LINKS

To create an image as a link, start by adding an image tag and then add the link anchor tag, <A>, before and after the image which provides the link to any file or document.

Use following steps to add an image as a link:

1. Add an image tag, <IMG>, and SRC= attribute to the document.
```
<IMG SRC="C:/Water lilies.jpg">
```
2. Include alternative text using the ALT= attribute.
```
<IMG SRC="C:/Water lilies.jpg" ALT= "Water Lilies.">
```
3. Add remaining attributes you want to include, like HEIGHT= ,WIDTH= and BORDER= attribute.
```
<IMG SRC="C:/Water lilies.jpg" WIDTH="200" HEIGHT="200" BORDER="0"
ALT="Water Lilies.">
```
4. Add the link anchor tag, <A>, before and after the image tag, <IMG>.
```
<A> <IMG SRC="C:/Water lilies.jpg" WIDTH="200" HEIGHT="200" BORDER="0"
ALT="Water Lilies."> </A>
```
5. Add the HREF= attribute to the opening anchor tag to specify the URL, to which file the image to be linked.
```
<A HREF="C:\HomeBazar\Html\Home.htm"> <IMG SRC="C:/Water lilies.jpg"
WIDTH="200" HEIGHT="200" BORDER="0" ALT="Water Lilies."> </A>
```

The output is displayed in the browser as shown in following Fig. 6.7 containing the image link linked to the Home.htm document.

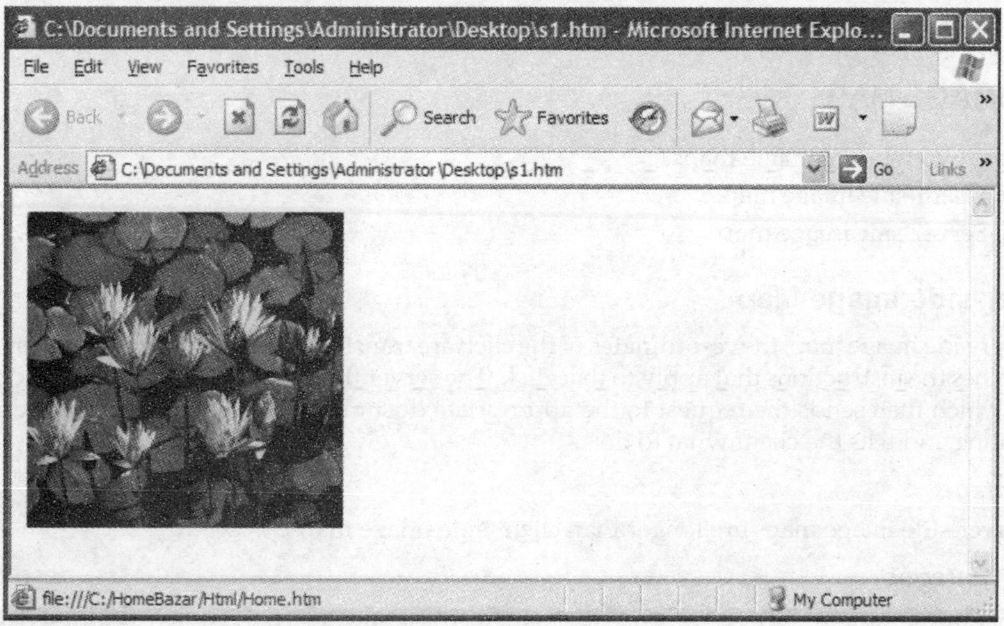

Fig. 6.7 *HTML document including Linked Image.*

The above image linked to the document, whose URL is displayed at the beneath of the web page on the status bar shown in above figure (file:///C:/HomeBazar/Html/Home.htm). After clicking the image, you switched to the document as shown in following Fig. 6.8.

Fig. 6.8

6.5 IMAGE MAP

There are two types of image maps:

1. Client-side image map
2. Server-side image map

Server-side Image Map

In server-side image map, the co-ordinates of the click are transferred to the server computer, which determines the instructions that apply to that click. The server then send the information back to the client, which then sends the request to the appropriate document. The server computer does the calculating and tells the client what to do.

Advantage

The server-side image maps are longer than client-side image maps.

Disadvantages

Server-side image maps responds slower than client-side image maps, it requires the input from the server. They needs supplementary software to process the image map.

Client-side Image Map

The client-side image map is faster because there is no back and forth communication between client and the server to process the map.

Client side image maps are more user friendly than the server-side image maps because when visitor moves the mouse pointer over an image map link within a document, the status bar displays the URL of the link. In contrast, when visitor moves the mouse pointer over an server-side image map link, the status bar displays only co-ordinate points of the mouse pointer.

Finally client-side image maps are better for you because you can use and test them before you can put the image map on the server. In contrast, server-side image maps do not work until they have been installed on the server, making testing more difficult.

Creating Client Side Image Maps

Creating Client Side Image Maps requires the following steps:

1. Defining the image area.
2. Creating the image map.
3. Activating the image map.

(a) Defining the Image Area

You can define image areas by using three shapes:

Circles

Rectangles

Polygons

You can create image map, by combining these shapes, which are drawn by using co-ordinate points.

(b) Creating the Image Map

To create an image map, include tags and attributes that tell the browser what to do when visitor clicks the defined map area as shown in following table.

Tags/Attributes	*Use*
<MAP>	Marks the map definition block within the HTML document.
NAME= "..."	Provides the name for the map definition block.
<AREA>	Defines the area within the block.
SHAPE= "..."	Identifies the shape of an area as CIRCLE, RECT, or POLY.
HREF= "..."	Specifies a target for area.
COORDS= "x1,y1,x2,y2,.."	Identifies the shape of an area.
ALT= "..."	Provides the alternating text describes each link.
USEMAP= "..."	Names the client side map definition to use. It is attribute of <IMG> tag.
ISMAP	Specifies that the image uses the server-side image map. It is also attribute of <IMG> tag.

Client-Side Image Map

To include client side image map, use following steps.

Within the HTML document, in opening and closing <BODY> elements, add opening and closing <MAP> tags.

```
<HTML>
<HEAD>
<TITLE> Client Side Image Map </TITLE>
</HEAD>
<BODY>
   <MAP >
   </MAP>
</BODY>
</HTML>
```

1. Give the name to the map by using NAME=attribute. It should be clear and descriptive.

```
<HTML>
<HEAD>
<TITLE> Client Side Image Map </TITLE>
</HEAD>
<BODY>
   <MAP NAME="CLIENTMAP">
   </MAP>
</BODY>
</HTML>
```

2. Add an <AREA> tag for one of the shapes. (Rectangle, circle and polygon)

```
<MAP NAME="CLIENTMAP">
   <AREA>
</MAP>
```

3. Add the SHAPE= attribute to the <AREA> tag and RECT as its value in this example.

```
<MAP NAME="CLIENTMAP">
   <AREA SHAPE="RECT">
</MAP>
```

4. Add the COORDS= attribute with the x1, y1, x2, y2 coordinates of the corner points of the rectangle.

```
<MAP NAME="CLIENTMAP">
  <AREA SHAPE="RECT" COORDS="0, 0, 50, 100">
</MAP>
```

5. Add the HREF= attribute pointing to the target file. You can use relative or absolute URLs in client side image maps. In this case, rectangular area links to the target file called 's1.htm'.

```
<MAP NAME="CLIENTMAP">
  <AREA SHAPE="RECT" HREF="C:\Documents and Settings\Administrator\Desktop\s1.htm"
  COORDS="0, 0, 50, 100">
</MAP>
```

6. Add ALT= attribute for describing link area.

```
<MAP NAME="CLIENTMAP">
  <AREA SHAPE="RECT" HREF="C:\Documents and Settings\Administrator\Desktop\s1.htm"
  COORDS="0, 0, 50,100" ALT="waterlilies">
</MAP>
```

(c) Use the Map

Add the image the HTML document and place the image map with its name that you have created on this image that is called using the map or activating the map.

The image tag, looks like this:

```
<IMG SRC="E:/Web Project/TempKop/HomeBazar/NewAds/DELTON.GIF" WIDTH="400"
HEIGHT="100" HSPACE="100" BORDER="1" >
```

To connect the image to the map that you have created in the previous section, simply add the USEMAP= attribute, as follows,

```
<IMG SRC="E:/Web Project/TempKop/HomeBazar/NewAds/DELTON.GIF" WIDTH="400"
HEIGHT="100" HSPACE="100" BORDER="1" USEMAP="#CLIENTMAP">
```

The result is shown in following Fig. 6.9.

The rectangular part of the image in the above figure is linked to the s1.html document as shown in following Fig. 6.10.

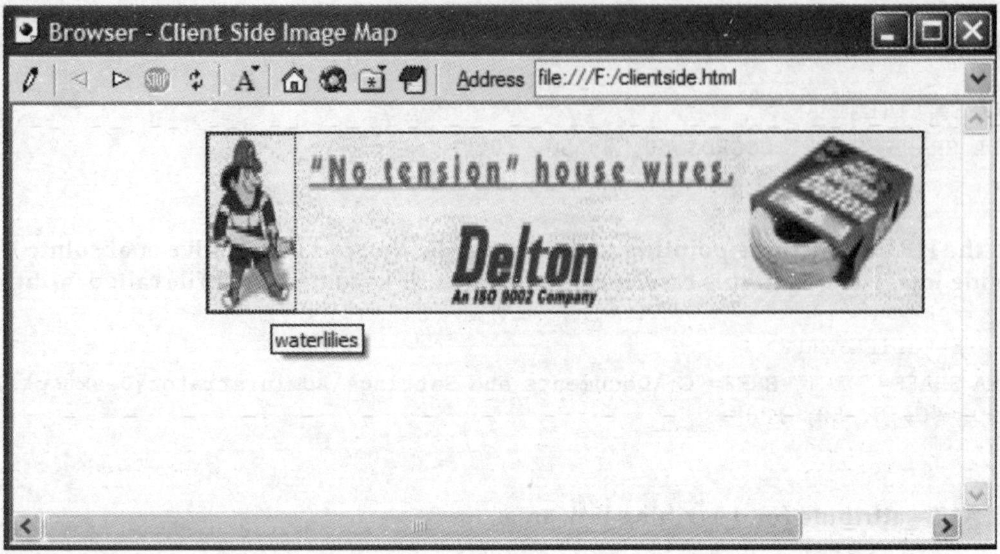

Fig. 6.9 *HTML document including Image map containing rectangular linked area.*

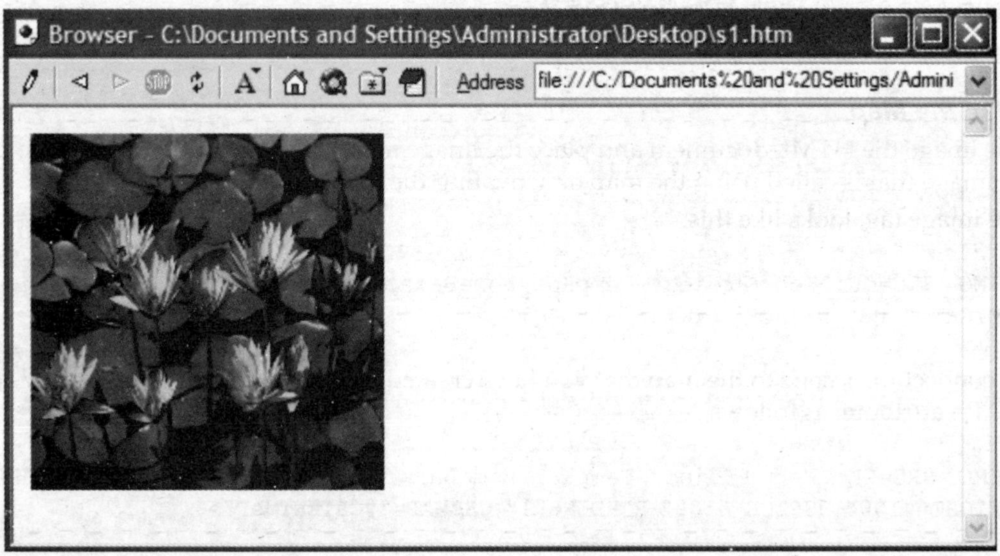

Fig. 6.10 *HTML document including Image after clicking rectangular area in the image map.*

Server-Side Image Map

Server-side image map is similar to that of client side image map; the only difference is in map file format. Each type of server can have different types of image map formats. There are different types of server-side image map formats, however in practice, only two server-map formats are used: NCSA (National Center for Supercomputing Application) and CERN (Centre European Research).

NCSA Image Map

The NCSA image map format is as follows:

method URL co-ordinates

where,

method is nothing but which area you want to place in the map. (Circle, Rectangle, Polygon)

URL is the address of the document you want to link to the area.

co-ordinates specify the area within the map.

The NCSA server-side map file is like this:

```
circle   /Link/DocumentB.html  100,100,40
rect   /Link/DocumentA.html  300,300,380,380
```

After creating this map file, save it with a map extension in the */Link* folder just below the server root where the rest of the documents resides.

Now use this image map file, by placing it in the image using ISMAP attribute.

```
<IMG SRC="E:/Web Project/TempKop/HomeBazar/NewAds/DELTON.GIF" WIDTH="400"
HEIGHT="100" HSPACE="100" BORDER="1" ISMAP>
```

Add anchor tag, <A>, with HREF= attribute around this image.

```
<A HREF= "http://.../Link/SLinl.map"><IMG SRC="E:/Web Project/TempKop/
HomeBazar/NewAds/DELTON.GIF"  WIDTH="400"  HEIGHT="100"  HSPACE="100"
BORDER="1" USEMAP="#CLIENTMAP" ISMAP></A>
```

If the client recognizes the client-side image map, it discards the server-side map. If the client can't recognize the client-side image map, it uses the server-side map.

CERN Image Map

The CERN image map format is as follows:

method co-ordinates URL

where,

method is nothing but which area you want to place in the map. (Circle, rectangle, polygon)

URL is the address of the document you want to link to the area.

co-ordinates specifies the area within the map.

The CERN server-side map file is like this:

```
circle  (100,100) 40  /Link/DocumentB.html
rect  (300,300) (380,380)   /Link/DocumentA.html
```

the difference between NCSA and CERN are that the co-ordinate pairs are enclosed within the parentheses, the co-ordinates are before URL and rectangle can use only two opposite co-ordinates rather than top-left and lower-right. The URLs are either absolute or relative.

PRACTICE

1. Include an image as links in the web page.

```
<HTML>
  <HEAD>
    <TITLE> IMAGE BORDER </TITLE>
  </HEAD>
  <BODY>
    <A  HREF="C:\HomeBazar\Html\Home.htm">  <IMG  SRC="C:/Water  lilies.jpg"
    WIDTH="200" HEIGHT="200" BORDER="0" ALT="Water Lilies."> </A>
  </BODY>
</HTML>
```

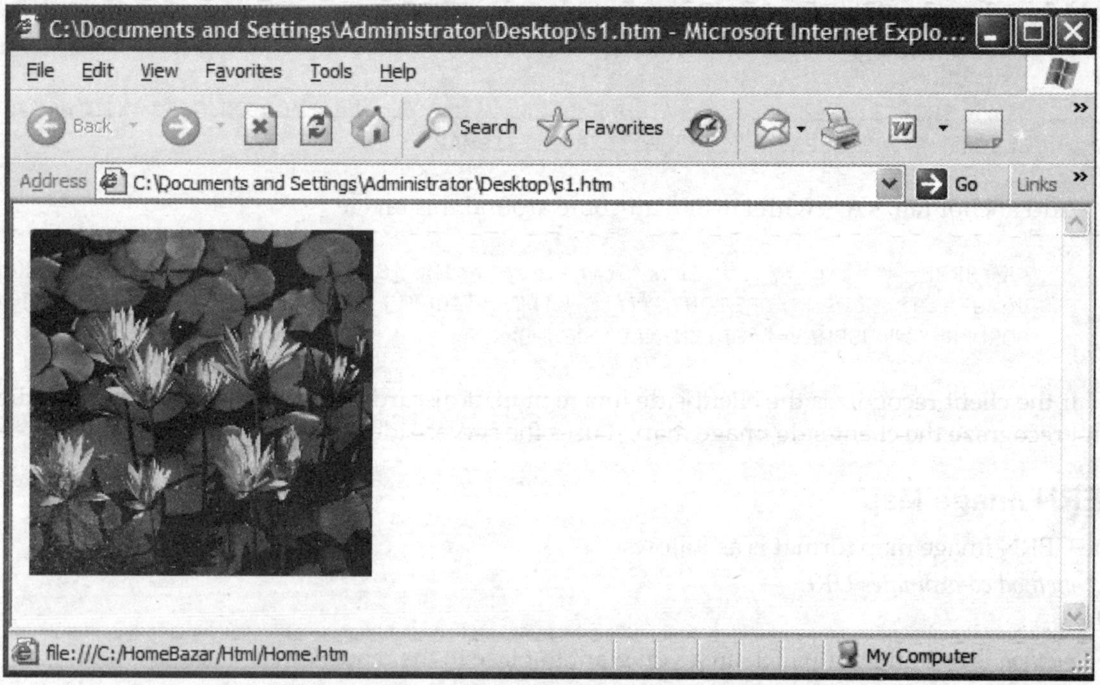

Fig. 6.11 *HTML document containing linked image*

The above image in Fig. 6.11 linked to the document, whose URL is displayed at the beneath of the web page on the status bar shown in above figure (file:///C:/HomeBazar/Html/Home.htm). After clicking the image, you switched to the document as shown in following Fig. 6.12.

2. Include an image in the web page with different attributes.

```
<HTML>
  <HEAD>
    <TITLE> IMAGE ATTRIBUTES </TITLE>
```

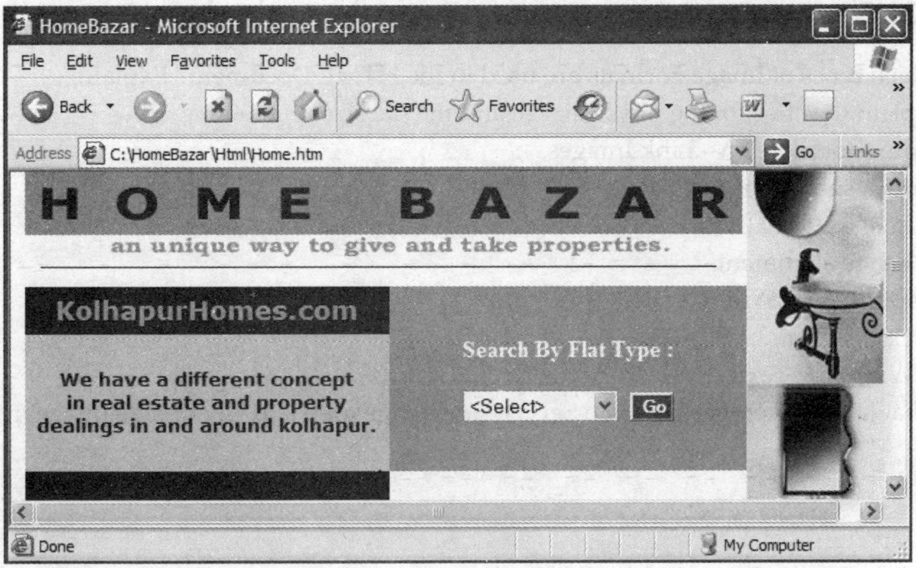

Fig. 6.12

```
  </HEAD>
  <BODY>
    <P>IMAGE HORIZONTAL SPACE, VERTICAL SPACE, ALIGNMENT, BORDER,HEIGHT, and WIDTH
    ATTRIBUTES
    <IMG SRC= "E:\sss\weblog_r3_c1.jpg" ALT="Weblog Logo" HSPACE=170 VSPACE=70
    HEIGHT=100 WIDTH=100 BORDER=5 ALIGN=CENTER></P>
  </BODY>
</HTML>
```

The output is displayed as shown in following Fig. 6.13.

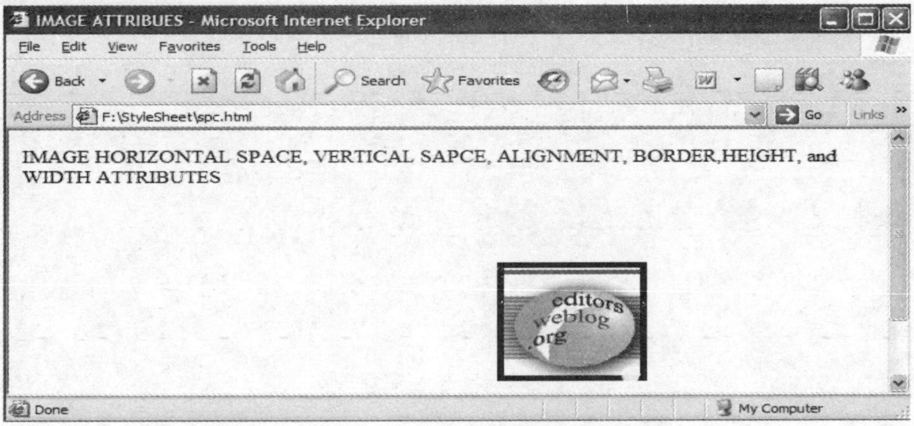

Fig. 6.13

QUESTIONS

1. Which types of Image Formats are used in the HTML Document? Explain.
2. Explain the effect of the physical size and the file size on the image.
3. Write short note on – Link Images.
4. Write a short note on–
   a. Image alternatives.
   b. Image alignment.
   c. Height and Width.
   d. HSPACE and VSPACE.
   e. Wrapping Text.
5. What is the difference between Server-side image map and Client-side image map?

□□□

7

Developing HTML Forms

Forms are effective means of making Web pages user-friendly. Forms are used in HTML for getting inputs from the user.

7.1 CREATING FORMS

Forms have two basic parts:

1. The part you can see (that a visitor fills out).
2. The part you can not see (that specifies how the server should process the information).

In this chapter we just see the first part that is, how visitor fills out the information in the form so that it is possible for the visitor how to interact with the Web pages.

For filling the information in the form, there are several types widgets i.e. controls consists in the forms, which are fields you can use to collect data:

- Submit and Reset buttons send the form information to the server for processing and returns the form to its original settings.
- Text fields are areas for text input, for inputting names, addresses etc.
- Select lists are lists from which visitors can select one or more items. It is used to present long list of choices.
- Check boxes allow visitors to select none, one, or more items from the list.
- Option buttons allow visitors to select only one item from the list, form example, gender, result etc.
- Text areas are areas for lengthy text input, as in open-ended commends or free form response.

To create a form, use the form element in the HTML document. It is written as <FORM>... </FORM> tag. This tag marks a form within the HTML document. To include various input fields i.e. controls in the form, use the input empty element. It is written as <INPUT>. It sets an area in a form for visitor to input.

7.2 FORM CONTROLS

Form controls are the input fields, which we include in the form by using various attributes in the <INPUT> tag. Following table shows the input tag and its attributes:

Tags/Attributes	Use
<FORM>	Marks a form within the HTML document. It is the fundamental tag or container tag which contains other form tags.
<INPUT>	Sets an area in a form for visitor to input.
TYPE= "..."	Set the type of input field. Possible values are TEXT, CHECKBOX, PASSWORD, RADIO, FILE, HIDDEN, IMAGE, SUBMIT and RESET.
NAME= "..."	Processes form result.
VALUE= "..."	Provides content associated with NAME= "...". Use this attribute with radio buttons and check boxes because they do not accept other input. You can use this attribute with text fields to provide initial input.
SRC= "..."	Indicates the image source file which is used in IMAGE type button.
SIZE= n	Sets the visible size for a field. Use this attribute with text input field.

1. Text Controls

(a) Text Fields

This is used for single line text entry field, in conjunction with SIZE and MAXLENGTH attributes. To include a text field, use following statement:

```
<INPUT TYPE=TEXT NAME= "..."  VALUE= "...">
```

For example, to include text field, use above statement in form area in the HTML document as follows:

```
<HTML>
  <HEAD><TITLE>TEXT FIELD</TITLE><HEAD>
  <BODY>
  <FORM>
    First Name : <INPUT TYPE=TEXT NAME="FNAME"><BR>
    Last Name : <INPUT TYPE=TEXT NAME="LNAME">
  </FORM>
  </BODY>
<HTML>
```

The output is displayed in browser as shown in following Fig. 7.1 containing the text fields.

(b) Text Areas

This is used for multiple-lines text entry field, in conjunction with SIZE and MAXLENGTH attributes. To include a text areas, use following statement:

```
<INPUT TYPE=TEXTAREA NAME= "..."  VALUE= "...">
```

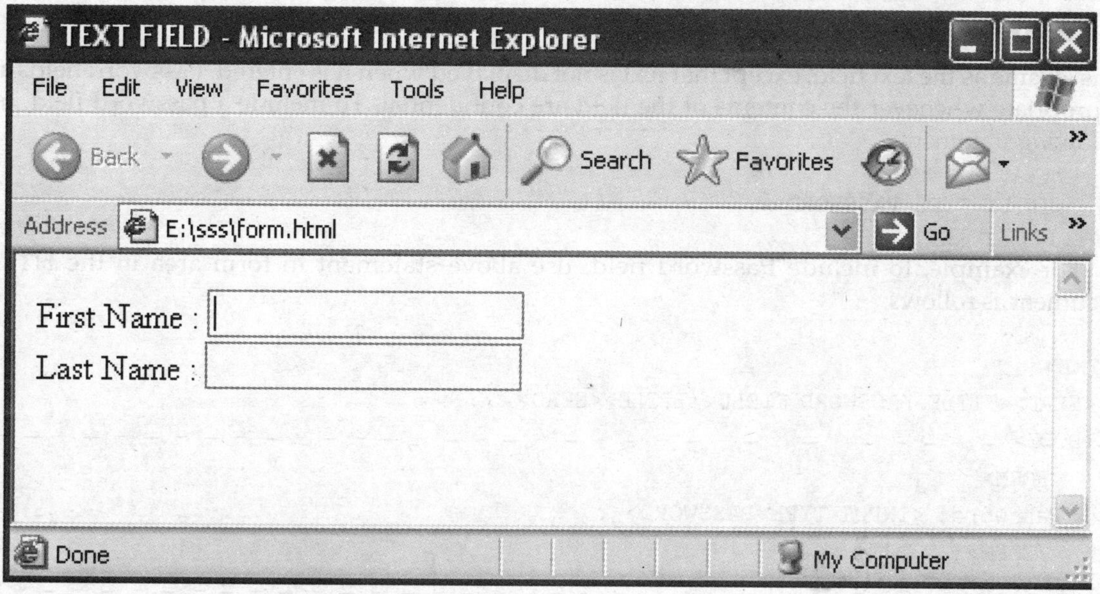

Fig. 7.1 *HTML document including form containing text fields.*

Or you can use < TEXTAREA > </TEXTAREA> tag to include the text area in the document. The user can enter more than one line in it. For Example,

```
< TEXTAREA ROW=8 COLUMN=24 NAME= "…"> < /TEXTAREA >
```

It is displayed in browser as shown in following Fig. 7.2 containing the text box fields.

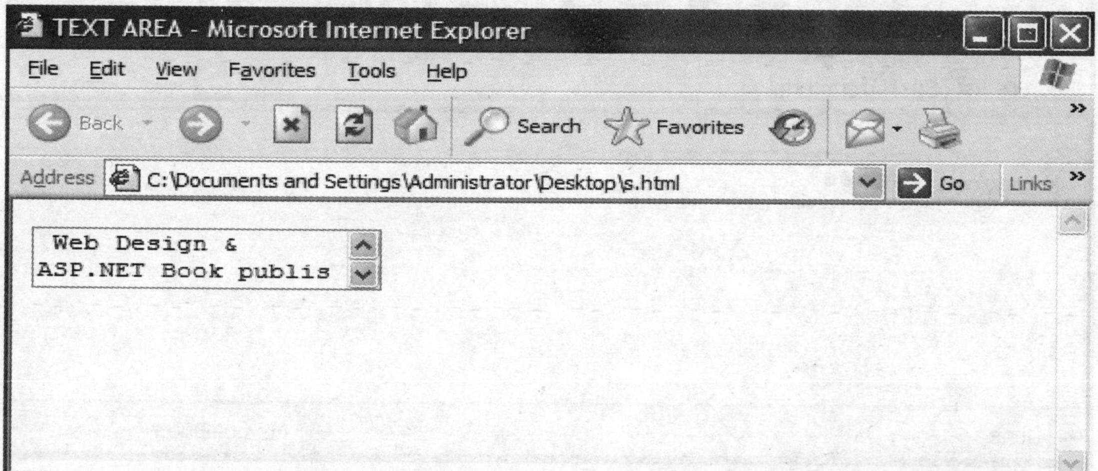

Fig. 7.2 *HTML document including form containing textarea field.*

2. Password Field

This is same as the text field, except that text is not displayed when it is entered. Password fields are appropriate whenever the contents of the field are confidential. To include a password field, use following statement:

```
<INPUT TYPE=PASSWORD>
```

For example, to include Password field, use above statement in form area in the HTML document as follows:

```
<HTML>
  <HEAD><TITLE>PASSWORD FIELD</TITLE><HEAD>
  <BODY>
    <FORM>
    Password: <INPUT TYPE=PASSWORD>
    </FORM>
  </BODY>
<HTML>
```

The output is displayed in browser as shown in following Fig. 7.3 containing the password field.

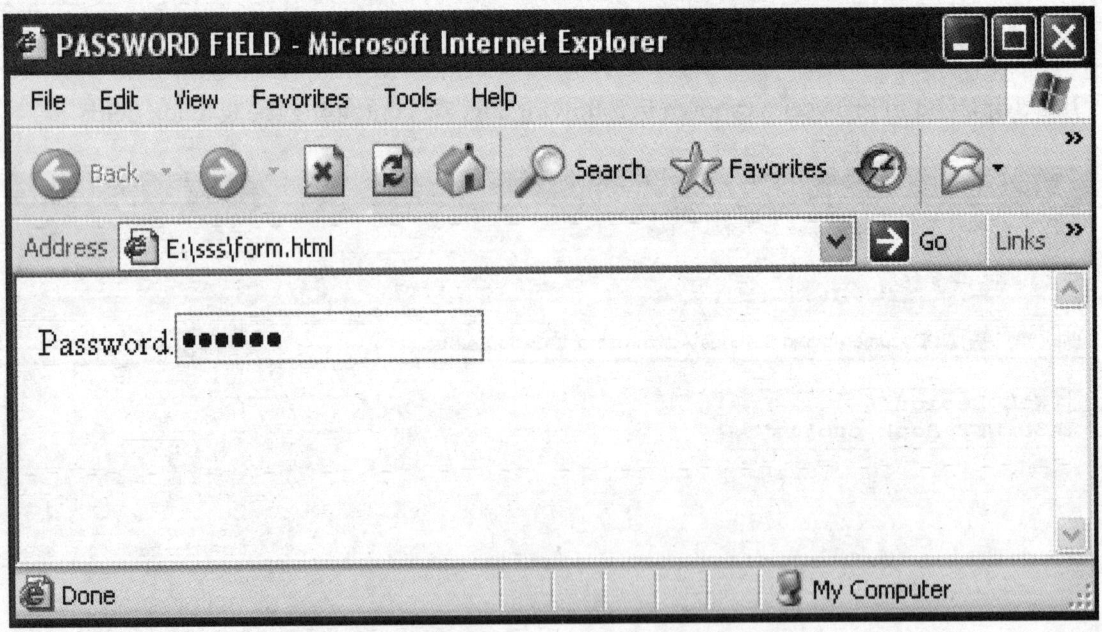

Fig. 7.3 *HTML document including form containing password field.*

3. Option Field

This control is a small round button in a group of buttons from which you can select only one at a time. This control is also called Radio Button Control. To include option fields, use following statement:

```
<INPUT TYPE=RADIO NAME= "..."  VALUE= "...">
```

For example, to include Option field, use above statement in form area in the HTML document as follows:

```
<HTML>
  <HEAD><TITLE>RADIO FIELD</TITLE><HEAD>
  <BODY>
    <FORM>
    Blue: <INPUT TYPE=RADIO NAME= "A" VALUE= "BLUE">
    <BR>
    Red: <INPUT TYPE=RADIO NAME= "B" VALUE= "RED">
    </FORM>
  </BODY>
<HTML>
```

The output is displayed in browser as shown in following Fig. 7.4 containing the option button controls.

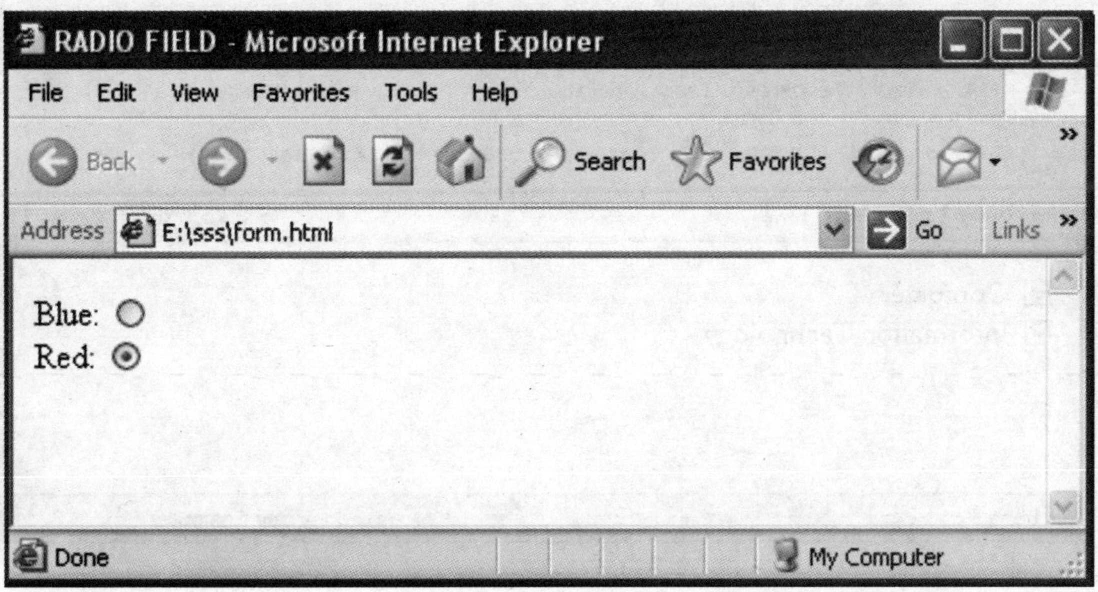

Fig. 7.4 *HTML document including form containing radio fields.*

4. Checkbox Field

This control is a small square box that represents an on and off status. This is used to select none, one, or more items from the list. Each checkbox works independently from others; visitors can select or deselect any combinations of checkboxes. To include option fields, use following statement:

```
<INPUT TYPE=CHECKBOX NAME= “...” VALUE= “...”>
```

For example, to include Checkbox field, use above statement in form area in the HTML document as follows:

```
<HTML>
  <HEAD><TITLE>CHECKBOX FIELD</TITLE><HEAD>
  <BODY>
    <FORM>
      <INPUT TYPE= CHECKBOX NAME= “A” VALUE= “COMPUER”> Computer
      <BR>
      <INPUT TYPE= CHECKBOX NAME= “B” VALUE= “IT”> Information Technology
    </FORM>
  </BODY>
<HTML>
```

The output is displayed in browser as shown in following Fig. 7.5 containing the checkbox controls.

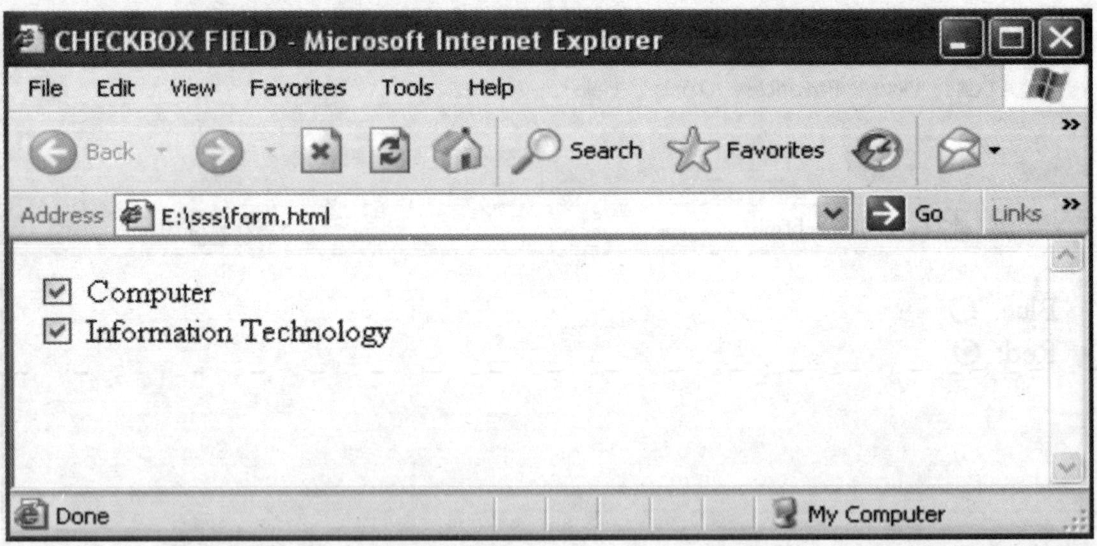

Fig. 7.5 *HTML document including form containing checkbox fields.*

5. Submit Button Control

This control is a push button or command button control that you click to submit a form. To include a Submit Button Control, use the following statement:

```
<INPUT TYPE=SUBMIT NAME= "..." VALUE= "...">
```

For example, to include Submit Button Control, use above statement in form area in the HTML document as follows:

```
<HTML>
  <HEAD><TITLE>SUBMIT CONTROL</TITLE><HEAD>
  <BODY>
    <FORM>
      <INPUT TYPE= SUBMIT NAME= "A" VALUE= SUBMIT>
    </FORM>
  </BODY>
<HTML>
```

The output is displayed in browser as shown in following Fig. 7.6 containing the submit button.

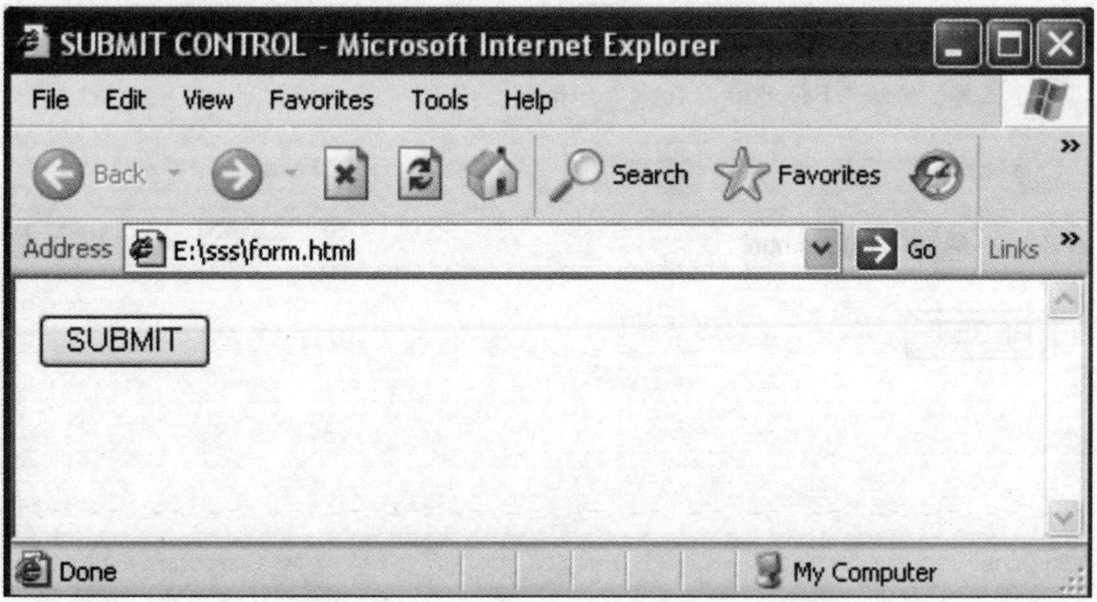

Fig. 7.6 *HTML document including form containing submit button.*

6. Reset Button Control

This control is a push button or command button control that you click to clear a form. To include a Reset Button Control, use the following statement:

```
<INPUT TYPE=RESET NAME= "..."  VALUE= "...">
```

For example, to include Reset Button Control, use above statement in form area in the HTML document as follows:

```
<HTML>
  <HEAD><TITLE>RESET CONTROL</TITLE><HEAD>
  <BODY>
    <FORM>
      <INPUT TYPE= RESET NAME= "A" VALUE= RESET>
    </FORM>
  </BODY>
<HTML>
```

The output is displayed in browser as shown in following Fig. 7.7 containing the reset button.

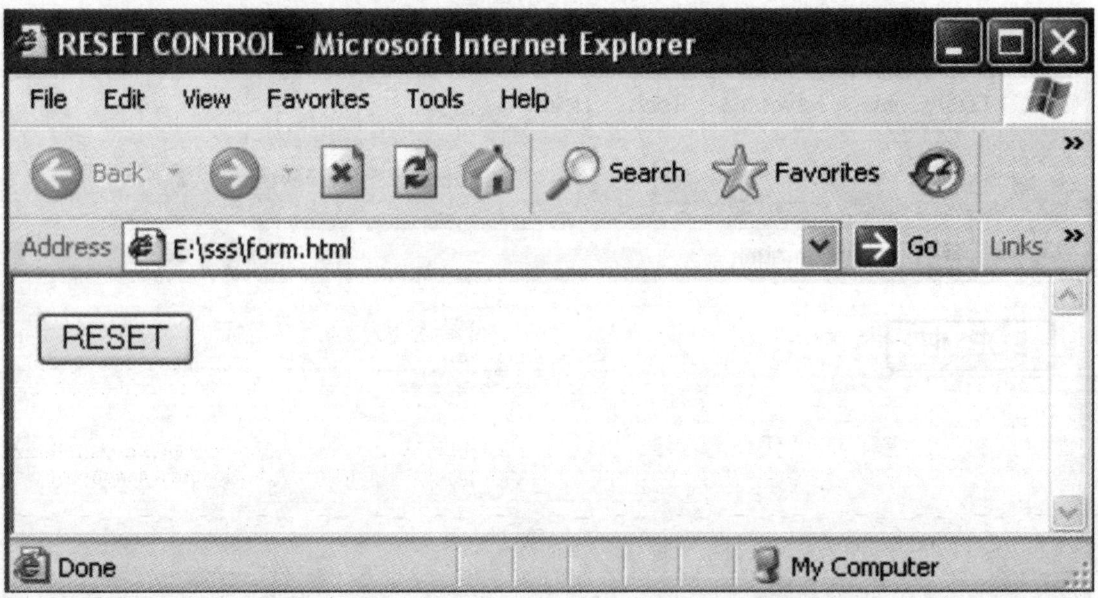

Fig. 7.7 *HTML document including form containing reset field.*

7. Hidden Control

This control is a field that is not displayed on the form. It used to transfer information between the client and the server. To include a Hidden Control, use the following statement:

```
<INPUT TYPE=HIDDEN NAME= "..."  VALUE= "...">
```

8. File Field

This field allows visitors to upload files. To include a File Control, use the following statement:

```
<INPUT TYPE=FILE>
```

For example, to include File Control, use above statement in form area in the HTML document as follows:

```
<HTML>
  <HEAD><TITLE>FILE CONTROL</TITLE><HEAD>
  <BODY>
    <FORM>
      <INPUT TYPE= FILE>
    </FORM>
  </BODY>
<HTML>
```

The output is displayed in browser as shown in following Fig. 7.8 containing the file control to upload the file.

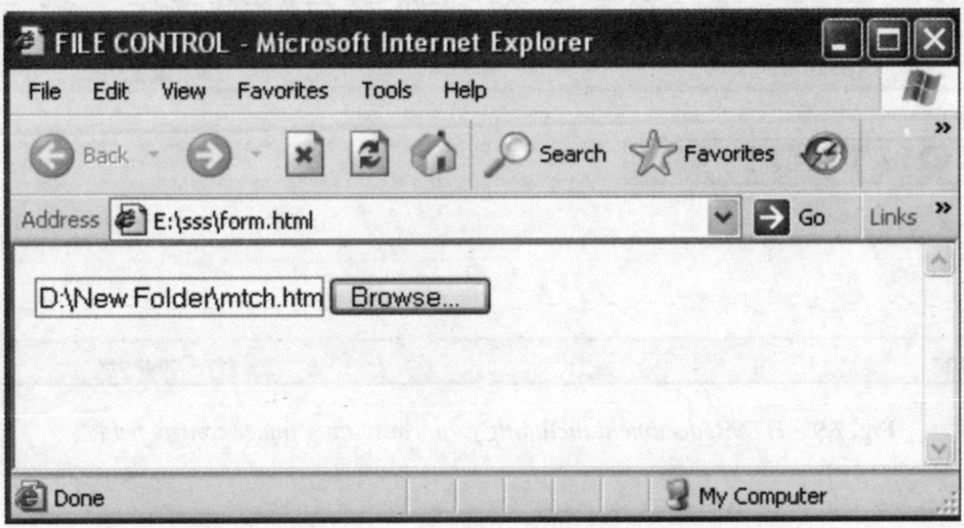

Fig. 7.8 *HTML document including form containing file field.*

9. Image Control

This control is used to add image button on the browser. To include a Image Button Control, specify the INPUT element, TYPE= "SUBMIT" and SRC attribute that defines URL of an image, as in following statement:

```
<INPUT TYPE=IMAGE SRC="…">
```

For example, to include Image Control, use above statement in form area in the HTML document as follows:

```
<HTML>
  <HEAD><TITLE>IMAGE CONTROL</TITLE><HEAD>
  <BODY>
    <FORM>
      <INPUT TYPE= IMAGE SRC="C:\Documents and Settings\88888\Desktop\se
      project\amol\project\contact1.jpg">
    </FORM>
  </BODY>
<HTML>
```

The output is displayed in browser as shown in following Fig. 7.9 containing the image.

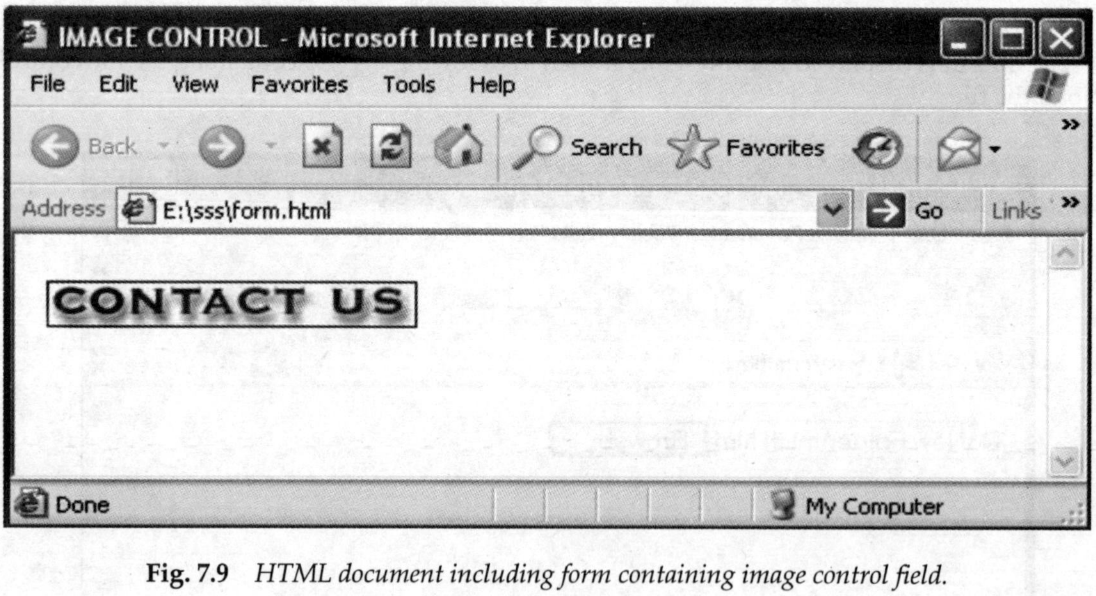

Fig. 7.9 *HTML document including form containing image control field.*

7.3 FORMS CONTROL SELECTION AND OPTION PROCESSING

Selection and Option Processing Control

Selection and Option Processing Control is a menu type control, sometimes called pull down menu that allows visitors to select single or multiple responses. The table following describes the tags and attributes used to create Selection and Option Processing Control.

Tags/Attributes	*Use*
<SELECT>	Sets an area in the form for select field that can look like a drop-down list or a larger select field.
NAME= "..."	Gives name for this field.
SIZE= "n"	Sets the visible size for the select field. The default value 1 creates the drop down list. You can change 2 or more if you more options to be visible.
MULTIPLE	Sets select field to accept more than one selection. Displays the field as list box.
<OPTION>	Includes an item in the select field. The </OPTION> is optional.
VALUE= "..."	Provides a name to the item like NAME= attribute.
SELECTED	Lets you to specify the default selection of an item, which will appear when the form is loaded or reset.

To include a Selection and Option Processing Control in the browser, use the following statements:

```
<SELECT>
  <OPTION>...</OPTION>
  <OPTION>...</OPTION>
  <OPTION>...</OPTION>
  .
  .
</SELECT>
```

For example, to include Selection and Option Processing Control (Drop-Down List Control), use SELECT and OPTION elements with their attributes as follows:

```
<HTML>
  <HEAD>
    <TITLE> Drop-Down List Control </TITLE>
  </HEAD>
  <BODY>
  <SELECT NAME="A">
    <OPTION>RED</OPTION>
    <OPTION>GREEN</OPTION>
```

```
    <OPTION SELECTED>BLUE</OPTION>
  </SELECT>
  </BODY>
</HTML>
```

The output is displayed in browser as shown in following Fig. 7.10.

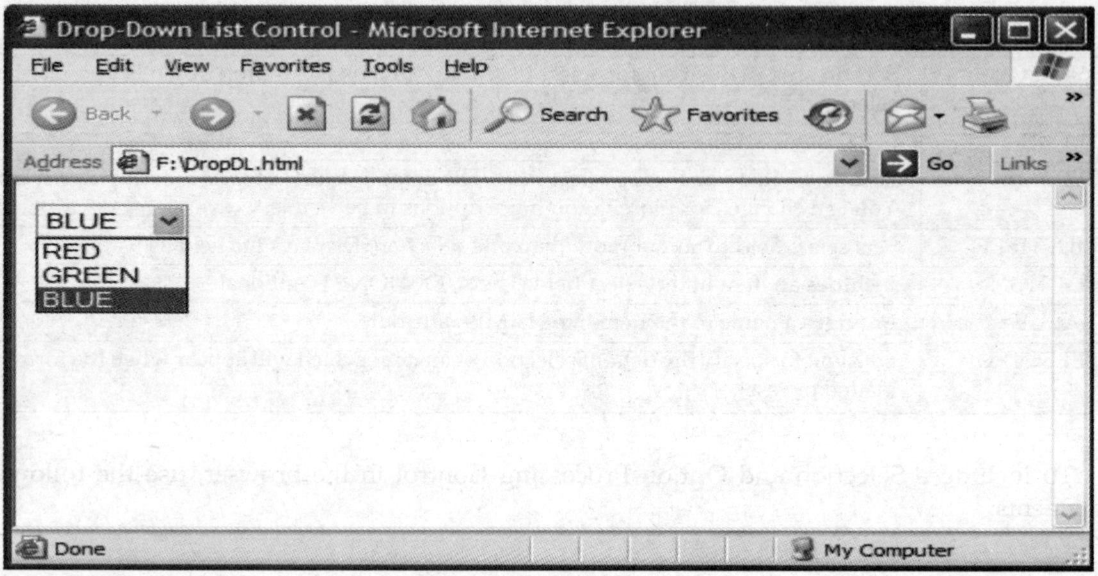

Fig. 7.10 *HTML document including form containing selection and option processing fields.*

And to include Selection and Option Processing Control (List Box Control), use SELECT and OPTION elements with their attributes as follows:

```
<HTML>
  <HEAD>
    <TITLE> List Box Control </TITLE>
  </HEAD>
  <BODY>
  <SELECT NAME="A" MULTIPLE>
    <OPTION>RED</OPTION>
    <OPTION>GREEN</OPTION>
    <OPTION SELECTED>BLUE</OPTION>
  </SELECT>
  </BODY>
</HTML>
```

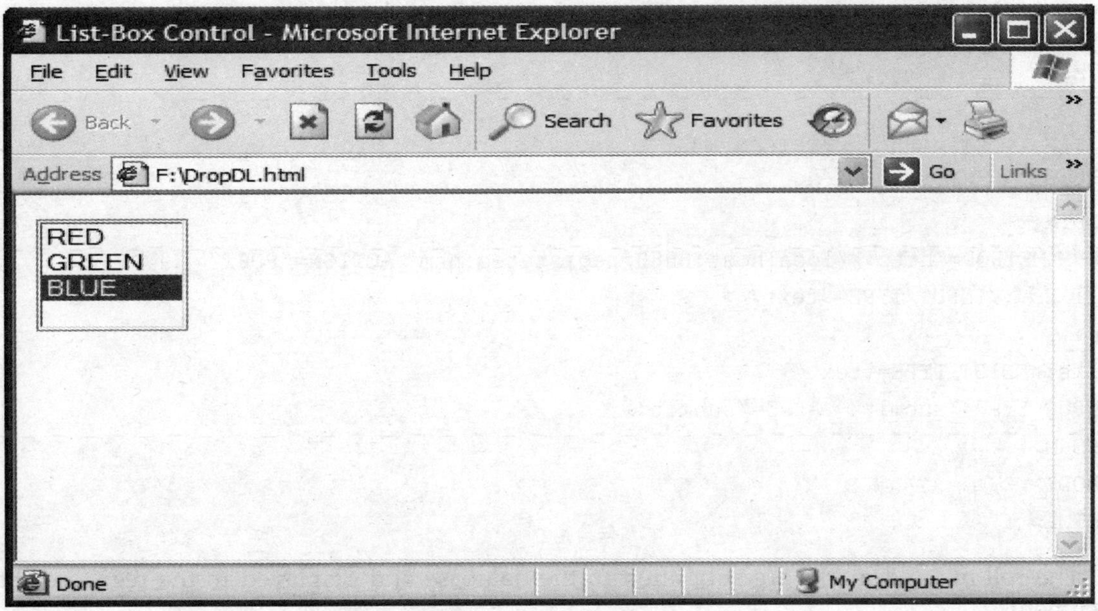

Fig. 7.11 *HTML document including form containing list-box field.*

7.4 PROCESSING A FORM

Once the information is filled in the form and clicks the submit button, the browser with which the user is viewing and editing the form transfers the information from user's computer to the URL specified in the *action* attribute in the <FORM> tag. The form handling program loads the form into the database. The <FORM> tag will use *method* attribute to specify the HTTP or CGI protocol by which form is submitted to the server, which contains the program that process the form.

The *method* attribute has two values: GET and POST. METHOD= "GET" appends the submitted information to the URL named by the *action* attribute which is displayed in the address bar of the browser. METHOD= "POST" does not appends the submitted information to the URL named by the *action* attribute which is displayed in the address bar of the browser. It simply sends the form to the server for processing. The table following describes the use of *action* and *method* attributes in the FORM element:

Tag/Attributes	*Use*
<FORM>	Marks a form within an HTML document.
ACTION= "..."	Indicates the program on the HTTP server that will process the output from the form.
METHOD= "..."	Tells the browser how to send data to the server, with either GET method or POST method.

For example, to post Roll No. and Marks to registered.htm write code as follows:

```
<HTML>
<HEAD>
<TITLE> POST Method </TITLE>
</HEAD>
<BODY>
<FORM METHOD="http://localhost:8080/registered.htm" ACTION="POST">
Roll No.:<INPUT TYPE="text" >
<BR>
Marks:<INPUT TYPE="text">
<INPUT TYPE="submit" VALUE="submit">
</FORM>
</BODY>
</HTML>
```

The roll no. and marks are submitted to the database and displayed in the registered.htm document.

PRACTICE

Create HTML form.

```
<HTML>
  <HEAD>
    <TITLE> HTML FORM </TITLE>
  </HEAD>
  <BODY>
    <FORM>
      <INPUT TYPE= CHECKBOX NAME= "A" VALUE= "COMPUER"> Computer
      <BR>
      <INPUT TYPE= CHECKBOX NAME= "B" VALUE= "IT"> Information Technology
      <BR>
      <INPUT TYPE=RADIO NAME= "A1" VALUE= "BLUE"> Male
      <BR>
      <INPUT TYPE=RADIO NAME= "B1" VALUE= "RED"> FEMALE
      <BR>
      Roll No.:<INPUT TYPE="text" >
      <BR>
      Marks:<INPUT TYPE="text" MAXLENGTH=10>
      <BR>
      <INPUT TYPE="submit" VALUE="submit">
      <INPUT TYPE= RESET NAME= "R" VALUE= RESET>
```

```
      </FORM>
   </BODY>
</HTML>
```

The output of this HTML document is shown in following Fig. 7.12.

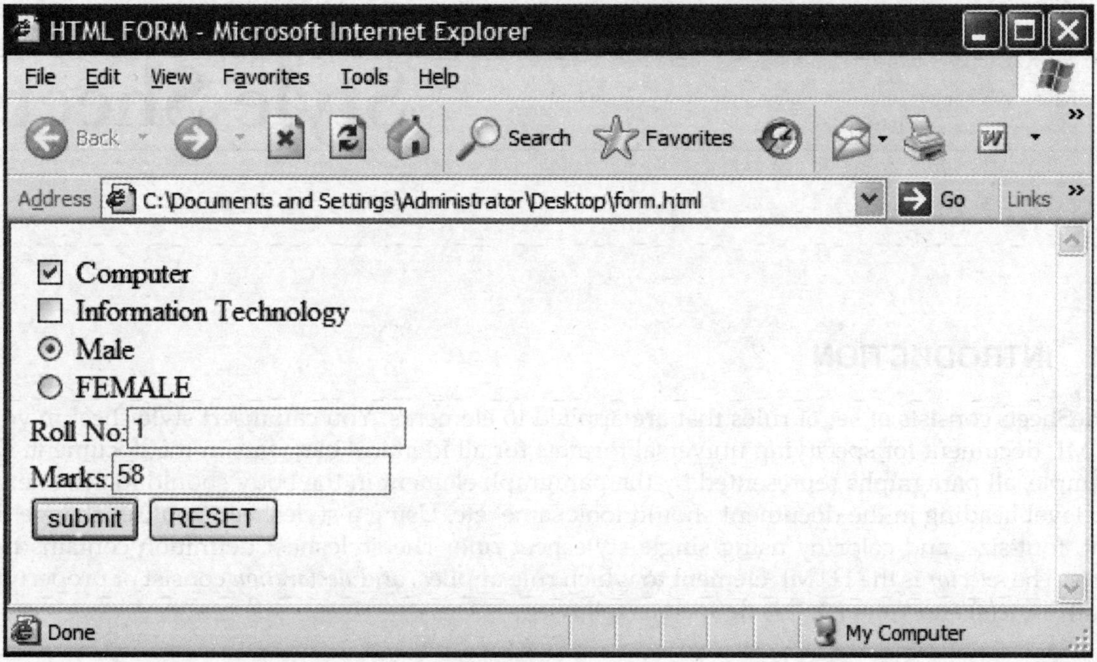

Fig. 7.12

QUESTIONS

1. How to create forms in the HTML document?
2. Write a Short note on—
   a. Text Control.
   b. Password Field.
   c. Option Field.
   d. Check Box Field.
   e. Submit Button Field.
   f. Reset Button Field.
   g. Image Control.
   h. Hidden Control.
   i. File Field.
3. Explain Selection and Option Processing System.
4. How to process the Form?

□□□

8

Style Sheets

8.1 INTRODUCTION

StyleSheets consists of set of rules that are applied to elements. You can insert style sheet in your HTML document for specifying universal formats for all identical elements in the document. For example, all paragraphs represented by the paragraph element in the body should look same; all top level heading in the document should look same, etc. Using a stylesheet, you can change the font, font-size, and color by using single stylesheet rule. The stylesheet definition contains two parts: The *selector* is the HTML element to which rule applies, and *declaration* consist of property(s) or attribute(s) and value(s). It is defined as follows:

```
Element/selector {attribute1: value1; attribute2: value2;….attributeN: valueN}
```

8.2 ADDING STYLE SHEET TO YOUR DOCUMENT

As stylesheet carry the formatting information, you associate it with HTML documents in following ways:

1. Embedding Style Sheet in HTML document by defining it between the opening and closing HEAD element.
2. Storing Style Sheet in separate document and either link or embed the style sheet to associate it with HTML document.
3. Using inline style sheet.

Embedding Style Sheet

It is the easiest methods of the four methods. Embedding Style Sheet means inserting the <STYLE> tags, along with style information, between the <HEAD> tags. Like this,

```
<HTML>
  <HEAD>
    <TITLE> Style Sheet </TITLE>
    <STYLE>
    <!–
```

```
        ...
        -->
        </STYLE>
    </HEAD>
    <BODY>

    </BODY>
</HTML>
```

Embedding style sheet makes maintaining or updating styles easy because you don't have to work with two or more documents (the style sheet document and the HTML document). You simply open the HTML document and insert the Style Sheet code in the head element.

To embed a style sheet in an HTML document, apply the tags and attributes shown in following table between the <HEAD> tags.

Tags/Attributes	*Use*
<STYLE>	Specifies the style sheet area within an HTML document.
<!– .... –>	A comment that hides the style sheet contents from non style capable browsers.
TYPE= "text/css"	Specifies the type of style sheet. By default it is "text/css" for cascading style sheet, and "text/jss" for javascript style sheet.

For example, to embed the style sheet and to display the paragraph text green using this type of style sheet, use the following steps:

1. Start with document header.

```
<HTML>
    <HEAD>
        <TITLE> Style Sheet </TITLE>
    </HEAD>
    <BODY>

    </BODY>
</HTML>
```

2. Insert opening and closing <STYLE> tags within the opening and closing <HEAD> tags.

```
<HTML>
    <HEAD>
        <TITLE> Style Sheet </TITLE>
        <STYLE TYPE= "text/css">
        </STYLE>
```

```
  </HEAD>
  <BODY>

  </BODY>
</HTML>
```

3. **Add the comment (<!– … –>) tags to hide the contents from non style capable browsers.**

```
<HTML>
  <HEAD>
    <TITLE> Style Sheet </TITLE>
    <STYLE TYPE= "text/css">
    <!–

    –>
    </STYLE>
  </HEAD>
  <BODY>

  </BODY>
</HTML>
```

4. **Insert the style information or style definition within the comment (<!– … –>) tags.**

```
<HTML>
  <HEAD>
    <TITLE> Style Sheet </TITLE>
    <STYLE TYPE= "text/css">
    <!–
    P {color: green }
    –>
    </STYLE>
  </HEAD>
  <BODY>
    <P>Embedding Style Sheet Example</P>
  </BODY>
</HTML>
```

After opening this HTML document in Internet Explorer, the text in paragraph "Embedding Style Sheet Example" is displayed in Green color as shown in following Fig. 8.1.

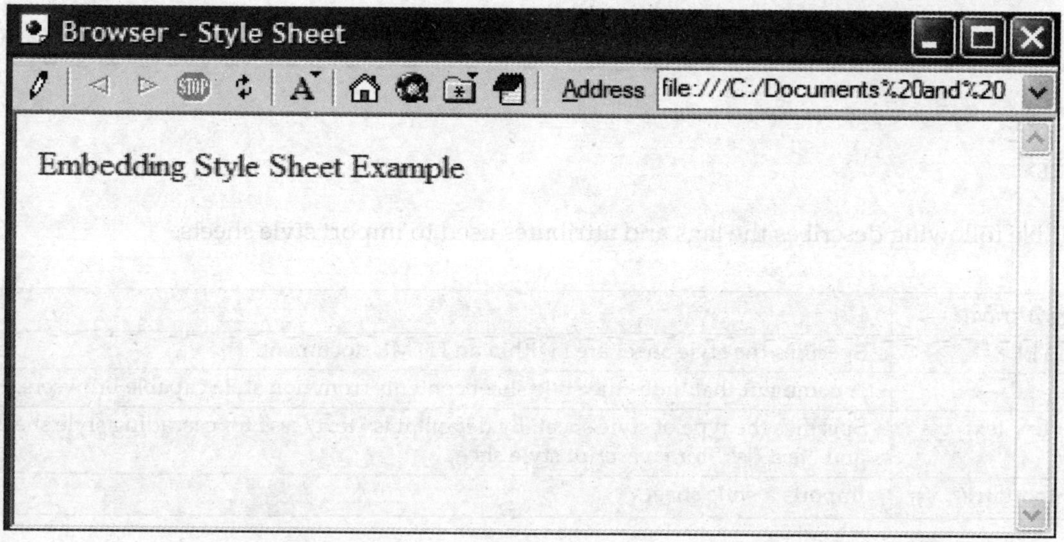

Fig. 8.1 *HTML document with embedding style sheet.*

Linking to a Style Sheet

Linking to a Style Sheet, means create a separate style sheet in a plain text file, including only style definitions. This separate style sheet file can apply to one or number of HTML documents.

After you create the separate style sheet document, you can apply it to the HTML document(s) using either of these methods:

Importing.

Linking.

Importing

Using importing method, multiple style sheet pages each has a specific task can import in single HTML document. For example, you can develop a style sheet page that applies color to paragraph in the document, one that applies color to heading in the document.

Importing Style Sheet means applying the style sheet pages (.css files), along with style information, to HTML document. Like this,

```
<HTML>
  <HEAD>
    <TITLE> Style Sheet </TITLE>
    <STYLE TYPE= "text/css">
    <!-
    @import url('abc.css');
    @import url('xyz.css');
    ->
    </STYLE>
```

```
  </HEAD>
  <BODY>

  </BODY>
</HTML>
```

Table following describes the tags and attributes used to import style sheets.

Tags/Attributes	*Use*
<STYLE>	Specifies the style sheet area within an HTML document.
<!– .... –>	A comment that hides the style sheet contents from non style capable browsers.
TYPE= "text/css"	Specifies the type of style sheet. By default it is "text/css" for cascading style sheet, and "text/jss" for javascript style sheet.
@import url('...');	Imports a style sheet.

For example, to display the paragraph text with green and heading with blue color by using import style sheets, use the following steps:

1. Start with complete style section or style sheet.

```
<HTML>
  <HEAD>
    <TITLE> Importing Style Sheet. </TITLE>
    <STYLE TYPE= "text/css">
    <!–
    ...
    –>
    </STYLE>
  </HEAD>
  <BODY>
    <H1>Importing Style Sheet Example.</H1>
    <P> Importing Style Sheet means applying the style sheet pages (.css files),
    along with style information, to HTML document.</P>
  </BODY>
</HTML>
```

2. Within a style sheet, add a statement which imports one style sheet page (ParagraphColor.css) containing (P {color: green}) statement, which provides green color to the paragraph text within the HTML document.

```
<HTML>
  <HEAD>
    <TITLE> New Document </TITLE>
    <STYLE TYPE= "text/css">
    <!–
    @import url('ParagraphColor.css');
    –>
    </STYLE>
  </HEAD>
  <BODY>
    <H1>Importing Style Sheet Example.</H1>
    <P> Importing Style Sheet means applying the style sheet pages (.css files),
    along with style information, to HTML document.</P>
  </BODY>
</HTML>
```

3. Within a same style sheet, add another statement which imports second style sheet page (HeadColor.css) containing (H1 {color: blue }) statement, which provides blue color to the heading within the HTML document.

```
<HTML>
  <HEAD>
    <TITLE> New Document </TITLE>
    <STYLE TYPE= "text/css">
    <!–
    @import url('ParagraphColor.css');
    @import url('HeadColor.css');
    –>
    </STYLE>
  </HEAD>

  <BODY>
    <H1>Importing Style Sheet Example.</H1>
    <P> Importing Style Sheet means applying the style sheet pages (.css files),
    along with style information, to HTML document.</P>
  </BODY>
</HTML>
```

The output is displayed as shown in following Fig. 8.2.

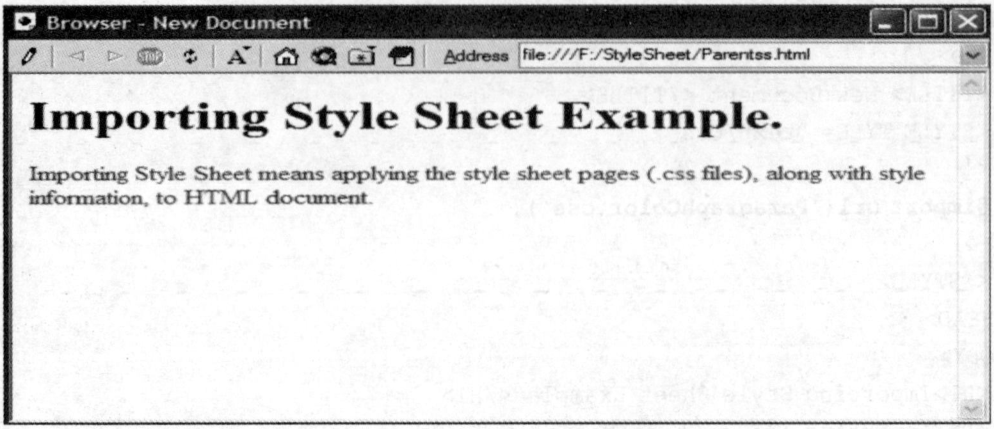

Fig. 8.2 *HTML document with importing style sheet.*

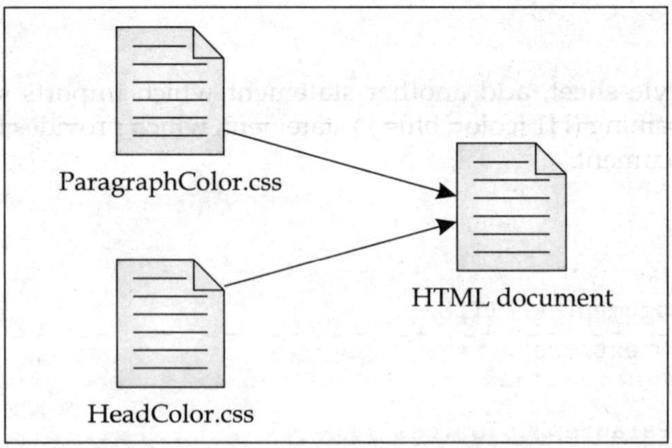

Fig. 8.3 *Importing style sheet.*

Linking

This method gives a visitors a choice of style sheets to use for a specific page.

Table following describes the tags and attributes used to link style sheets.

Tags/Attributes	*Use*
<LINK>	References a Style Sheet.
REL=StyleSheet	Specifies that the referenced file is a Style Sheet. You can use Alternate Style Sheet to reference optional Style Sheet.
TYPE= "text/css"	Specifies the type of style sheet. By default it is "text/css" for cascading style sheet, and "text/jss" for javascript style sheet.
HREF= "URL"	Identifies the style sheet source as standard URL.
TITLE= "..."	Names the Style Sheet.

For example, to display heading with blue color by using linking style sheets, use the following steps:

1. Within the head of HTML document, instead of using <STYLE> section, add <LINK> tag.

```
<HTML>
  <HEAD>
    <TITLE> Linking Style Sheet Document.</TITLE>
    <LINK>
  </HEAD>
  <BODY>
    <H1>Linking Style Sheet Example.</H1>
    <P> This method gives visitors a choice of style sheets to use for a specific
    page. </P>
  </BODY>
</HTML>
```

2. Specify REL and TYPE values of Style Sheet and text/css respectively to link to the standard Style Sheet.

```
<HTML>
  <HEAD>
    <TITLE> Linking Style Sheet Document.</TITLE>
    <LINK REL="StyleSheet"  TYPE= "text/css">
  </HEAD>
  <BODY>
    <H1>Linking Style Sheet Example.</H1>
    <P> This method gives visitors a choice of style sheets to use for a specific
    page. </P>
  </BODY>
</HTML>
```

3. Specify the address of the Style Sheet (HeadColor.css) containing (H1 {color: blue }) statement, within the HREF= attribute. Specify either a relative URL or absolute URL. Here in this example, a relative URL is used, because both Style Sheet and HTML document are within the same folder.

```
<HTML>
  <HEAD>
    <TITLE> Linking Style Sheet Document.</TITLE>
    <LINK REL="StyleSheet" HREF="HeadColor.css" TYPE= "text/css">
  </HEAD>
```

```
   <BODY>
      <H1>Linking Style Sheet Example.</H1>
      <P> This method gives visitors a choice of style sheets to use for a specific
      page. </P>
   </BODY>
</HTML>
```

The output is displayed as shown in following Fig. 8.4.

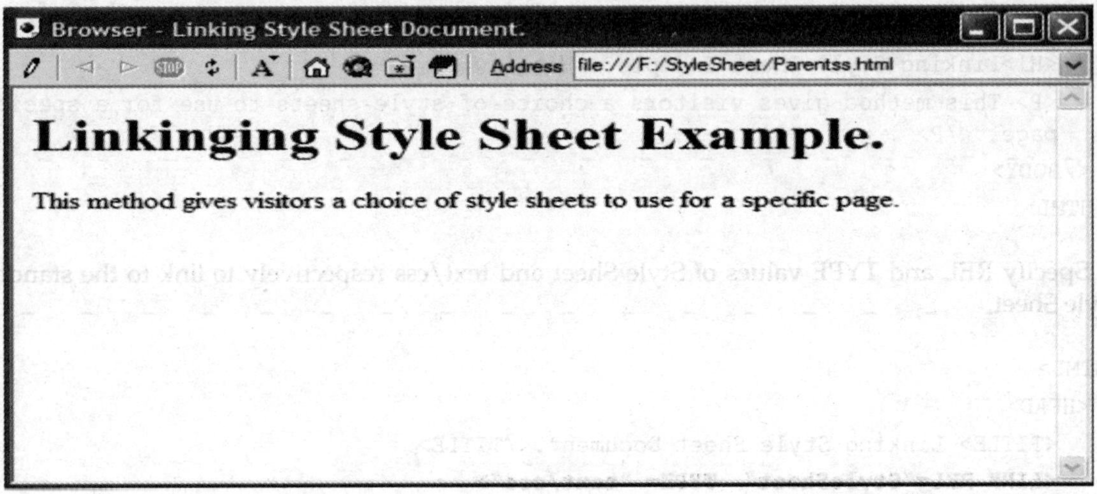

Fig. 8.4 *HTML document with linking style sheet.*

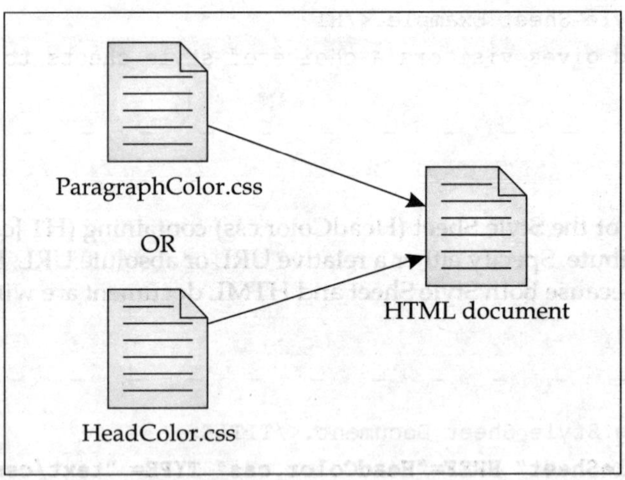

Fig. 8.5 *Linking style sheet.*

Using Inline Style Sheet

Including inline style sheet definitions throughout an HTML document is similar to applying an attributes to HTML tags. You can apply an inline style definition to the specific element or tag in the HTML document. Inline style sheet would not apply it's definition throughout an HTML document. It is time consuming. The table following shows the tags and attributes you use to apply inline styles.

Tags/Attributes	*Use*
Any HTML tag	All HTML tags within and including <BODY> can support style definitions.
STYLE= " ... "	Used for inline style definitions which you apply as an attribute to HTML tags. Provide style definition within quotes.

For example, to apply color and alignment attributes to a specific paragraph within the HTML document, use style definition within the <P> tag.

```
<HTML>
  <HEAD>
    <TITLE> Inline Style Sheet </TITLE>
  </HEAD>
  <BODY>
    <P STYLE="align: right; color: green">Including inline style sheet definitions
    throughout an HTML document is similar to applying an attributes to HTML tags.
    You can apply an inline style definition to the specific element or tag in the
    HTML document. Inline style sheet would not apply it's definition throughout an
    HTML document. It is time consuming.
    </P>

    <P>apply color and alignment attributes to a paragraph, use style definition
    within the  tag.</P>
  </BODY>
</HTML>
```

The output is shown in browser as shown in following Fig. 8.6.

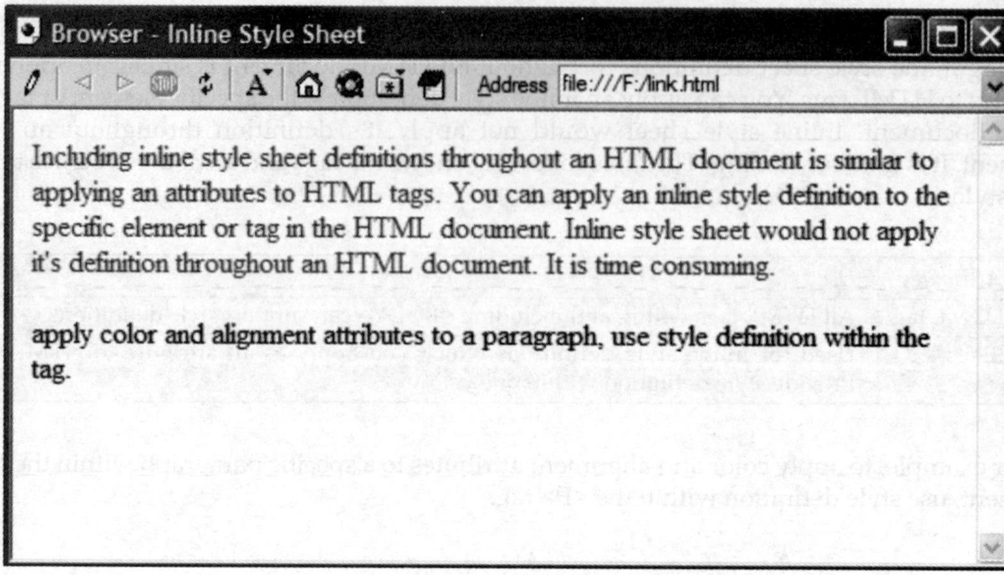

Fig. 8.6 *HTML document with inline style sheet.*

8.3 STYLE SHEET PROPERTIES

Text Properties

To establish text properties for text blocks not of individual characters, use the properties and values shown in following Table.

Property	*Value*
word-spacing	measurement.
letter-spacing	measurement.
text-decoration	none, overline, underline, line-through, blink.
vertical-align	baseline, super, sub, top, text-top, middle-bottom, text-bottom.
text-transform	none, capitalize, uppercase, lowercase.
text-align	left, right, center and justify.
text-indent	measurement or %

Now, apply some of the above properties to the text blocks. For example, to align text paragraph to right side of the web page with spacing between letters of 5 pixels, use following steps:

1. Within the style block, add a P selector.

```
<HTML>
  <HEAD>
    <TITLE> Style Sheet.</TITLE>
    <STYLE>
    <!–
    P
    –>
```

```
    </STYLE>
  </HEAD>
  <BODY>
    <H1>Text Properties.</H1>
    <P>Text Properties of Style Sheet.</P>
  </BODY>
</HTML>
```

2. Add brackets.

```
<HTML>
  <HEAD>
    <TITLE> Style Sheet.</TITLE>
    <STYLE>
    <!–
    P{ }
    –>
    </STYLE>
  </HEAD>
  <BODY>
    <H1>Text Properties.</H1>
    <P>Text Properties of Style Sheet.</P>
  </BODY>
</HTML>
```

3. Add the text-align property with a value 'right' and letter-spacing property with a value of 5 pixels. Separate these two properties with semicolon (;).

```
<HTML>
  <HEAD>
    <TITLE> Style Sheet.</TITLE>
    <STYLE>
    <!–
    P{text-align: right; letter-spacing:5px }
    –>
    </STYLE>
  </HEAD>
  <BODY>
    <H1>Text Properties.</H1>
    <P>Text Properties of Style Sheet.</P>
  </BODY>
</HTML>
```

The output is displayed in browser as shown in following Fig. 8.7 containing the paragraph with the text alignment right and spacing between the letters of 5 pixels.

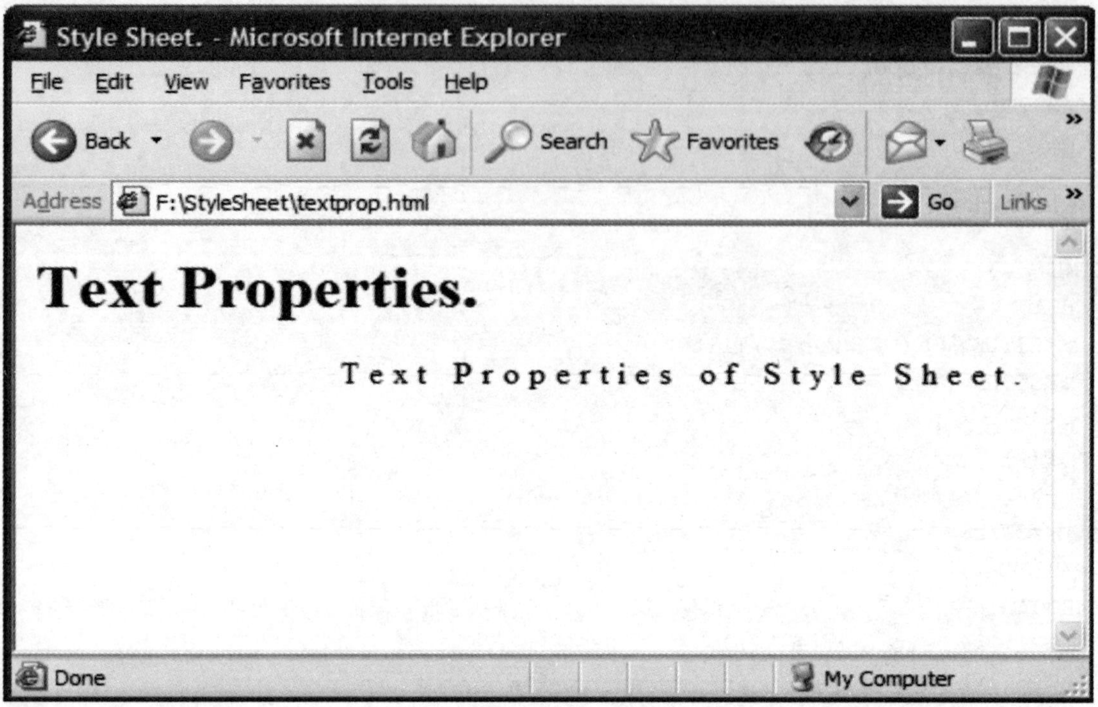

Fig. 8.7 *HTML document containing style sheet with text properties.*

Color and Background Properties

To establish color and background properties for the sample document and or for any block level elements, use the attributes and the values shown in following table.

Property	*Value*
color	#rrggbb
background-color	#rrggbb, transparent
background-image	url(...)
background-repeat	repeat, repeat-x, repeat-y, no-repeat
background	any or all the above properties

To include background color pink, add the color and background properties to the <BODY> element as follows:

1. Within the style block, add the BODY selector.

```
<HTML>
  <HEAD>
    <TITLE> Style Sheet.</TITLE>
    <STYLE>
    <!-
    BODY{ }
    ->
    </STYLE>
  </HEAD>
  <BODY>
    <H1>Color and Background properties.</H1>
    <P>Color and Background properties of Style Sheet.</P>
  </BODY>
</HTML>
```

2. Add background-color attribute and the value, which specifies the #ff00ff color.

```
<HTML>
  <HEAD>
    <TITLE> Style Sheet.</TITLE>
    <STYLE>
    <!-
    BODY{background-color: #ff00ff }
    ->
    </STYLE>
  </HEAD>
  <BODY>
    <H1>Color and Background properties.</H1>
    <P>Color and Background properties of Style Sheet.</P>
  </BODY>
</HTML>
```

The output is displayed in browser as shown in following Fig. 8.8 containing the heading and paragraph with background-color pink (#ff00ff) for whole document.

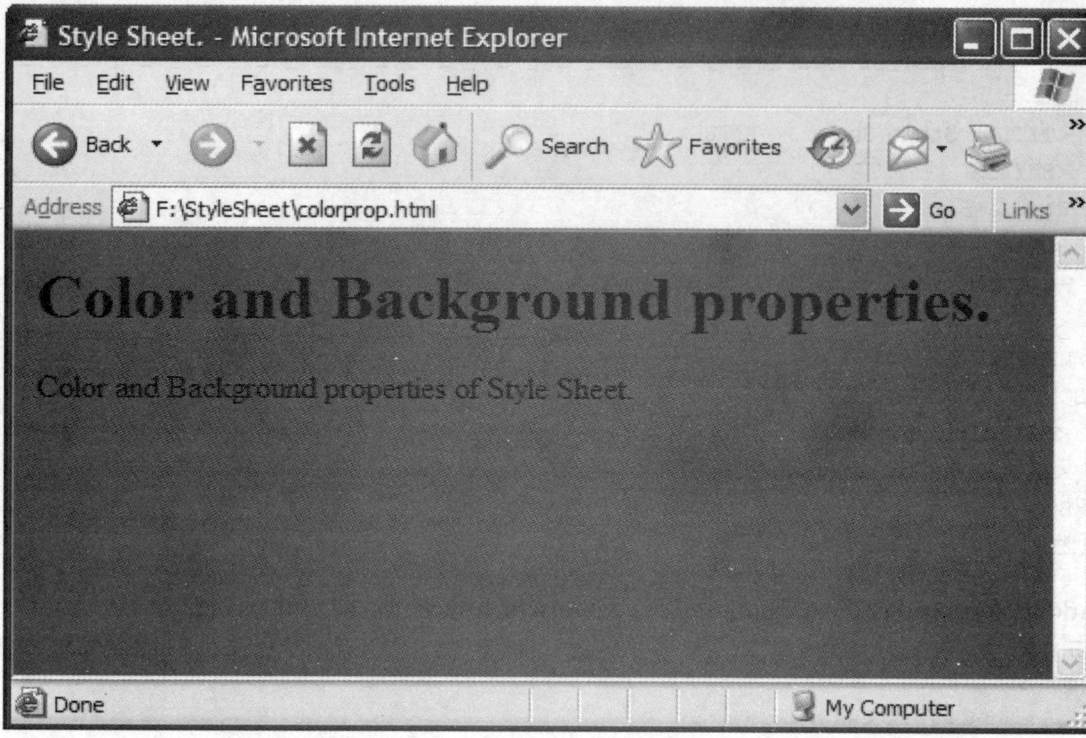

Fig. 8.8 *HTML document containing style sheet with color and background properties.*

Box Properties

To establish box properties for the sample document and or for any text, such as for giving border/box to important information, use the attributes and the values shown in following table.

Property	*Value*
margin-top	measurement, or percentage of parent
margin-right	measurement, or percentage of parent
margin-bottom	measurement, or percentage of parent
margin-left	measurement, or percentage of parent
margin	measurement, or percentage of parent
border-width	measurement, thick, medium, thin
border-color	#rrggbb
border-style	none, dotted dashed, solid, double, groove, ridge, inset, outset
border	any or all of above attributes
width	measurement, or percentage
height	measurement, or percentage
float	right, left, none
clear	right, left, none, both

To establish box properties for the heading (<H1>) element, add it to the <H1> element as follows:

1. Within the style block, add the H1 selector.

```
<HTML>
  <HEAD>
    <TITLE> Style Sheet.</TITLE>
    <STYLE>
      <!–
      H1{ }
      –>
    </STYLE>
  </HEAD>
  <BODY>
    <H1> Box properties.</H1>
    <P> Box properties of Style Sheet.</P>
  </BODY>
</HTML>
```

2. Add margin-top attribute with value 30%, border-style attribute with value solid and border-width attribute with value 4.

```
<HTML>
  <HEAD>
    <TITLE> Style Sheet. </TITLE>
    <STYLE>
    <!–
    H1 {margin-top: 30%; border-style: solid; border-width: 4px}
    –>
    </STYLE>
  </HEAD>
  <BODY>
    <H1>Box properties.</H1>
    <P>Box properties of Style Sheet.</P>
  </BODY>
</HTML>
```

The output is displayed in browser as shown in following Fig. 8.9 containing heading with border style solid, border width 4 pixels thick and 30% margin from the top.

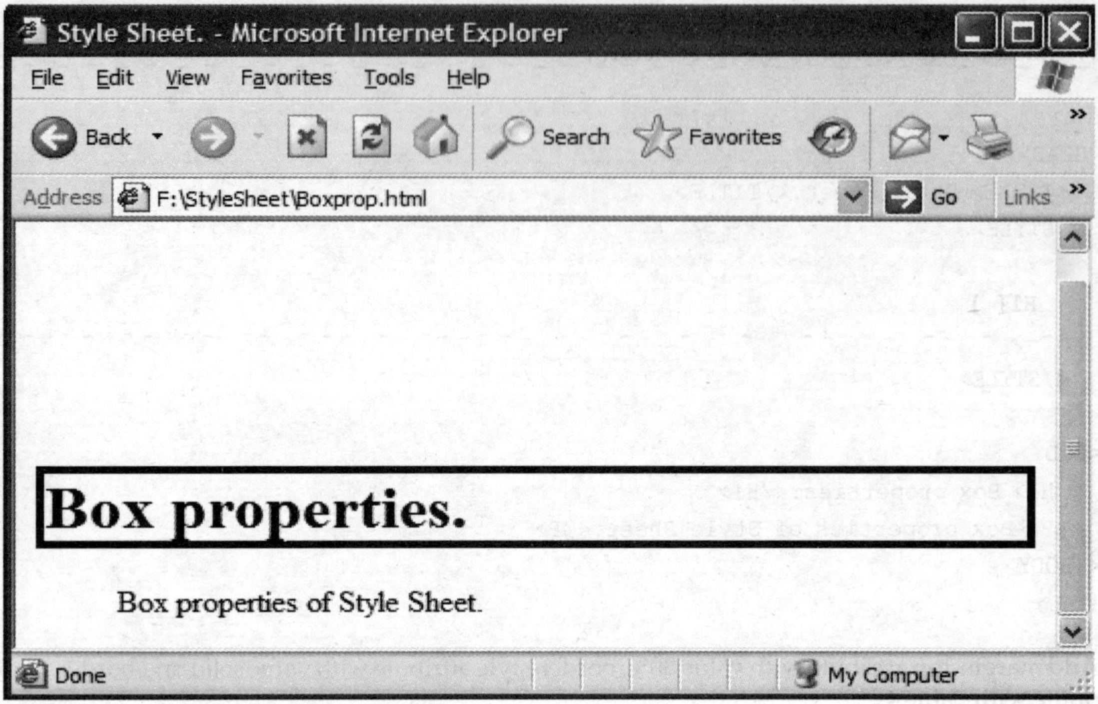

Fig. 8.9 *HTML document containing style sheet with box properties.*

Font Properties

To establish font properties for the sample document and or for any block level elements, use the attributes and the values shown in following table.

Property	*Value*
font-family	Times New Roman, Arial, serif, sans-serif, monospace
font-style	normal, italic, oblique
font-variant	normal, small-caps
font-weight	Normal, bold, bolder, lighter, 100, 200, 300, 400, 500, 600, 700, 800, 900
font-size	xx-small, x-small, small, medium, large, x-large, xx-large, or size measurement
font	any or all the above properties

To establish font properties for the sample document, add it to the <BODY> element as follows:

1. Within the style block, add the BODY selector.

```
<HTML>
  <HEAD>
    <TITLE> Style Sheet.</TITLE>
    <STYLE>
    <!–
    BODY{ }
    –>
    </STYLE>
  </HEAD>
  <BODY>
    <H1> Font properties. </H1>
    <P> Font properties of Style Sheet. </P>
  </BODY>
</HTML>
```

2. Add font-family attribute and the value, which specifies the Sans-serif and font-style attribute with value italic.

```
<HTML>
  <HEAD>
    <TITLE> Style Sheet.</TITLE>
    <STYLE>
    <!–
    BODY {font-family: sans-serif; font-style: italic}
    –>
    </STYLE>
  </HEAD>
  <BODY>
    <H1> Font properties.</H1>
    <P> Font properties of Style Sheet.</P>
  </BODY>
</HTML>
```

The output is displayed in browser as shown in following Fig. 8.10 containing heading and paragraph with font-family sans-serif and font-style italic.

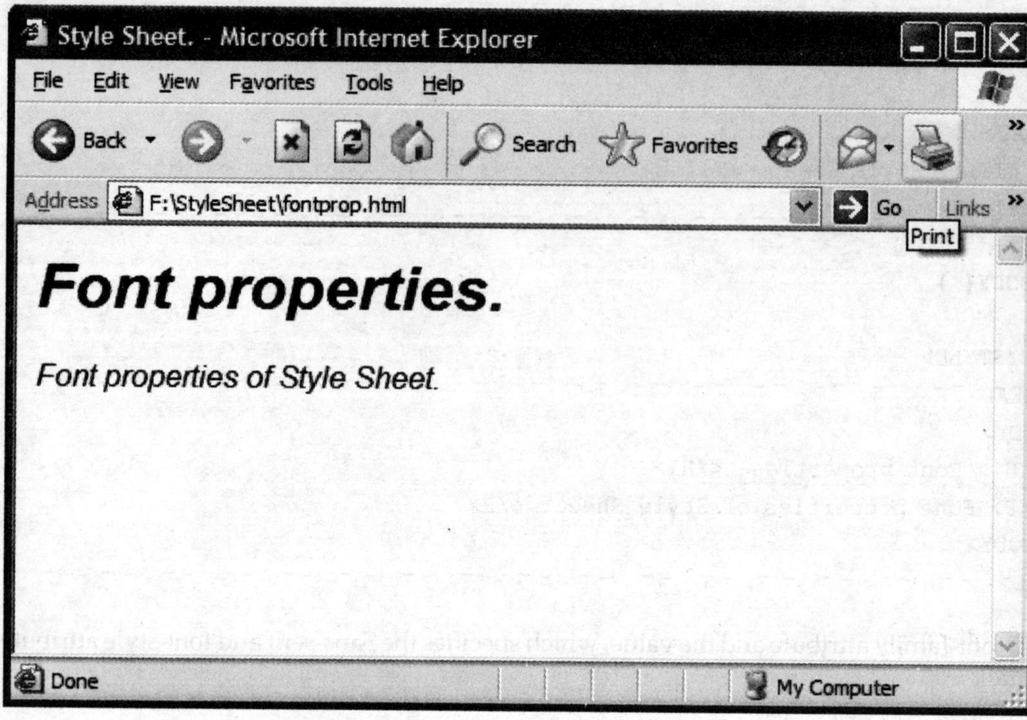

Fig. 8.10 *HTML document containing style sheet with font properties.*

PRACTICE

Create web Page and apply the style rules.

```
<HTML>
  <HEAD>
  <TITLE> Style Sheet.</TITLE>
  <STYLE>
    <!-
    BODY{background-color: #00ff00;font-family : sans-serif; font-style: italic}
    P{text-align: right; letter-spacing:5px }
    H1{margin-top: 30%; border-style: solid; border-width: 4}
    ->
  </STYLE>
  </HEAD>
  <BODY>
    <H1>Color and Background properties.</H1>
    <P>Color and Background properties of Style Sheet.</P>
```

```
  </BODY>
</HTML>
```

The Output is displayed in following Fig. 8.11.

Fig. 8.11

QUESTIONS

1. How to Embed Style-Sheet in the HTML Document?
2. How to Embed Style-Sheet in the HTML Document?
3. How to use inline Style-Sheet in the HTML Document?
4. Explain Text properties of the Style Sheet in the HTML Document.
5. Explain Box properties of the Style Sheet in the HTML Document.
6. Explain Font properties of the Style Sheet in the HTML Document.
7. Explain Color and Background properties of the Style Sheet in the HTML Document.

□□□

9

Introduction to Scripting

The scripts are small sections of programming code that make your Web pages more dynamic and interactive. A script can display different values for a variable, result of calculations of other variables, or display the date, time or both values.

HTML 4.0 supports a set of built-in intrinsic events that trigger a script when there an action such as the click of a mouse button, the press of a keyboard key, click of a form button etc. intrinsic events are attributes of HTML elements.

The HTML document can include client-side scripts, which are run on the browser which is located on the client computer. In HTML document the beginning and end of script is marked by the <SCRIPT> start tag and </SCRIPT> end tag, respectively.

Two scripts – VBScript and JavaScript – you can use as scripting or programming language in your pages.

Purpose:

1. Scripts may be evaluated, as a document loads, to modify the contents of the document dynamically.
2. Scripts process input as it is entered.
3. Scripts may be triggered by events that affect the document such as loading, uploading, mouse movement, etc.
4. Scripts may be linked to form controls (*e.g.* buttons) to produce graphical user interface.

9.1 SCRIPTING LANGUAGES VBSCRIPT AND JAVASCRIPT

VBScript

To make your document dynamic or interactive you include VBScript scripts within your HTML document. VBScript scripts either run on the client computer or sever; therefore both HTML (uses client side browser) and ASP (uses server-side browser) support VBScript.

You can use VBScript script within the HEAD or BODY sections of your Web document.

A document that includes a VBScript script requires a special handling: it must be processed by an application that understands VBScript (such as Internet Explorer 4.0 or greater).

In HTML document, you identify the name of the scripting language and state the location at which the script should run, and embed the scripts using the SCRIPT element. For example:

```
<SCRIPT LANGUAGE= "VBSCRIPT">
<!–
   ...
//–>
<SCRIPT>
```

In above example, the <SCRIPT> start tag and </SCRIPT> end tag mark the beginning and the end of the script. The LANGUAGE attribute names the scripting language. The <! – and – //> delimiters represents comments. In this delimiters you include the VBScript statements. Remember that these statements does not ends with semicolon (;).

VBScript Constants

A constant is a value that never changes. VBScript has predefined intrinsic constants: Empty, Nothing, Null, True, and False. You can specify constant by using the const statement as follows:

```
Const pi = 3.145
```

VBScript Variables

A variable is a value that always changes. VBScript provides three statements with which you can declare variables - Dim, Private, and Public. You can specify variable by using these statements as follows:

```
Dim a
Private b
Public c
```

VBScript Operators

VBScript provides three types of operators with which you can calculate and test values.

1. Arithmetic operators: — Plus (+), Minus (–), Multiplication (*), Division (/)
2. Comparison operator: — Equal to (=), less than (<), greater than (>), less than or equal to (<=), greater than or equal to (>=)
3. Logical operators: - Not, And, Or, Xor, Eqv, Imp.

VBScript Control Statements

Conditional control statements

VBScript supports two types of conditional control statements: If…Then…ElseIf…Then…End If and Select Case.

The syntaxes are:

To check single condition;

```
If (Condition) Then
  Else
EndIf
```

To check multiple conditions;

```
If (Condition1) Then
  ElseIf (Condition2) Then
  ElseIf (Conditionn) Then
  EndIf
```

To reduce complications to check multiple conditions, use select… case statement.

```
Select (expression)
  Case 1:
  …
  Case 2:
  …
  Case n:
  …
  Case Default:
  …
End Select
```

Looping control statements

Looping control statements repeatedly executes the statements within the loop until a particular value reached or particular conditional remains or becomes true. VBScript supports four types of looping control statements: Do … Loop, While … Wend, For Each … Next, and For… Next

The syntaxes are:

```
For i = 1 To 10 Step 1
  Statement 1
  Statement 2
  Statement n
Next

Do
  Statement 1
  Statement 2
  Statement n
```

```
While(Condition)

Do until (condition)
   Statement 1
   Statement 2
   Statement n
Loop
```

Displaying text in the Browser

VBScript has *document* object with a *write* method for displaying text in the browser window. The write method accepts a string value that it displays in the browser. For example,

```
document.write("This is my first VBScript program.")
```

The following HTML document contains VBScript included in BODY tags to display a string message.

```
<HTML>
  <HEAD>
    <TITLE> VBScript </TITLE>
  </HEAD>
  <BODY>
    <SCRIPT LANGUAGE="VBSCRIPT">
    <!-
    document.write("This is my First VBScript program.")
    //->
    </SCRIPT>
  </BODY>
</HTML>
```

The output is displayed as shown in following Fig. 9.1.

In the following HTML document, you include VBScript code in BODY tags for performing arithmetic operation.

```
<HTML>
  <HEAD>
    <TITLE> VBScript </TITLE>
  </HEAD>
  <BODY>
    <SCRIPT LANGUAGE="VBSCRIPT">
    <!-
```

Fig. 9.1 *HTML document including VBscript displaying text.*

```
    Dim a,b,c
    a = 2
    b = 3
    c = a + b
    document.write("Addition of a,b and c= " & c)//two strings are connected with &
    sign
    </SCRIPT>
  </BODY>
</HTML>
```

The output is displayed as shown in following Fig. 9.2.

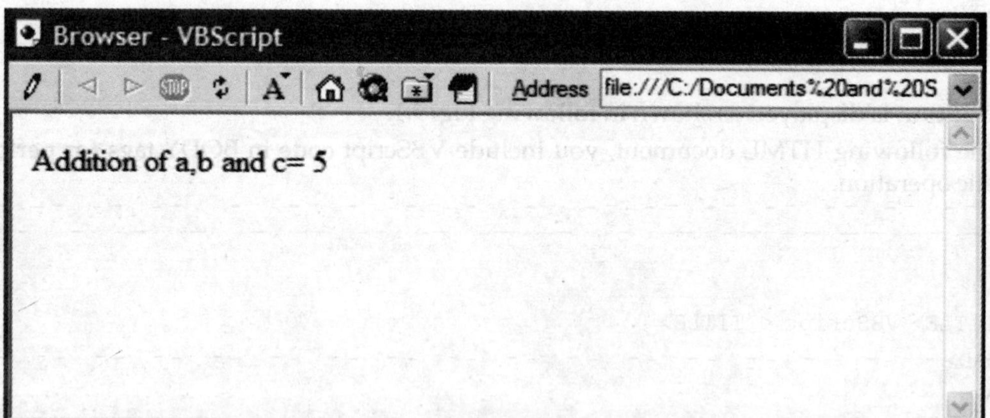

Fig. 9.2 *HTML document including VBscript performing arithmetic operation.*

In the following HTML document, you include VBScript code in BODY tags which performs looping operation.

```
<HTML>
  <HEAD>
    <TITLE> VBScript Program </TITLE>
  </HEAD>
  <BODY>
    <SCRIPT LANGUAGE="VBSCRIPT">
    <!–
    document.write("Odd Numbers between 1 to 10: - ")
    For i = 1 To 10 Step 2
    document.write(i)
    document.write(",  ")
    Next
    </SCRIPT>
  </BODY>
</HTML>
```

The output is displayed as shown in following Fig. 9.3.

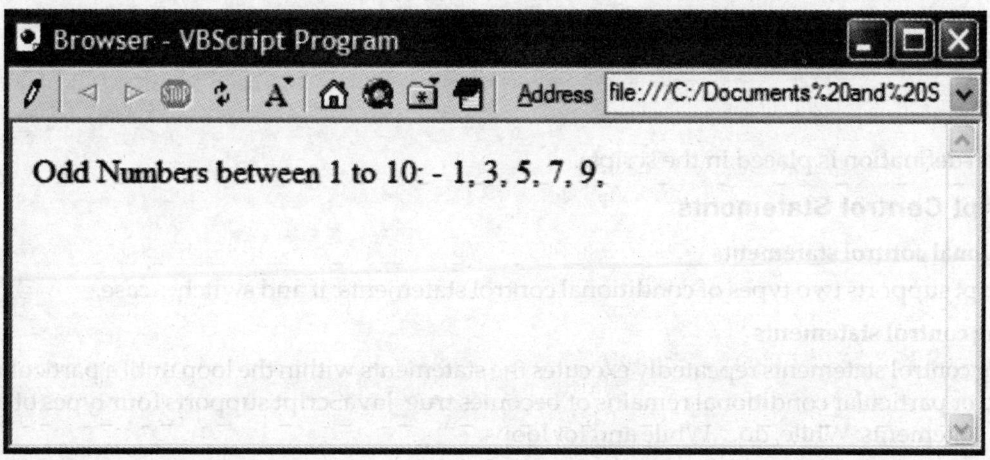

Fig. 9.3 *HTML document including VBscript performing loop control operation.*

JavaScript

JavaScript is a scripting language that is created by Netscape Communication and Sun Microsystems. JavaScript is easier and simpler to use and it is less sophisticated, less complex than a real programming language. JavaScript allows wed browser to produce dynamic documents and enables programmers to call routines written in Java, C and C++.

Variable Declaration

A variable is a value that always changes. JavaScript variables are declared by using *var* keyward followed by variable name. Variable declaration ends with semicolon. For example;

```
var varable_name;
or
var variable_name=value;
```

JavaScript Operators

JavaScript provides three types of operators with which you can calculate and test values.

1. Arithmetic operators: – Plus (+), Minus (-), Multiplication (*), Division (/)
2. Comparison operator: – Equal to (=), less than (<), greater than (>), less than or equal to (<=), greater than or equal to (>=)
3. Logical operators: – Not, And, Or, Xor, Eqv, Imp.
4. Increment (++) and decrement (– –) operators

Use of Functions

Functions are defined by using *function* keyward followed by the name of the function and paramenters in paranthesis. The block of function is enclosed in opening and closing curly brackets in which JavaScript code is written. For example,

```
function function_name(parameter list)
{
  .....     ;
}
```

Function defination is placed in the scripts.

VBScript Control Statements

Conditional control statements

JavaScript supports two types of conditional control statements: if and switch...case.

Looping control statements

Looping control statements repeatedly executes the statements within the loop until a particular value reached or particular conditional remains or becomes true. JavaScript supports four types of looping control statements: While, do...While and for loops.

Displaying text in the Browser

JavaScript has *document* object with a *write* method for displaying text in the browser window. The write method accepts a string value that it displays in the browser. For example,

```
document.write("This is my first JavaScript Example.");
```

The following HTML document contains JavaScript included in BODY tags to display a string message.

```
<HTML>
  <HEAD>
    <TITLE> JavaScript Program </TITLE>
  </HEAD>
  <BODY>
    <SCRIPT LANGUAGE="JavaScript">
    <!–
    document.write("This is my first JavaScript Example.");
    //–>
    </SCRIPT>
  </BODY>
</HTML>
```

The output is displayed as shown in following Fig. 9.4.

Fig. 9.4 *HTML document including Javascript displaying message.*

In the following HTML document, you include JavaScript code in BODY tags for performing arithmetic operation.

```
<HTML>
  <HEAD>
    <TITLE> JavaScript Program </TITLE>
  </HEAD>
  <BODY>
    <SCRIPT LANGUAGE="JavaScript">
    <!–
    var a,b,c;
```

```
    a = 2;
    b = 3;
    c = a + b;
    document.write("Addition of a,b and c= "+ c);//two strings are connected with +
sign
    //->
    </SCRIPT>
  </BODY>
</HTML>
```

The output is displayed as shown in following Fig. 9.5.

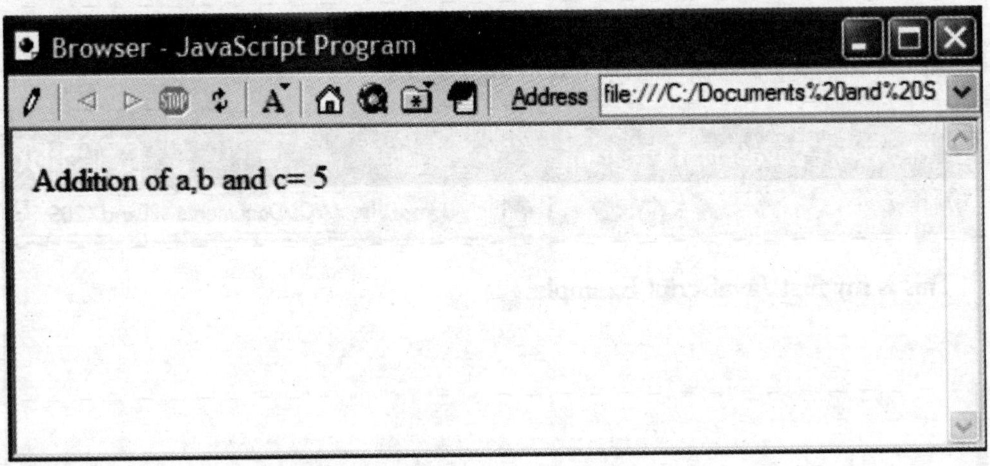

Fig. 9.5 *HTML document including Javascript performing arithmetic operation.*

In the following HTML document, you include VBScript code in BODY tags which performs looping operation.

```
<HTML>
  <HEAD>
    <TITLE> JavaScript Program </TITLE>
  </HEAD>
  <BODY>
    <SCRIPT LANGUAGE="JavaScript">
    <!-
    document.write("Numbers 1 to 10 are : - ")
    var i;
    for(i = 1; i <= 10; i++ )
```

```
        {
          document.write(i);
          document.write(", ");
        }
        //->
        </SCRIPT>
    </BODY>
</HTML>
```

The output is displayed as shown in following Fig. 9.6.

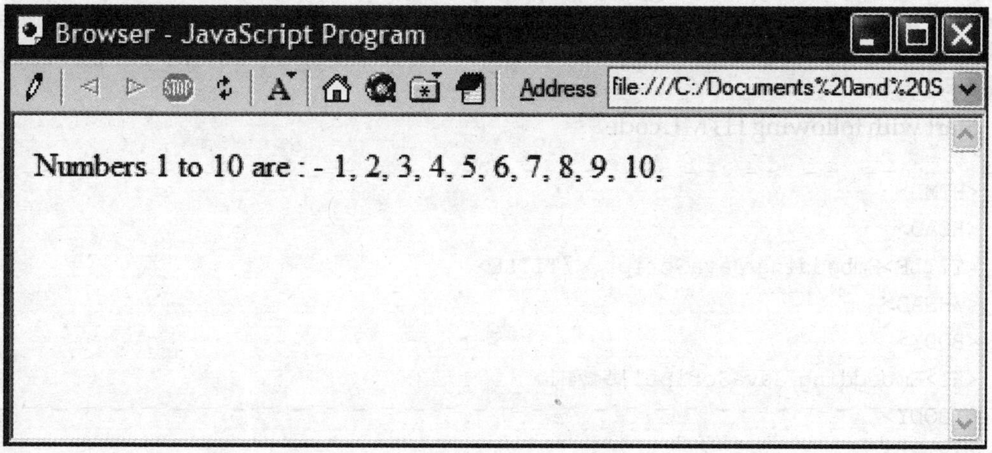

Fig. 9.6 *HTML document including VBScript performing loop control operation.*

9.2 JAVASCRIPT TERMINOLOGY

To work with the JavaScript, you need to be familiar with the following terminology:

Object: An object is a thing – a check box on form, the form itself, an image, a document, a link, or even a browser window. Some objects are built into JavaScript and are not necessarily part of your Web page. For example, the Date object provides a wide range of date information. You can think of objects as the nouns in the JavaScript language.

Property: A property describes an object. Properties can be anything from the color to number of items, such as radio buttons, within an object. When visitors select an item in a form, they change form's properties. You can think of properties as the adjectives in the JavaScript language.

Method: A method is an instruction. The method available for each object describes what you can do with the object. For example, using a method, you can convert text in an object to all uppercase or to all lowercase letters. Every object has a collection of methods, and every method belongs to an at least one object. You can think of methods as the verbs in the JavaScript language.

Statement: A statement is a JavaScript language sentence. Statements combine the objects, properties and methods (nouns, adjectives and verbs).

Function: A function is a collection of statements that perform actions. Function contains one or more statements and thus can be considered the paragraphs of the JavaScript language.

Events: An events occurs when something happens on your page, such as visitor submitting a form or clicking the mouse on the object or moving the mouse cursor over an object.

Event handler: An event handler waits for something to happen—such as mouse moving over a link—and then launches a script based on that event. For example, the onMouseOver event handler performs an action when visitor moves the mouse pointer over the object.

9.3 EMBEDDING JAVASCRIPT

Embedding JavaScript means including JavaScript within the document body, (that is, including JavaScript script in the <BODY> tag) the browser performs the actions as it reads the page. If the <BODY> tag includes a JavaScript script, the first task the browser completes is running the script.

Let us embed the JavaScript script that displays the result of the addition of contents of two variables.

1. Start with following HTML code.

```
<HTML>
<HEAD>
<TITLE>Embedding JavaScript.</TITLE>
</HEAD>
<BODY>
<H1>Embedding JavaScript!!!</H1>
</BODY>
</HTML>
```

2. Add <SCRIPT> tags within the body.

```
<BODY>
<H1>Embedding JavaScript!!!</H1>
<SCRIPT>
<!- -
a=3
b=2
c= a+b
document. write("Result in c =" +c);
- ->
</SCRIPT>
</BODY>
```

9.4 ADDING JAVA SCRIPT BLOCK IN HEADER

If you want to use JavaScript frequently within the document, place it in the document's <HEAD> tag. Like this:

```
<HTML>
<HEAD>
<SCRIPT TYPE= "text/javascript">
<!-
...
//->
</SCRIPT>
</HEAD>
<BODY>
</BODY>
<HTML>
```

Here in this script define any function and call that function from the document body. For example;

```
<HTML>
<HEAD>
<SCRIPT TYPE= "text/javascript">
  <!-
    function Display() {document.write ("Adding Java Script Block in Header");}
  //->
</SCRIPT>
</HEAD>
<BODY>
</BODY>
<HTML>
```

To call the function Display() from the document body, and again <SCRIPT> tags within <BODY> tags, as follows:

```
<HTML>
<HEAD>
<SCRIPT TYPE= "text/javascript">
  <!-
    function Display() {document.write ("Adding Java Script Block in Header");}
  //->
```

```
</SCRIPT>
</HEAD>
<BODY>
<SCRIPT TYPE= "text/javascript">
  <!-
    Display()
  //->
</SCRIPT>
</BODY>
<HTML>
```

The output is shown in following Fig. 9.7

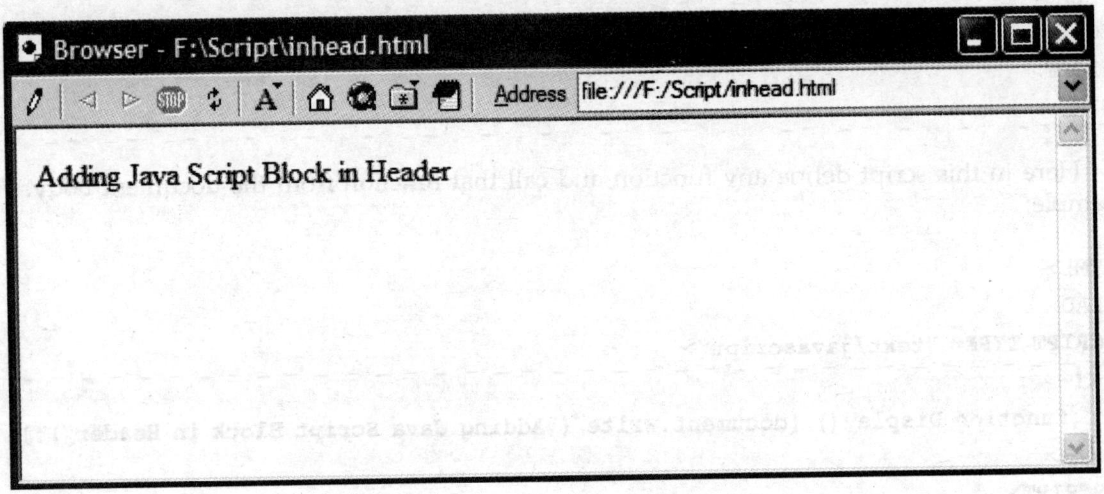

Fig. 9.7 *Adding JavaScript block in header.*

9.5 LINKING JAVA SCRIPT

If you place script function in separate file and refer to that file from your document, then this method is called as linking JavaScript. The linked file is simply text file that includes variable declarations and functions. You can link this file to other documents. This file has .JS extention.

For example, the function *Display()* is written in separate file named *linkfun.js* which contains the following text:

```
document.write ("Linking Java Script");
```

You can then link to script with the following code from the document head as follows:

```
<HTML>
<HEAD>
```

```
<SCRIPT SRC="linkfun.js" TYPE= "text/javascript">
  <!–
  //–>
</SCRIPT>
</HEAD>
<BODY>
</BODY>
<HTML>
```

The output is shown in following Fig. 9.8

Fig. 9.8 *Linking JavaScript.*

So by including this reference by using SRC= attribute in <SCRIPT>, you can access any function from any document.

9.6 MOUSE EVENTS

HTML 4.0 supports a set of built-in intrinsic events that trigger a script when there is an action such as the click of a mouse button, the press of a keyboard key, click of a form button etc. intrinsic events are attributes of HTML elements.

JavaScript event handlers react to visitor action by running statements or calling JavaScript functions (moving their mouse, clicking a button, or selecting an option buttons on a form). For example, with the onMouseOver and onMouseOut event handlers, you can change the information on the status bar of you browser, you can display the result by calculating the contents of the variables, etc.

Events are the attributes of HTML elements; you can use many elements with most elements. But others are limited to one or two. This is illustrated in following example:

1. Start with an HTML document that includes a Head element (<H1>).

```
<HTML>
  <HEAD>
    <TITLE>
    Mouse Events
    </TITLE>
  </HEAD>
  <BODY>
    <H1>Click Me!!!</H1>
  </BODY>
</HTML>
```

2. Add the onMouseOver= event handler to the <H1> tag.

```
<H1 onMouseOver = " ">Click Me!!! </H1>
```

3. Add window.status= to the event handler. Window.status= attribute specifies what appears in the status bar.

```
<H1 onMouseOver = "window.status= 'HTML 4.0' ">Click Me!!!</H1>
```

So when you move mouse pointer over Click Me!!! HEAD element, 'HTML 4.0' message is displayed on the browser's status bar.

4. Add another event handler onMouseOut= to the <H1> tag.

```
<H1 onMouseOver = "window.status= 'HTML 4.0' " onMouseOut= " ">Click Me!!!
</H1>.
```

Add another window.status= to this event handler.

```
<H1 onMouseOver = "window.status= 'HTML 4.0' " onMouseOut= "window.status=
'Netscapes Navigator' ">Click Me!!! </H1>.
```

So when you move mouse pointer over 'Click Me!!!' HEAD element, 'HTML 4.0' message is displayed on the browser's status bar, and when mouse pointer is out from the 'Click Me!!!' HEAD element, 'Netscape's Navigator' message is displayed on the status bar.

So your HTML program becomes as follows:

```
<HTML>
<HEAD>
<TITLE>
Mouse Events
```

```
</TITLE>
</HEAD>
<BODY>
<H1 onMouseOut="window.status='Netscapes Nevigator'"
onMouseOver="window.status='HTML 4.0'">Click Me!!!</H1>
</BODY>
</HTML>
```

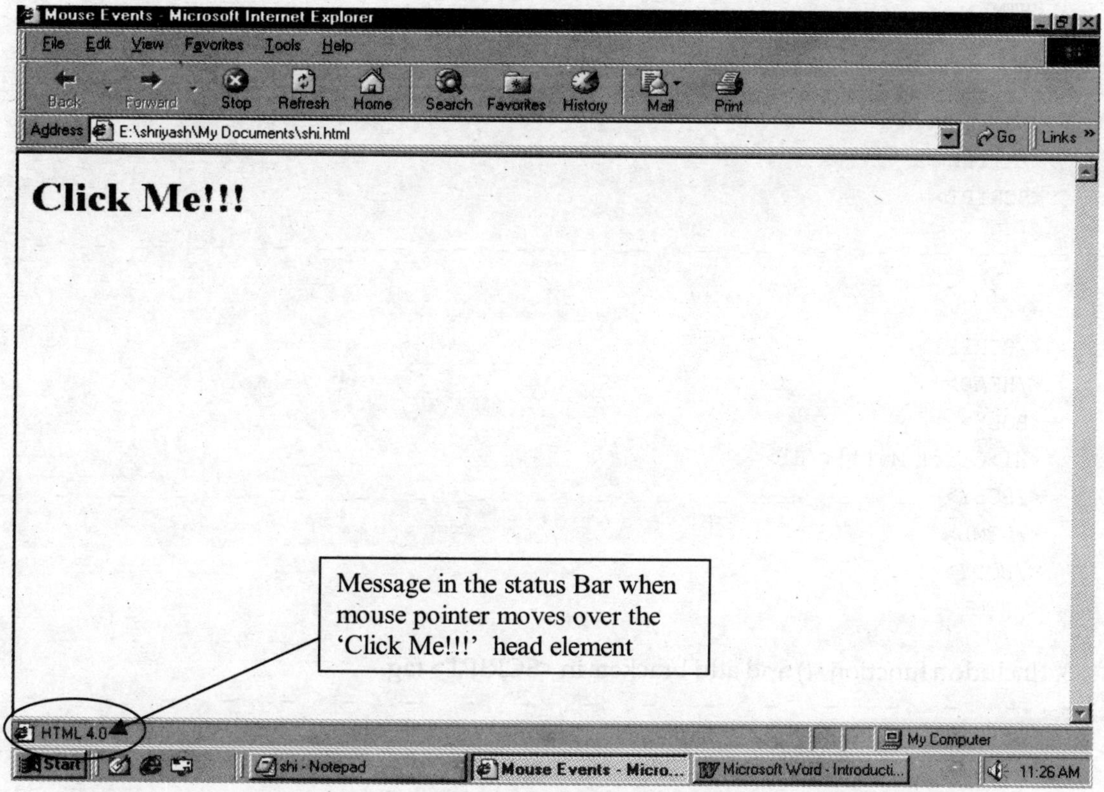

Fig. 9.9 *OnMouseOver and OnMouseOut event showing windows status in status bar.*

You can also display these message by using function in script as follows:

1. Start with an HTML document that includes a HEAD element (<H1>).

```
<HTML>
<HEAD>
<TITLE>
Mouse Events
</TITLE>
</HEAD>
```

```
<BODY>
<H1>Click Me!!!</H1>
</BODY>
</HTML>
```

2. In an HTML document, add the <SCRIPT> and comment tags anywhere in the document i.e. either in <HEAD> tag or <BODY> tag.

```
<HTML>
<HEAD>
<TITLE>
Mouse Events
</TITLE>
<SCRIPT>
<!–


–>
</SCRIPT>
</HEAD>
<BODY>
<H1>Click Me!!!</H1>
</BODY>
</HTML>
</BODY>
</HTML>
```

3. Include a function s() and add brackets in <SCRIPT> tag.

```
<SCRIPT>
<!–
function s()
{

}
–>
</SCRIPT>
```

4. Add window.status= statement to set the status bar.

```
<SCRIPT>
<!–
```

```
function s()
{
window. status= "HTML 4.0"
}
->
</SCRIPT>
```

5. Now you need only to call the script from the HEAD element in the document with an onMouseOver statement.

```
<H1 onMouseOver="s()">Click Me!!!</H1>
```

So your HTML program becomes as follows:

```
<HTML>
<HEAD>
<TITLE>
Mouse Events
</TITLE>
<SCRIPT>
<!-
function s()
{
window. status="HTML 4.0"
}
->
</SCRIPT>
</HEAD>
<BODY>
<H1 onMouseOver="s()">Click Me!!!</H1>
</BODY>
</HTML>
</BODY>
</HTML>
```

9.7 ONCLICK, ONCHANGE, AND ONSUBMIT EVENT HANDLERS

onClick Event Handler

This event fires when object is clicked on. This event performs action on button, radio button, checkbox, submit button, and reset button. For example, following HTML document includes a button, which invokes the a() function when it is clicked. That a() function is defined in the JavaScript containing a write method to display a string in the document.

```
<HTML>
  <HEAD>
    <TITLE> OnClick Event Handler </TITLE>

    <SCRIPT LANGUAGE="JavaScript">
    <!-
      function a()
      {
      document.write ("Use of onClick Event in  Java Script");
      }

    //->
    </SCRIPT>
  </HEAD>
  <BODY>
    <FORM onSubmit="b();">
      <INPUT TYPE="button" VALUE="Display" onClick="a();">
    </FORM>
  </BODY>
</HTML>
```

The output is shown in following Fig. 9.10(a).

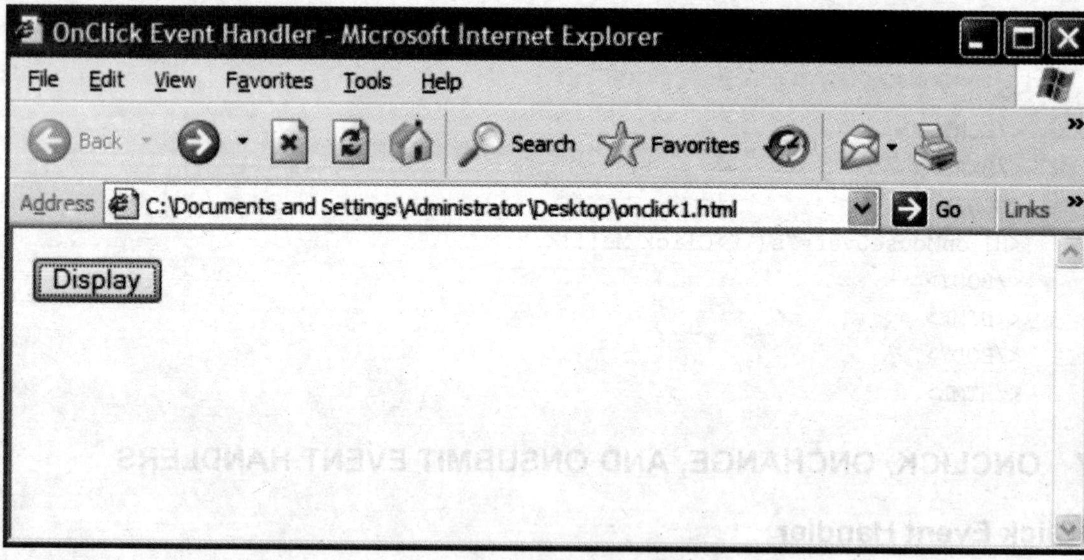

Fig. 9.10(a) *OnClick event on button shows following result.*

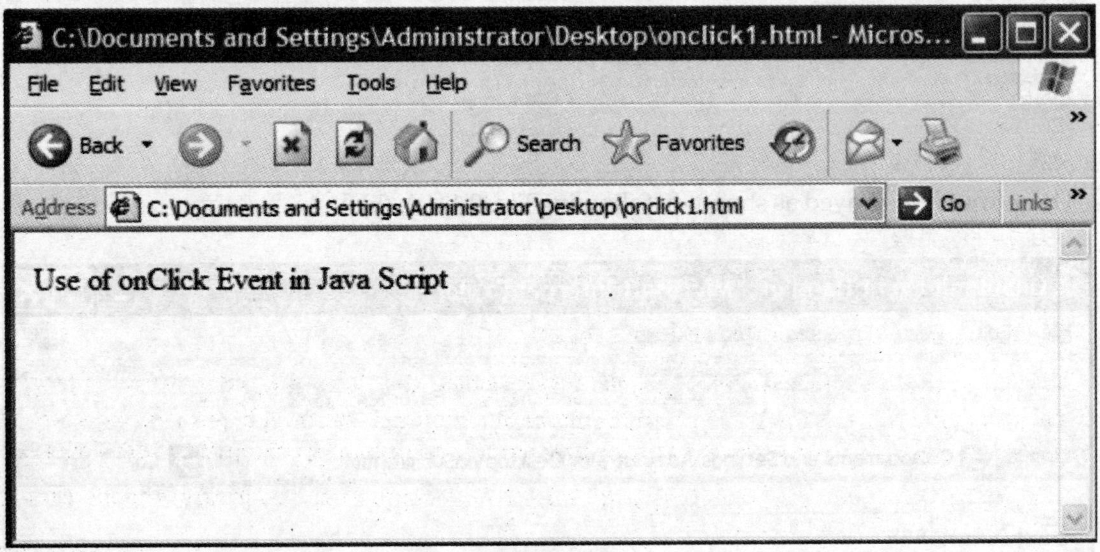

Fig. 9.10(b)

onSubmit Event Handler

This event fires when Submit button is clicked. This event submits the all information in the document to the server. For example, following HTML document includes a Submit button, which invokes the b() function, calling from the FORM element for submitting all information in it, when it is clicked. That b() function is defined in the JavaScript containing a write method to display a string in the document.

```
<HTML>
  <HEAD>
    <TITLE> OnSubmit Event Handler </TITLE>
    <SCRIPT LANGUAGE=”JavaScript”>
    <!–

      function b()
      {
      document.write (“Use of onSubmit Event Handler in Java Script”);
      }
    //–>
    </SCRIPT>
  </HEAD>
  <BODY>
    <FORM onSubmit=”b();”>
      First Name:<INPUT TYPE=”text”>
      <BR>
```

```
    Last Name:<INPUT TYPE="text">
    <INPUT TYPE="submit" VALUE="submit">
  </FORM>
 </BODY>
</HTML>
```

The output is displayed as shown in following Fig. 9.11(a), (b).

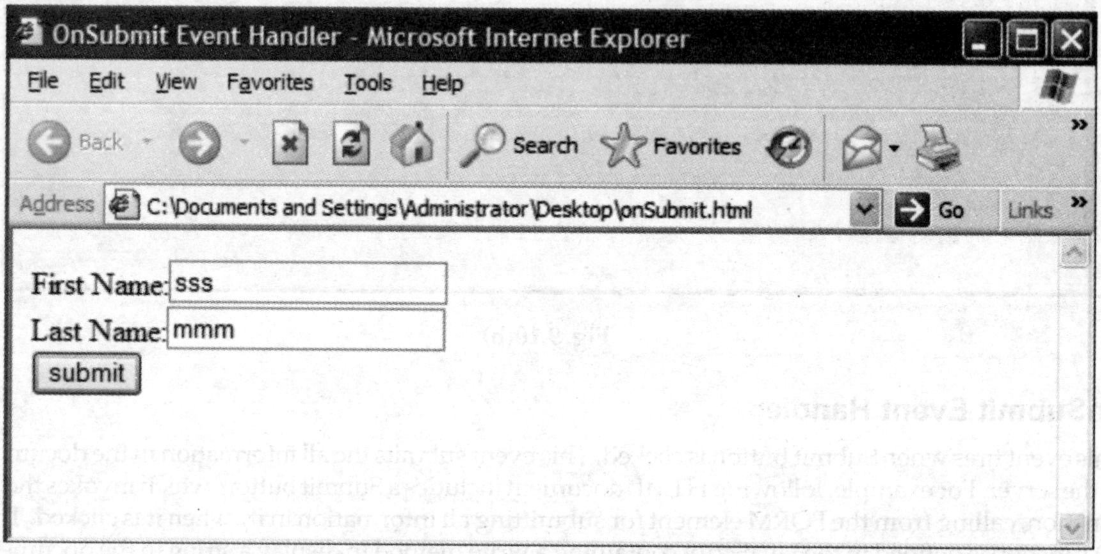

Fig. 9.11(a) *OnSubmit event on "Submit" button shows following result.*

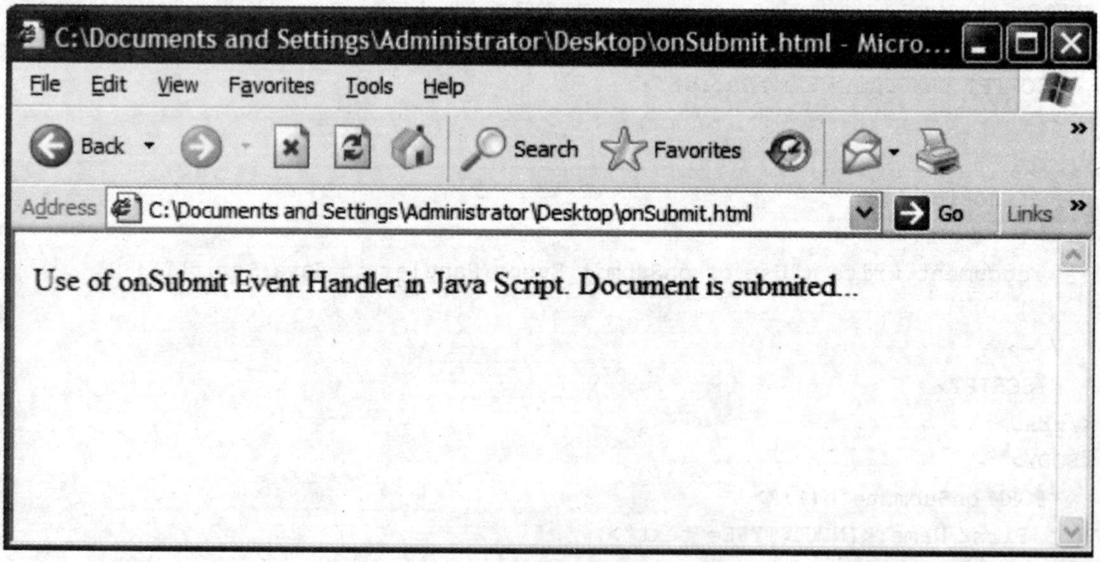

Fig. 9.11(b)

onChange Event Handler

This event fires when text is changed in an object. This event performs action on Text, Password, and TextArea object. For example, following HTML document includes a button, which invokes the a() function when it is clicked. That a() function is defined in the JavaScript containing a write method to display a string in the document.

```
<HTML>
<HEAD>
<TITLE> OnSubmit Event Handler </TITLE>
<SCRIPT LANGUAGE="JavaScript">
<!-

    function b()
    {
    document.write ("Use of onChange Event Handler in Java Script");
    }
//->
</SCRIPT>
</HEAD>
<BODY>
<FORM>
Name:<INPUT TYPE="text" onChange="b();">
</FORM>
</BODY>
</HTML>
```

The output is displayed as shown in following Fig. 9.12(a), (b).

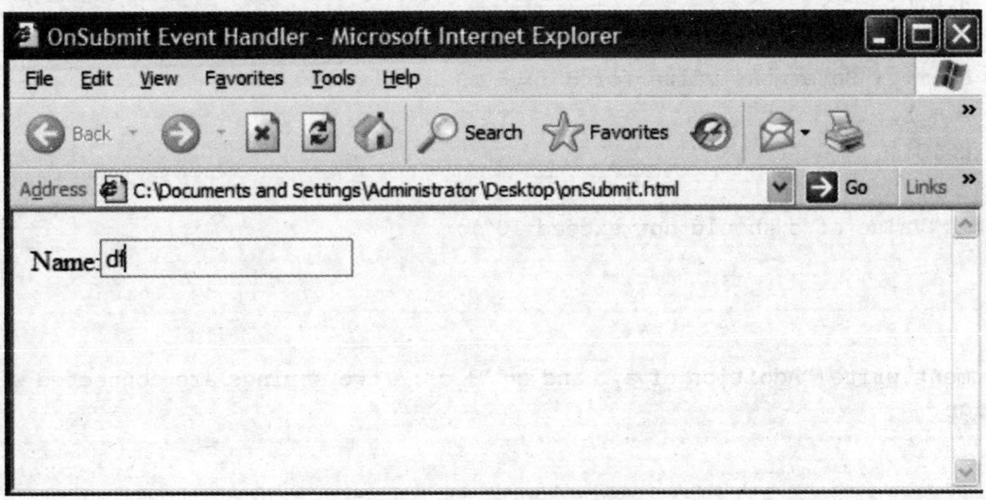

Fig. 9.12(a) *OnChange event on "textbox" shows following result.*

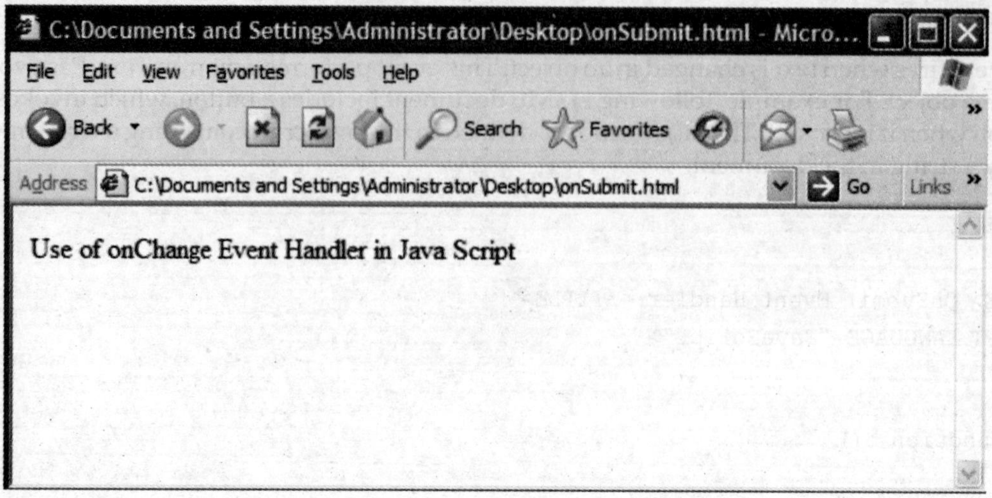

Fig. 9.12(b)

PRACTICE

Design a Web Application using Embedded JavaScript.

```
<HTML>
  <HEAD>
    <TITLE> JavaScript Program </TITLE>
  </HEAD>
  <BODY>
    <SCRIPT LANGUAGE="JavaScript">
    <!–
      var a,b,c;
      a = Prompt("Enter the value for A");
      b = Prompt("Enter the value for B");
      c = a + b;
      if (c>10)
      {
      Alert("Value of c should not exceed 10");
      }
      Else
      {
      document.write("Addition of a,b and c= "+ c);//two strings are connected with
      + sign
      }
    //–>
```

```
    </SCRIPT>
  </BODY>
</HTML>
```

The Output is shown in following Fig. 9.13(a), (b) & (c).

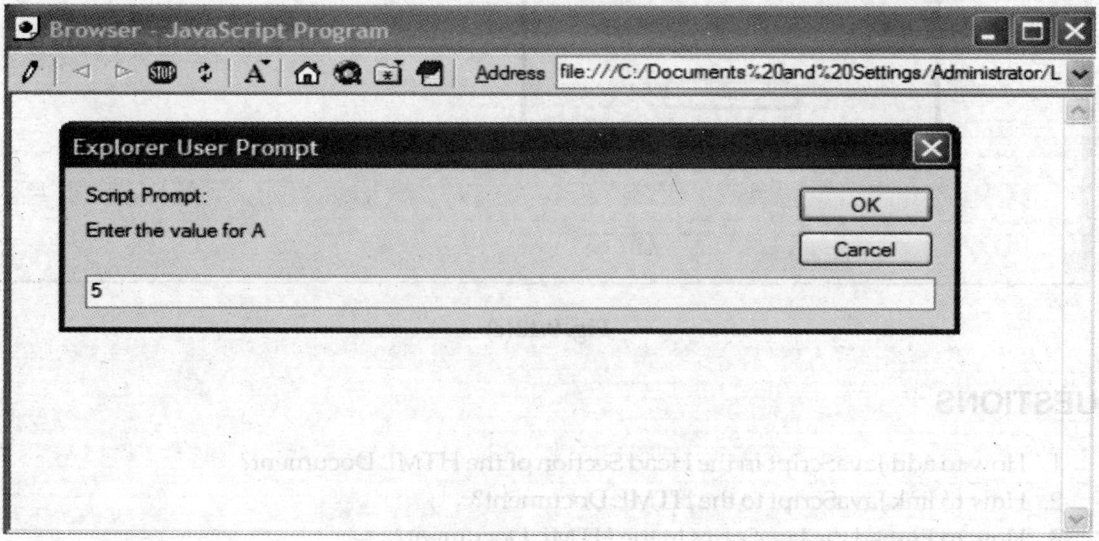

Fig. 9.13(a)

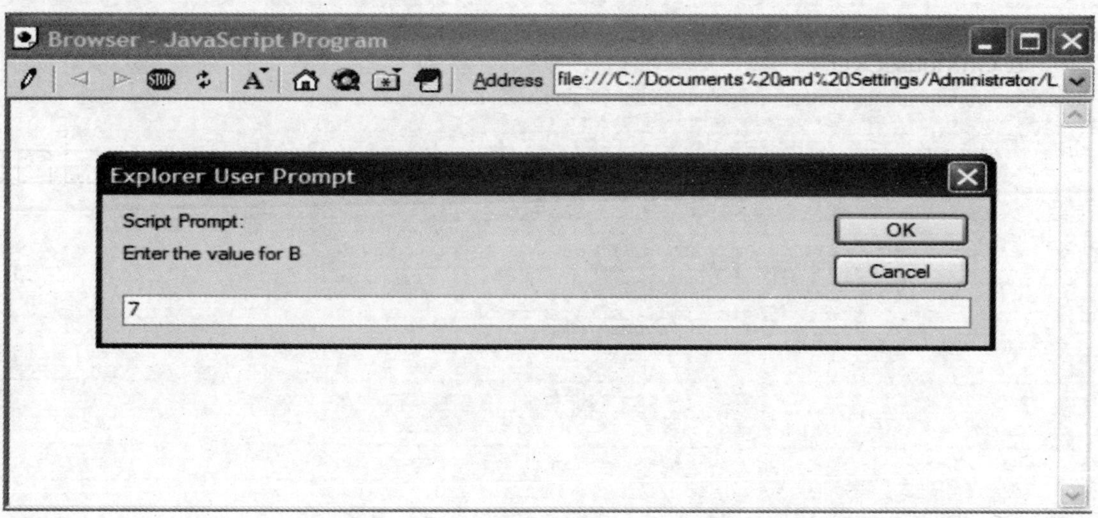

Fig. 9.13(b)

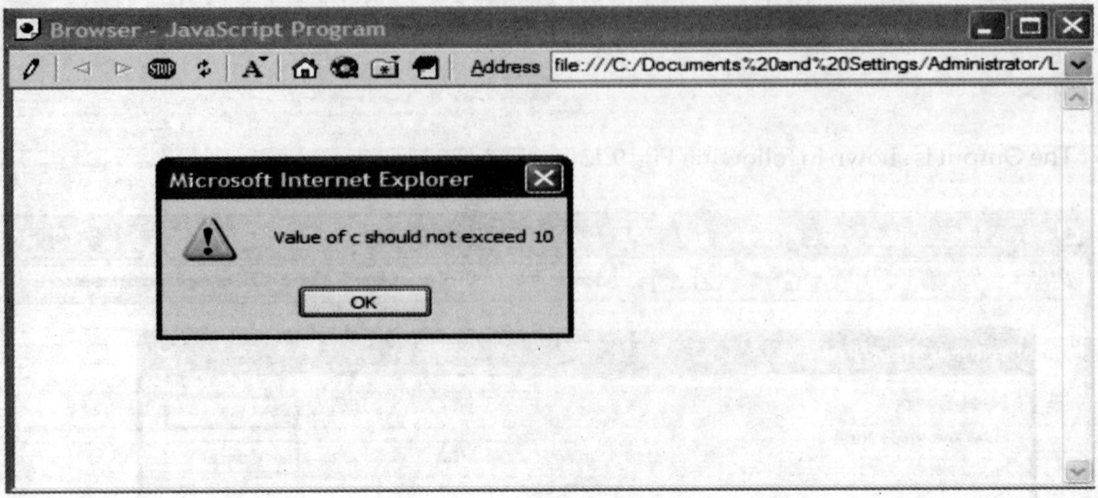

Fig. 9.13(c)

QUESTIONS

1. How to add JavaScript in the Head Section of the HTML Document?
2. How to link JavaScript to the HTML Document?
3. How to Embed the JavaScript in the HTML Document?
4. Explain mouse events used in the JavaScript.
5. Writc a Short note on—
   a. OnClick
   b. OnMouseOver

□□□

10

Including Multimedia

10.1 ADDING SOUNDS

Adding sounds can produce some fun effects, Web page sounds come in two types:

1. Sounds that play when visitors access the page.
2. Sounds that play when visitors click something.

Sounds that play when visitors access the page are called background sounds and can be a short tune or one that plays the entire time a visitor is at the page.

Sounds that play when visitors clicks on something *i.e.* on control box shown in following Fig. 10.1.

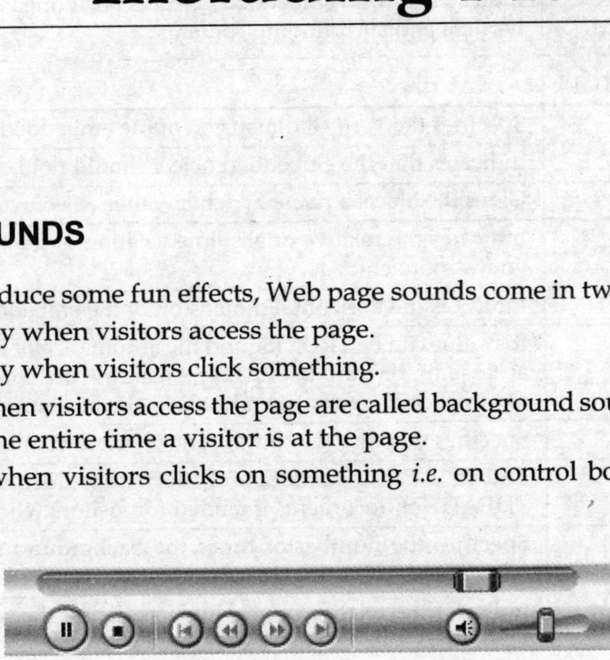

Fig. 10.1 *Sound Control Box.*

Sound File Formats

Sound file comes in one of the following four formats:

MIDI (Musical Instrument Digital Interface): A MIDI file contains a synthesized music. MIDI files are small files. If you have a MIDI capable musical instrument (Keyboard) and a little skill, you can create your own MIDI files.

AIFF (Audio Interchange File Format): An AIFF contains a recorded sound sample, which can be a music or a sound effect. This format is most common on Macintosh and usable on most other systems.

AU (AUdio): An AU file also provides acceptable – but not great-quality sample sound. These files are accessible on wide range of browsers and computer systems.

WAV (WAVe): A WAV file provides a very good quality sampled sound, but is usable almost exclusively on Windows computers.

MP3 (Media Player version 3): An MP3 file provides an outstanding sound, but is usable only through browser plug-ins.

If you have sound card and microphone, you can record your own sounds and you can find thousands or millions of sample sounds on the web.

When you have a sound file, use following HTML tags and attributes in table:

Tags/Attributes	*Use*
<EMBED>	Places an embedded object into a document.
ALIGN={LEFT,RIGHT, CENTER,ABSBOTTOM, ABSMIDDLE,BASELINE, BOTTOM, TEXTTOP,TOP}	Indicates how an embedded object is positioned relative to the document borders and surrounding contents.
HEIGHT= "n"	Specifies the vertical dimension of the embedded object.
HIDDEN	Indicates that the embedded object should not be visible.
NAME= "..."	Gives the object a name by which other objects can refer to it.
SRC= "URL"	Indicates the relative or absolute location of the file containing the object you want to embed.
WIDTH= "n"	Indicates the horizontal dimension of the embedded object.
AUTOSTART= "..."	It's value can be TRUE (Sound file automatically opens when Web page is accessed.) or can be FALSE (Visitors do something *i.e.* sound file automatically opens when he clicks the button.)
HIDDEN= "..."	Specifies whether the sound control box is visible in the Web page.
<BGSOUND>	Embed a background sound file within documents/use in document <HEAD> of documents intended for visitors who use Internet Explorer.
LOOP= "{n, INFINITE}"	Specifies the number of times the background sound file repeats. The value INFINITE is the default.
SRC= "URL"	Indicates the relative or absolute location of the sound file.

We can link Sound files or we can embed them in the Web page.

Linking video file is done as follows:

```
<A HREF="F:\catia smp\sound.wav">Catia Sound</A>
```

Include this statement in HTML document as follows:

```
<HTML>
  <HEAD>
    <TITLE> Linking Sound File</TITLE>
  </HEAD>
  <BODY>
    <A HREF="F:\catia smp\sound.wav">Catia Sound</A>
  </BODY>
</HTML>
```

The output is displayed in browser as shown in following Fig. 10.2.

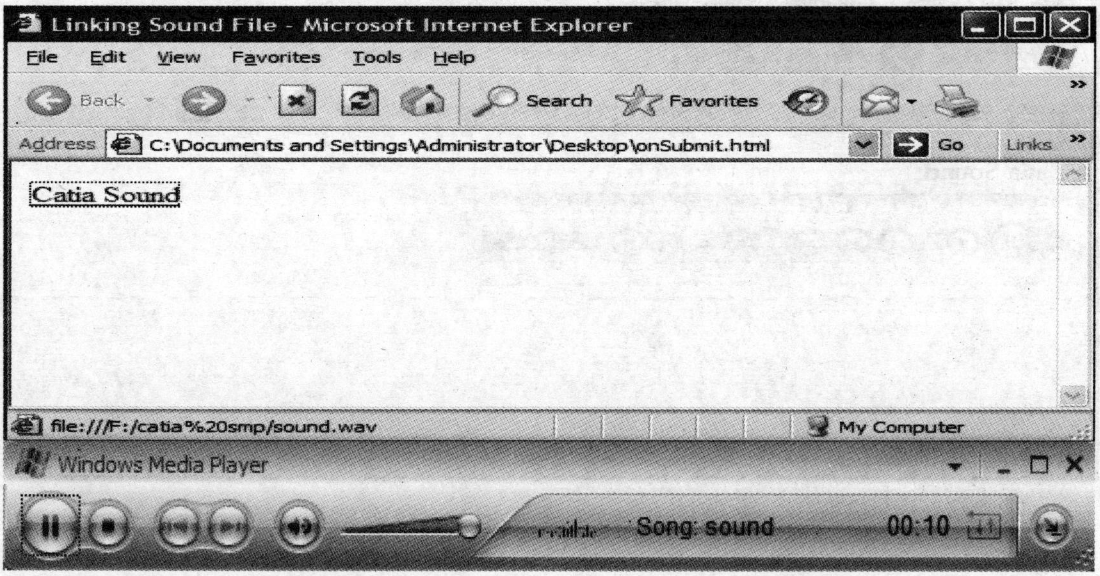

Fig. 10.2 *HTML Document Containing Link to Video File.*

When Sound files are linked, visitors can choose whether to view them.

Embedding Sound file is done by adding <EMBED> tag in <BODY> tags as follows:

```
<BODY>
<EMBED SRC="F:\catia smp\sound.wav">
</BODY>
```

Include these statements in HTML document as follows:

```
<HTML>
  <HEAD>
    <TITLE> Linking Sound File</TITLE>
  </HEAD>
  <BODY>
    Catia Sound: <BR>
    <EMBED SRC="F:\catia smp\sound.wav">
  </BODY>
</HTML>
```

The output is displayed in browser as shown in following Fig. 10.3.

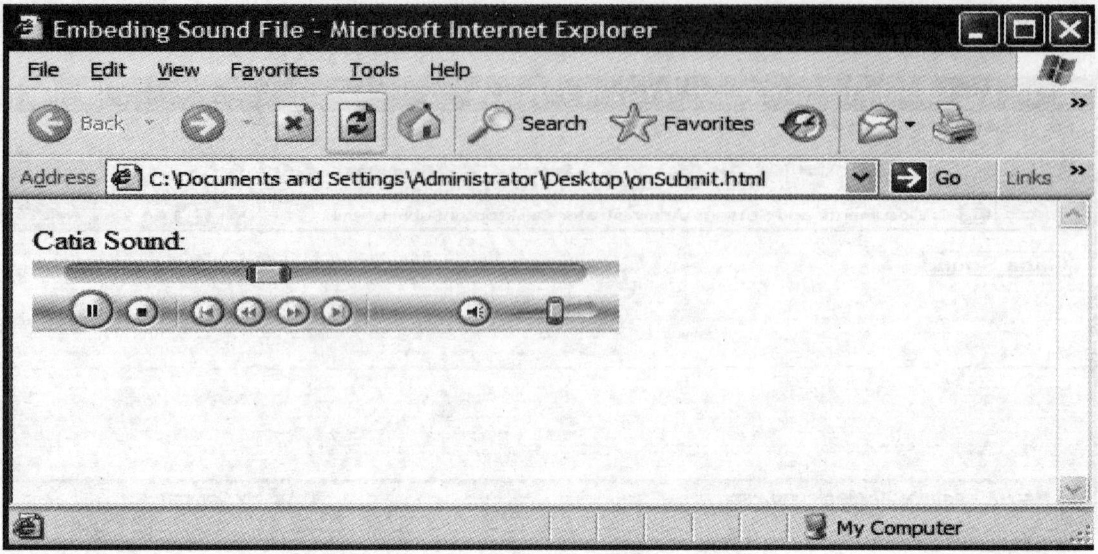

Fig. 10.3 *Sound Control Box in browser.*

10.2 ADDING VIDEO

Video is the one of the most interesting multimedia element in the HTML. In order to clear the complex concept or to show a certain process, it is essential to add video in your Web page. Add video in Web page using video files.

Video file comes in one of the following formats:

AVI (Audio Video Interleave): This format is more widely available. It is a good choice if your visitors will almost exclusively be using Windows.

MPEG (Motion Picture Expert Group): This format is the most widely supported, and the viewers are available for most platforms. Because it is highly compressed and usable, MPEG is the best universal choice.

QuickTime: This format, originally a Macintosh standard, is now available for windows standard. It provides a good quality if your visitors have the plug-in and use personal computers.

If you have a video file, use following HTML tag and attributes in table:

Tags/Attributes	*Use*
<EMBED>	Places an embedded object into a document.
ALIGN={LEFT,RIGHT, CENTER,ABSBOTTOM, ABSMIDDLE,BASELINE, BOTTOM, TEXTTOP,TOP}	Indicates how an embedded object is positioned relative to the document borders and surrounding contents.
HEIGHT= "n"	Specifies the vertical dimension of the embedded object.
HIDDEN	Indicates that the embedded object should not be visible.

NAME= "..."	Gives the object a name by which other objects can refer to it.
SRC= "URL"	Indicates the relative or absolute location of the file containing the object you want to embed.
WIDTH= "n"	Indicates the horizontal dimension of the embedded object.
AUTOSTART= "..."	It's value can be TRUE (video file automatically opens when Web page is accessed.) or can be FALSE (Visitors do something *i.e.* video file automatically opens when he clicks the button.)

We can link video files or we can embed them in the Web page.

Linking video file is done as follows:

```
<A HREF="F:\catia smp\CATIA_P3Splash.avi">Catia Video</A>
```

Include this statement in HTML document as follows:

```
<HTML>
  <HEAD>
    <TITLE> Linking Video File</TITLE>
  </HEAD>
  <BODY>
    <A HREF="F:\catia smp\CATIA_P3Splash.avi">Catia Video</A>
  </BODY>
</HTML>
```

The output is displayed in browser as shown in following Fig. 10.4.

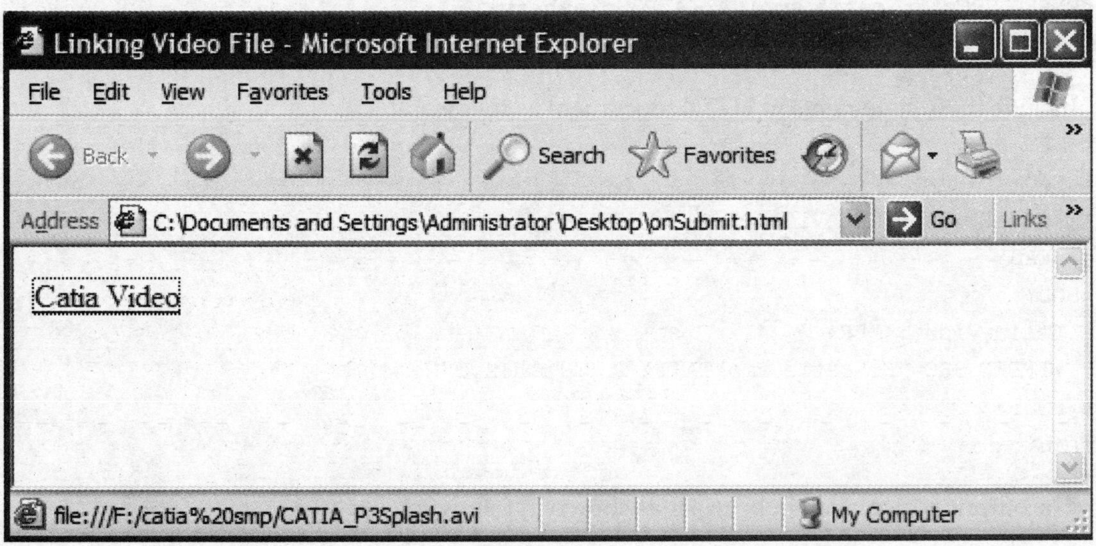

Fig. 10.4 *HTML document containing link to video file*

Fig. 10.5 *Video File Playing after Link is Clicked.*

When video files are linked, visitors can choose whether to view them.

Embedding video file is done by adding <EMBED> tag in <BODY> tags as follows:

```
<BODY>
  <EMBED SRC="F:\catia smp\CATIA_P3Splash.avi">
</BODY>
```

Include these statements in HTML document as follows:

```
<HTML>
  <HEAD>
    <TITLE> Embeding Video File</TITLE>
  </HEAD>
  <BODY>
    Catia Video:</BR>
    <EMBED SRC="F:\catia smp\CATIA_P3Splash.avi">
  </BODY>
</HTML>
```

The output is displayed in browser as shown in following Fig. 10.6.

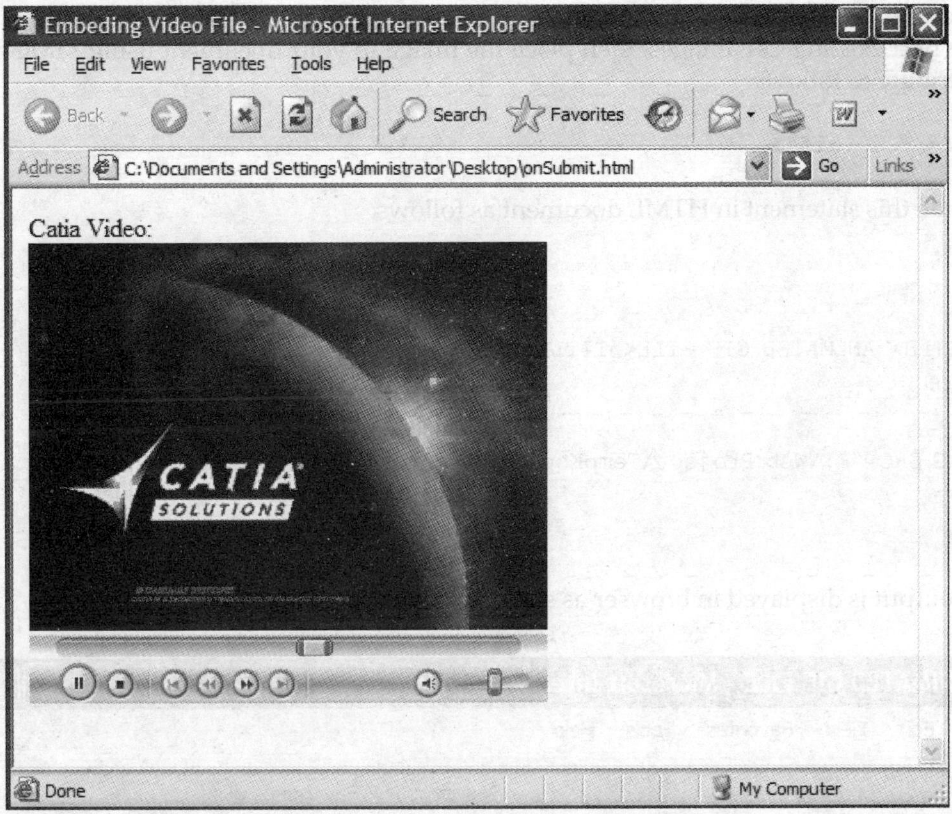

Fig. 10.6 *Video Control Box in browser.*

Further you can specify other attributes such as HEIGHT, WIDTH, AUTOSTART etc.

10.3 ANIMATED GIF

One of the most simple multimedia element is an animated GIF, which is a file that includes a bunch of images stacked together to give the illusion of movement. Animated GIFs are similar to those little cartoon booklets. When you quickly whirred through the pages, cartoon seemed to move. Animated GIFs work the same way. One of the most recent software available is macromedia flash version 5 and onwards.

Table following describes the use of tags and attributes to include animated GIF in the HTML document.

Tags/Attributes	*Use*
<IMG>	Inserts an Image in an HTML document.
SRC= "…"	Specifies the location of the image file.
ALT= "…"	Provides the alternate text for the visitors who don't view the image.

For example, to include the animated GIF images in your web page, first create a new GIF image or find existing GIF images, then place the image in your document using <IMG> tag and SRC= attribute as follows:

```
<IMG SRC= "   .gif">
```

Include this statement in HTML document as follows:

```
<HTML>
  <HEAD>
    <TITLE> ANIMATED GIF FILE</TITLE>
  </HEAD>
  <BODY>
    <IMG SRC="E:\Web Project\TempKop\HomeBazar\Animation\WINDOW1.GIF">
  </BODY>
</HTML>
```

The output is displayed in browser as shown in following Fig. 10.7.

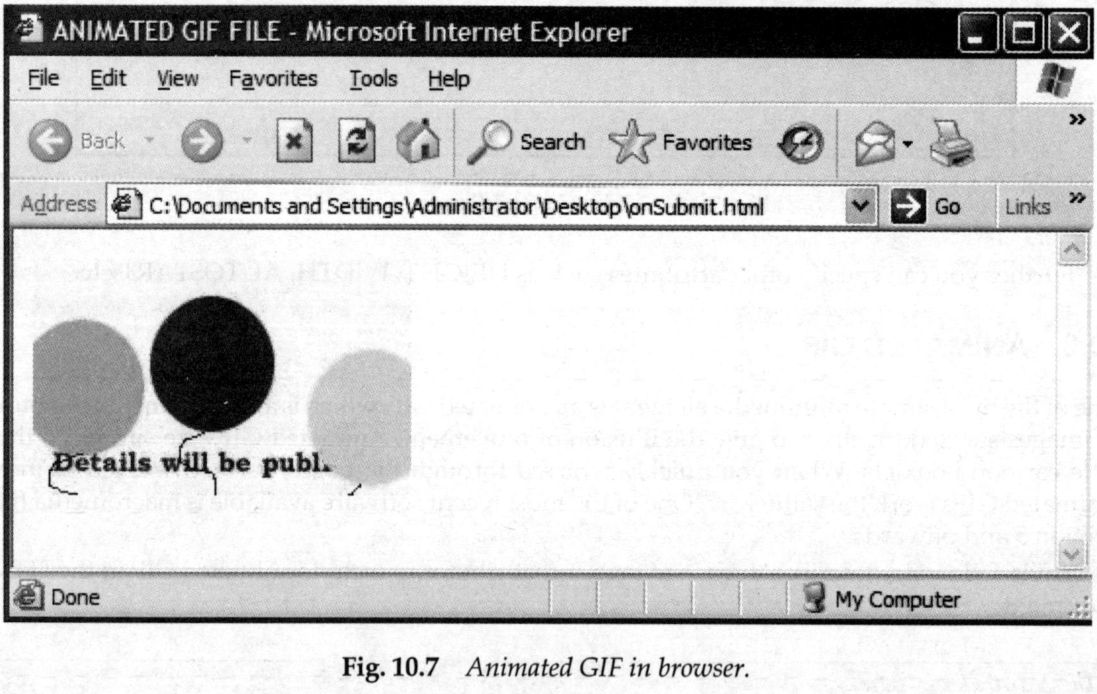

Fig. 10.7 *Animated GIF in browser.*

QUESTIONS

1. Explain how to embed Sounds in Web Pages.
2. Explain how to link Sounds in Web Pages.
3. Explain how to embed Video in Web Pages.
4. Explain how to link Video in Web Pages.
5. Explain how to use Animated GIF in Web Pages.

□□□

11

Beyond HTML

11.1 SGML

The SGML is a Standard Generalized Markup Language. It is the most powerful of three markup languages, HTML, SGML and XML. It provides the foundation for complex, large, or highly structured document sets. Using SGML, you can set up document rules or definition that let you to identify any structural part of the document such as headings, paragraph, and any other part.

SGML is a meta-language that is used to describe and define other markup languages. These languages are contained within a Document-Type-Definition, or DTD as a set of rules. SGML DTD is completely customizable, meaning that you can specify which tags and attributes may be contained in documents and what rules they must be follow. So SGML DTD is flexible.

The DTD defines the markup components of one or more documents with which it is associated. The components include elements, attributes and entities. An HTML document is always associated with predefined HTML DTD. However, an SGML document may or may not associate with a predefined DTD. For example, HTML DTD specifies that you can include maximum of six levels of heading (<H1> to <H6>) and that you can include at any point in the document.

Advantages of SGML

1. SGML capabilities are limitless; therefore SGML is ideal for extremely large or complex document sets.
2. Using SGML, you can custom-build SGML applications as per organization needs.
3. SGML is not linked to specific software, companies or versions.

Disadvantages of SGML

1. With SGML, you must have a complete DTD before you can start creating documents or contents.
2. The change in DTD's organization and structure, there is change of all existing documents.
3. SGML is very expensive to implement and use.
4. SGML specification accommodates unlimited numbers and combinations of tags and attributes plus different DTD's for different documents, which requires flexible and complex browsers.

11.2 XML

XML is an eXtended Markup language that combines the best of the features of the SGML and HTML. Like SGML, in XML you can develop your own markup tags that not only specify what each document is, but also establish each document structure and like HTML, XML documents are structured.

HTML's DTD is predefined; you can not edit any part of it. In contrast, you can create any number of DTDs for your XML documents. With XML you can define sets of custom elements to organize and describe information in a document, and then use style sheets to display it.

An XML document does not always require a DTD. A well formed document must follow XML rules, but is not necessarily associated with a DTD. On other hand a valid document must follow XML rules and always has an associated DTD. DTD is either internal or external. An internal DTD subset is a part of the document whose elements, attributes and other markup it defines. An external DTD subset is a separate document, which referred to from one or more documents.

The internal DTD subset is declared as follows:

```
<?xml version = "1.0"?>
<! DOCTYPE document [
  <! ELEMEMT h1 (#PCDATA)>
  <! ELEMEMT p (#PCDATA)>
]>
```

And, an external DTD subset is declared as follows:

```
<! DOCTYPE sss SYSTEM "abc.dtd" >
```

HTML and XML document looks same, with exception of the first line.

For example, XML document and it's DTD containing custom elements h1 & p are as follows:

```
<?xml version = "1.0"?>
<! DOCTYPE Document [
  <! ELEMEMT h1 (#PCDATA)>
  <! ELEMEMT p (#PCDATA)>
]>
<Document>
  <h1> Introduction to XML. </h1>
  <p> XML is an eXtended Markup language that combines the best of the features of
  the SGML and HTML. </p>
</Document>
```

Where Document is the main or root element and *h1* & *p* are the child elements.

Advantages of XML

XML gives the ability to provide context for words on the page. For example in traditional HTML you can use word *h1* from above internal DTD anywhere in the document.

Disadvantages of XML

1. XML is relatively new technology, and consequently there is no tools available quickly to develop and implement it.
2. Also due to new technology, not all browsers support it.

11.3 DYNAMIC HTML

Web page using dynamic HTML (DHTML), you can view new contents without reloading the page, change the screen colors with a mouse click and view animations without a plug-in.

Dynamic HTML expands on standard HTML by giving you a formatting control of Style Sheets with the interactive capabilities of scripting languages such as JavaScrript and VBScript. This is as follows as an example:

```
<HTML>
<HEAD>
<TITLE> Dynamic HTML </TITLE>
<STYLE>
<!–
H1{color: blue}
–>
</STYLE>
<SCRIPT LANGUAGE="JavaScript">
<!–
function a() {this. document. all. s. style. color =red}
//–>
</SCRIPT>
</HEAD>

<BODY>
<H1 ID=s>Dynamic HTML</H1>
<P onClick ="a()"> Click Me to change the color of above heading "Dynamic HTML"
</P>
</BODY>
</HTML>
```

By clicking on the paragraph text function *a()* will be invoked which is written in the script tag. The function *a()* contains " *this. document. all. s. style. color =red* " statement which specifies that from this document, to the appearance of all headings named with Id=s, assign color style red.

QUESTIONS

1. Write a Short note on—
   a. SGML.
   b. XML.
   c. Dynamic HTML.
2. What is the difference between HTML and XML?
3. What is Dynamic HTML? Explain?

□□□

12

Introduction to ASP.NET

12.1 TYPES OF APPLICATION

Internet Application

An Internet application is any application that uses the Internet in any way.

Types of Internet applications

- Web Applications
- Web-Services
- Internet-enabled Applications
- Peer-to-peer Applications

You can use Visual Studio .NET to create each of these types of applications.

Web Applications: These applications provide content from a server to client machines over the Internet. Users view the Web application through a Web browser.

Web-services: These components provide processing services from a server to other applications over the Internet.

Internet-enabled Applications: These are stand-alone applications that incorporate aspects of the Internet to provide online registration, help, updates, or other services to the user over the Internet.

Peer-to-peer Applications: These are stand-alone applications that use the Internet to communicate with other users running their own instances of the application.

Sources of Information

Table: *Sources of information about internet applications.*

Application type	*Use these topics in online help*
Web applications	ASP.NET, Web forms, *System.Web* namespace
Web services	ASP.NET, XML Web Services, *System.Web.Services* namespace
Internet-enabled applications	Microsoft Windows forms, HTML Help, WebBrowser control, *System.Net* namespace
Peer-to-peer applications	Accessing the Internet, pluggable protocols, System.Net and *System.Net.Sockets* namespace

12.2 HOW WEB APPLICATION WORKS

Web applications use client/server architecture.

The Web application resides on a server and responds to requests from multiple clients over the Internet, as shown in Fig. 12.1.

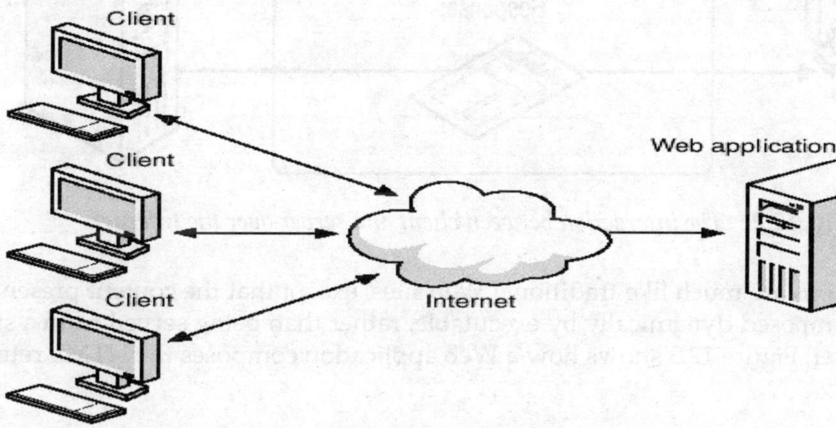

Fig. 12.1 *Web application resides on a server and responds to requests from multiple clients over the Internet.*

On the client side, the Web application is hosted by a browser.

The application's user interface takes the form of Hypertext Markup Language (HTML) pages that are interpreted and displayed by the client's browser.

On the server side, the Web application runs under Microsoft Internet Information Services (IIS).

IIS manages the application, passes requests from clients to the application, and returns the application's responses to the client. These requests and responses are passed across the Internet using Hypertext Transport Protocol (HTTP).

The executable portion of the Web application enables you to do many things that you can't do with a static Web site, such as:

- Collect information from the user and store that information on the server
- Perform tasks for the user such as placing an order for a product, performing complex calculations, or retrieving information from a database
- Identify a specific user and present an interface that is customized for that user
- Present content that is highly volatile, such as inventory, pending order, and shipment information

A *protocol* is a set of rules that describe how two or more items communicate over a medium, such as the Internet. Figure 12.2 shows how the client and server interact over the Internet.

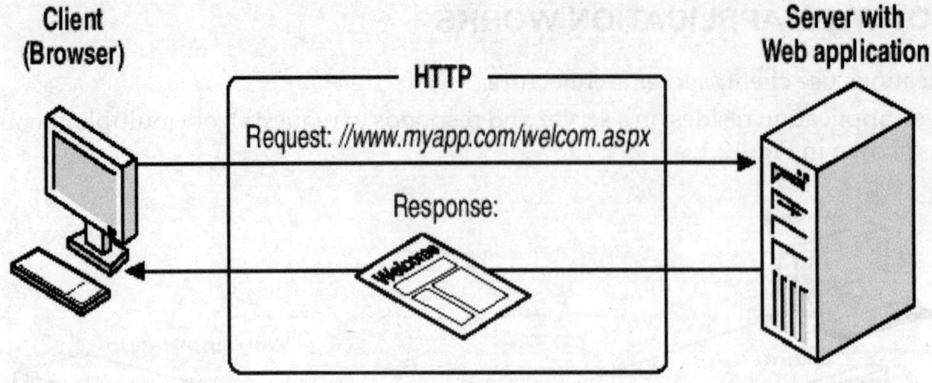

Fig. 12.2 *The interaction between client and server over the Internet.*

Web applications are much like traditional Web sites, except that the content presented to the user is actually composed dynamically by executable, rather than being served from a static page stored on the server. Figure 12.3 shows how a Web application composes the HTML returned to a user.

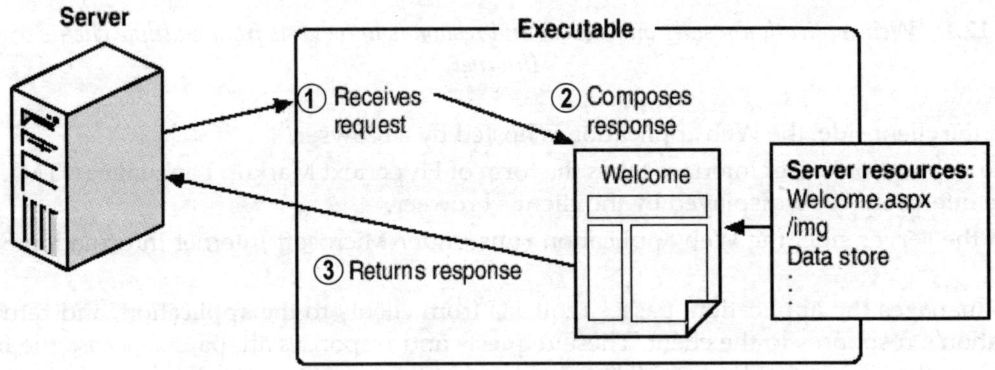

Fig. 12.3 *Web application composes the HTML returned to a user.*

12.3 WORKING WITH WEB FORMS IN ASP.NET

ASP.NET is used to create a web application. ASP stands for Active Server Pages. Web application contains the web forms or web pages that can be accessed using browser on the internet. These web pages are given the extension .aspx.

Before create web applications in ASP.NET, you need to install Microsoft Internet Information Services (ISS) version 5.0 or later in your system. IIS must be running on a Windows machine with the .NET framework installed so that your ASP.NET code can run.

To create a new Web application, select Project sub-option from New menu option in File menu item, which opens a New Project dialog box as shown in following Fig. 12.4, from which select ASP.NET Web Application icon.

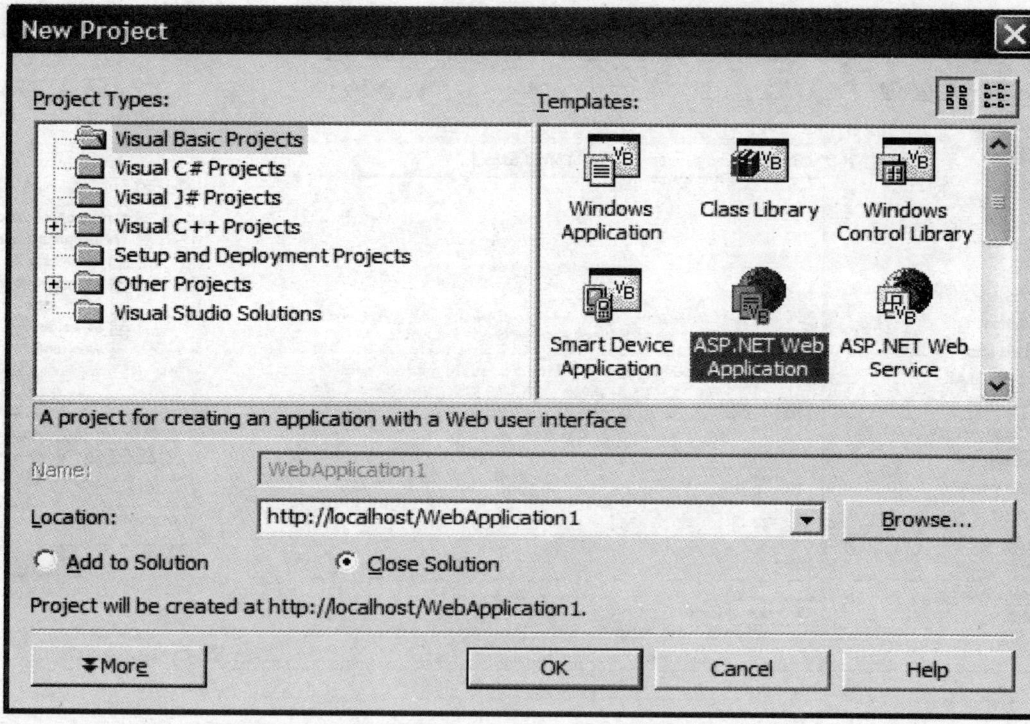

Fig. 12.4 *New Project Dialog Box for selecting projects.*

In this box, in Location field enter the location of the web server. By default, there is name of the local server, localhost and name of the virtual directory, WebApplication1. So the location of the web server is http://localhost/WebApplication1. Now in this directory you store your web application. For example, you create a WebApp1.aspx web form. You store this form in the location http://localhost/WebApplication1. That is the URL that gets launched when you run the application. For applications on the internet, the URL might look something like this:

```
http://localhost/WebApplication1/AebApp1.aspx
```

When you sure that what server you want to use, click OK button the new web application will be created which shown in following Fig. 12.5.

When Visual Studio .NET creates a new Web application project, it creates a new folder for the project and identifies the first Web form in the project (Webform1.aspx) as the start page. A start page is a page designated by Visual Studio as the first page to display in your application. All of the subordinate folders, such as/bin, are part of that application.

If your application design changes during development, or if you just want to quickly run the current page during debugging, you might want to change the start page of your application.

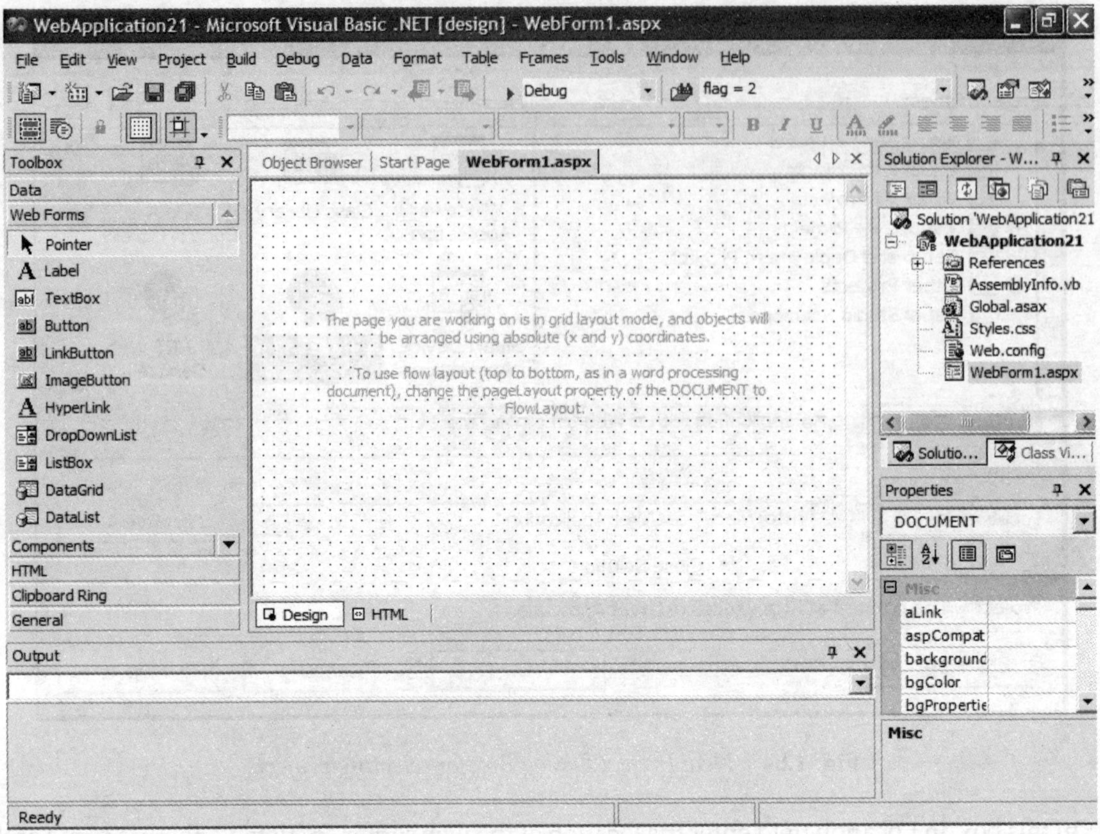

Fig. 12.5 *ASP.NET Integrated Development Environment.*

To set a different Web form or HTML page as the start page, do the following:

- In Solution Explorer, right-click the Web form or HTML page you want to specify as the start page of your application, and choose Set As Start Page on the shortcut menu.

When you are ready to deploy your Web application, you will usually want to set the application's start page as its default document in IIS. The IIS default document is the page that IIS displays if the user omits the document name as part of his or her requested address. By default, IIS specifies these default document file names: Default.htm, Default.asp, Index.htm, and Iisstart.asp.

The Files in a Web Forms Project

The Web form is only one of 11 files Visual Studio .NET generates when it creates a new Web forms project. Table describes the purpose of each of these project files. Visual Studio .NET creates these different files for each new Web application project. Only the files shown in bold are displayed in the Visual Studio .NET Solution Explorer.

Web Forms Project Files	
File name	*Contains*
AssemblyInfo.vb AssemblyInfo.cs	All of the attributes that are written into the compiled assembly, including version, company name, GUID, and so on.
Global.asax	The global events that occur in your Web application, such as when the application starts or ends. You can have only one Global.asax file per project, and it exists in the root folder of the project.
Global.asax.vb Global.asax.cs	The code used in Global.asax. This file is not shown in Solution Explorer.
Styles.css	The style definitions to use for the HTML generated by your project. This file appears only in Visual Basic .NET projects. For Visual C# projects, you can add it manually.
Web.config	The settings your Web server uses when processing this project. These settings specify how errors are reported, what type of user authentication to use, and so on.
Projectname.vsdisco	Descriptions of the Web Services that this project provides. This file is used for dynamic discovery of Web services (.asmx files) included in a Web application. This file is not shown in Solution Explorer.
WebForm1.aspx	The visual description of a Web form.
WebForm1.aspx.vb WebForm1.aspx.cs	The code that responds to events on the Web form. By default, this file is not shown in Solution Explorer.
WebForm1.aspx.resx	The Extensible Markup Language (XML) resources used by the Web form. This file is not shown in Solution Explorer.
Projectname.vbproj Projectname.csproj	The project file listing the files and settings used at design time. This file is not shown in Solution Explorer.
Projectname.vbproj.webinfo Projectname.csproj.webinfo	This file tracks the root virtual folder for the Web application. This file is not shown in Solution Explorer.

QUESTIONS

1. What are the Types of the Web Application? Explain.
2. How Web Application Works?
3. Explain Working with Web Forms in ASP.NET

□□□

13

Web Server Controls

These controls respond to user events by running event procedures on the server. Server controls have built-in features for saving data that the user enters between page displays. You use server controls to define the user interface of a Web form.

The following are the ASP.NET syntax and description that you use when creating a Web server control in a text or HTML editor.

13.1 LABEL WEB SERVER CONTROL

Displays static text on a Web Forms page and allows you to manipulate it programmatically.

Syntax:

```
<asp:Label
  id="Label1"
  Text="label"
runat="server"/>
      or
<asp:Label
  id="Label1" runat="server">
  Text
</asp:Label>
```

The important and widely used properties for the Label control is listed in following table.

Properties	*Use*
id= "..."	Sets identifier to the server control.
Text= "..."	Sets caption in Label control.

For Example, place the Label control on the web form from the toolbox as shown in following Fig. 13.1.

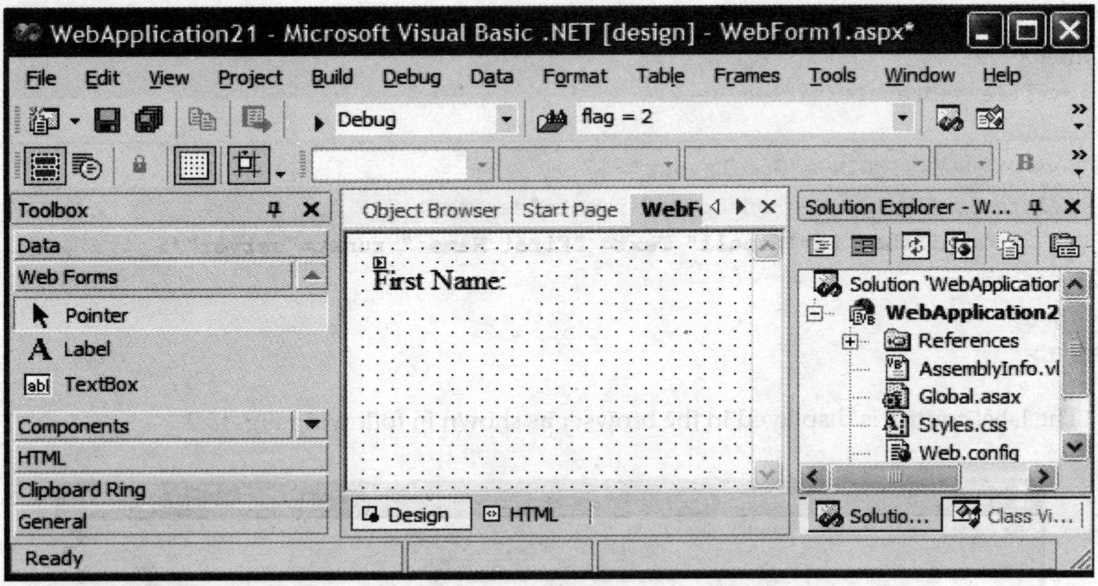

Fig. 13.1 *Placing of the Label control on the web form.*

When you add Label control on the web, it adds the following code to the ASPX file.

```
<%@ Page Language="vb" AutoEventWireup="false" Codebehind="WebLabel.aspx.vb"
Inherits="WebApplication12.WebForm2"%>
<!DOCTYPE HTML PUBLIC "-//W3C//DTD HTML 4.0 Transitional//EN">
<HTML>
  <HEAD>
    <title>WebLabel</title>
  </HEAD>
  <body MS_POSITIONING="GridLayout">
    <form id="Form1" method="post" runat="server">
      <asp:Label id="Label1" runat="server">First Name: </asp:Label>
    </form>
  </body>
</HTML>
```

Or

```
<%@ Page Language="vb" AutoEventWireup="false" Codebehind="WebLabel.aspx.vb"
Inherits="WebApplication12.WebForm2"%>
<!DOCTYPE HTML PUBLIC "-//W3C//DTD HTML 4.0 Transitional//EN">
```

```
<HTML>
  <HEAD>
    <title>WebLabel</title>
  </HEAD>
  <body MS_POSITIONING="GridLayout">
    <form id="Form1" method="post" runat="server">
        <asp:Label id="Label1" Text= "First Name:" runat="server"/>
    </form>
  </body>
</HTML>
```

The label control is displayed in the browser as shown in following Fig. 13.2.

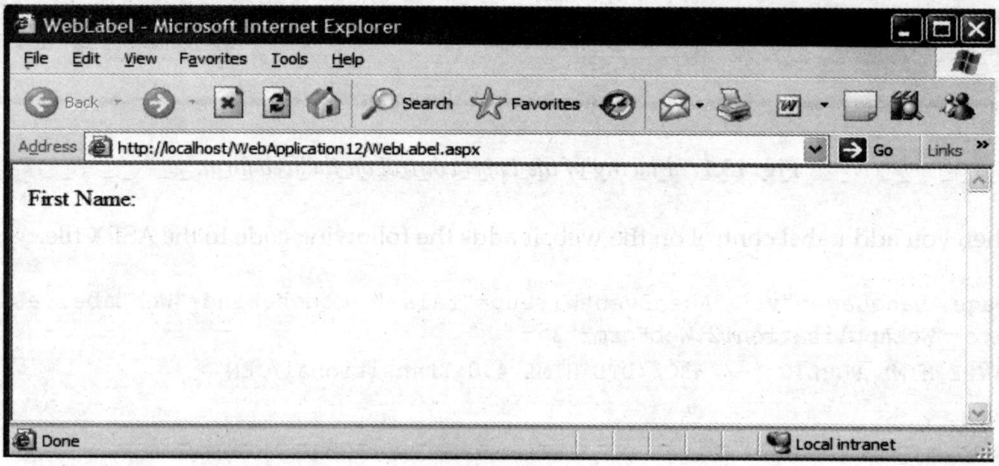

Fig. 13.2

13.2 TEXTBOX WEB SERVER CONTROL

Creates single-line and multiline text boxes.

Syntax:

```
<asp:TextBox
  id="value"
  AutoPostBack="True|False"
  Columns="characters"
  MaxLength="characters"
  Rows="rows"
  Text="text"
  TextMode="Single | Multiline | Password"
```

```
Wrap="True|False"
  OnTextChanged="OnTextChangedMethod"
runat="server"/>
```

The important and widely used properties for the Button control is listed in following table.

Properties	*Use*
id= "..."	Sets identifier to the server control.
Text= "..."	Sets caption in Button control.
AutoPostBack =" TRUE | FALSE "	Sets whether event will be automatically posted back to the server. It accepts TRUE and FALSE values.
Columns="..."	Sets the text box's width in characters.
MaxLength= "..."	Sets the maximum number of characters that may displayed in the text box.
TextMode="Single | Multiline | Password"	Sets whether a text box should be single line, multiline or password control.
Rows="..."	Sets a multiline text box's display height.
Wrap="True|False"	Sets whether text wraps in the text box.

The important and widely used events for the Button control is listed in following table.

Events	*Use*
OnTextChanged	Occurs when the text in the text box is changed.

For example, place the textbox controls on the web form from the toolbox as shown in following Fig. 13.3.

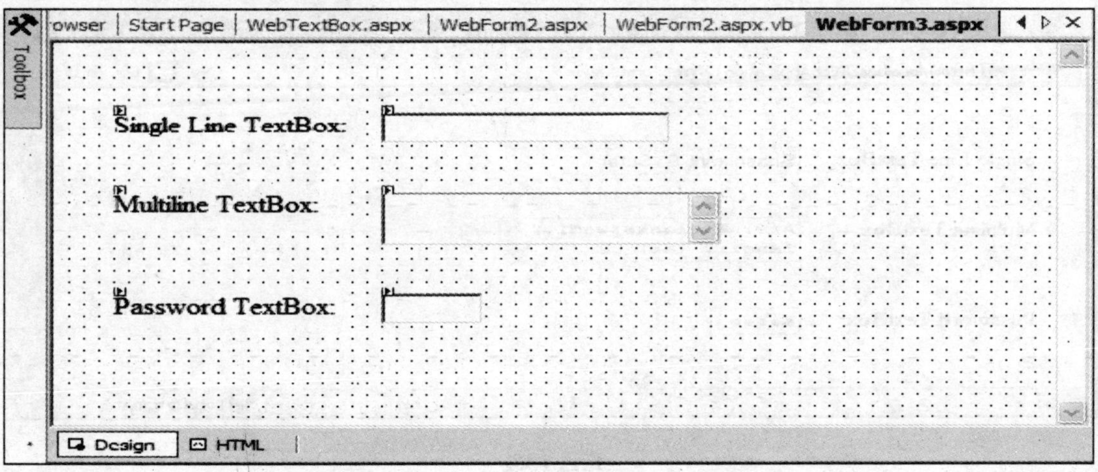

Fig. 13.3 *Placing of the TextBox controls on the web form.*

When you add TextBox controls on the web, it adds the following code to the ASPX file.

```
<%@ Page Language="vb" AutoEventWireup="false" Codebehind="WebForm3.aspx.vb"
Inherits="WebApplication12.WebForm3"%>
<!DOCTYPE HTML PUBLIC "-//W3C//DTD HTML 4.0 Transitional//EN">
<HTML>
      <HEAD>
         <title>WebTextBoxes</title>
     </HEAD>
     <body MS_POSITIONING="GridLayout">
         <form id="Form1" method="post" runat="server">
            <asp:textbox id="TextBox1" runat="server"></asp:textbox>
            <asp:textbox id="TextBox2" runat="server"
            TextMode="MultiLine"></asp:textbox>
            <asp:textbox id="TextBox3" Columns=5 MaxLength=5 runat="server"
            TextMode="Password"></asp:textbox>
            <asp:label id="Label1" runat="server">Single Line TextBox:</asp:label>
            <asp:label id="Label2" runat="server">Multiline TextBox:</asp:label>
            <asp:label id="Label3" runat="server">Password TextBox:</asp:label>
         </form>
      </body>
</HTML>
```

The Textbox controls are displayed in the browser as shown in following Fig. 13.4.

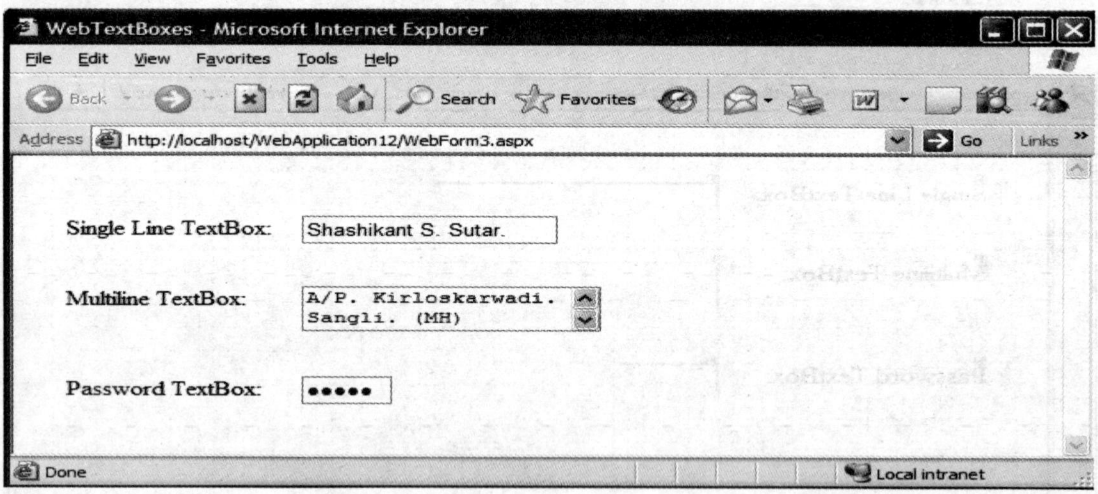

Fig. 13.4

13.3 BUTTON WEB SERVER CONTROL

Displays a push button control on the Web Forms page.

Syntax:

```
<asp:Button
   id="MyButton"
   Text="label"
   CommandName="command"
   CommandArgument="commandargument"
   CausesValidation="true | false"
   OnClick="OnClickMethod"
runat="server"/>
```

The important and widely used properties for the Button control is listed in following table.

Properties	*Use*
id= "..."	Sets identifier to the server control.
Text= "..."	Sets caption in Button control.
CommandName="..."	Sets command name associated with button.
CommandArgument="..."	Sets as an optional parameter.
CausesValidation= "..."	Sets a value indicating whether validation is performed when button is clicked.

The important and widely events used for the Button control is listed in following table.

Events	*Use*
OnClick	Occurs when button is clicked.
OnCommand	Occurs when command button is clicked.

For Example, place the Button control on the web forms from the toolbox as shown in following Fig. 13.5.

When you add button control on the web, it adds the following code to the ASPX file. Following code specifies that when you click on the button, the method Button1_Click is called which is written in the VBScript in the head section of the HTML document.

```
<%@Page Language="vb" AutoEventWireup="false" Codebehind="WebForm2.aspx.vb"
Inherits="WebApplication12.WebForm2"%>
<!DOCTYPE HTML PUBLIC "-//W3C//DTD HTML 4.0 Transitional//EN">
```

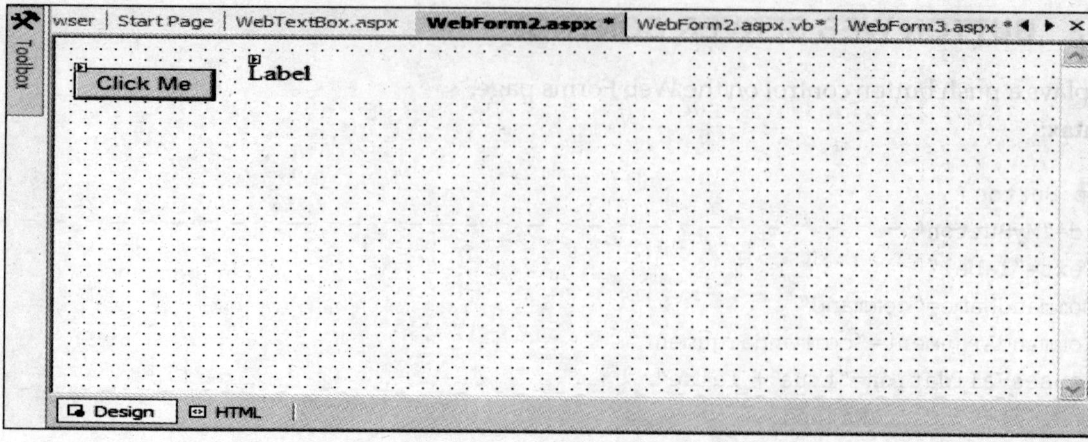

Fig. 13.5 *Placing of the Button control on the web form.*

```
<HTML>
<HEAD>
  <title>WebButton</title>
  <script language="vb" runat="server">
  Sub Button1_Click(ByVal sender As System.Object, ByVal e As System.EventArgs)
  Handles Button1.Click
    Label1.Text = "This is Button Control!!!"
  End Sub
  </script>
  </HEAD>
  <body MS_POSITIONING="GridLayout">
    <form id="Form1" method="post" runat="server">
    <asp:Button id="Button1" runat="server" Text="Click Me" OnClick=Button1_Click>
    </asp:Button>
    <asp:Label id="Label1" runat="server">Label</asp:Label>
    </form>
  </body>
</HTML>
```

The button control is displayed in the browser as shown in following Fig. 13.6.

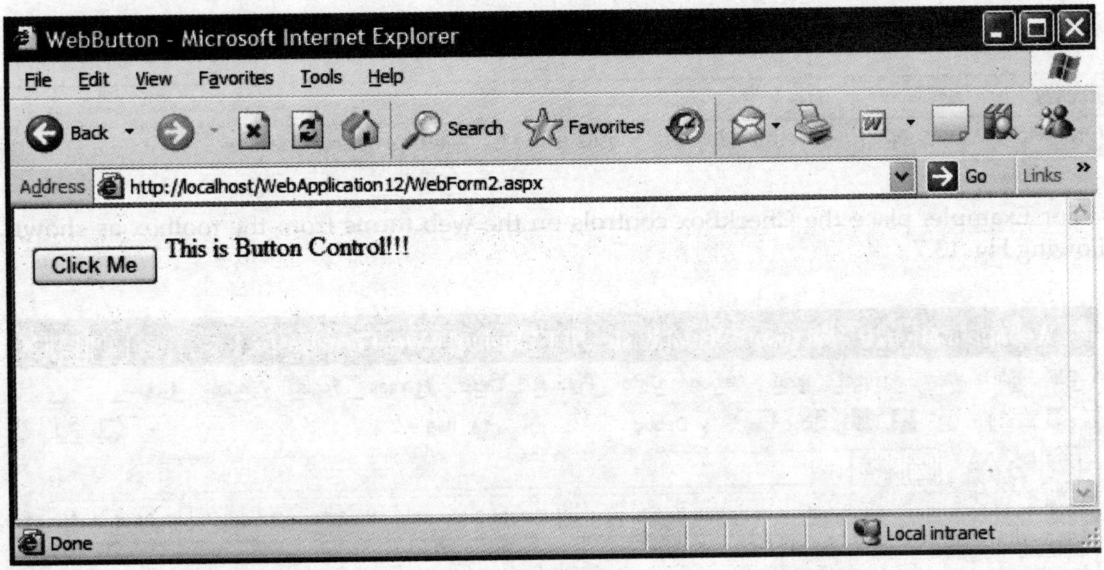

Fig. 13.6

13.4 CHECKBOX WEB SERVER CONTROL

Creates a check box control that allows the user to switch between a **true** or **false** state.

Syntax:

```
<asp:CheckBox
   id="CheckBox1"
   AutoPostBack="True|False"
   Text="Label"
   TextAlign="Right|Left"
   Checked="True|False"
   OnCheckedChanged="OnCheckedChangedMethod" runat="server"/>
```

The important and widely properties used for the CheckBox control is listed in following table.

Properties	*Use*
id= "…"	Sets identifier to the server control.
Text= "…"	Sets caption in CheckBox control.
AutoPostBack =" TRUE | FALSE "	Sets whether event will be automatically posted back to the server. It accepts TRUE and FALSE values.
Checked="True|False"	Sets whether checkbox displays a check.
TextAlign="Right|Left"	Sets the alignment of the text caption.
TextMode="Single | Multiline | Password"	Sets whether a text box should be single line, multiline or password control.

The important and widely events used for the CheckBox control is listed in following table.

Events	*Use*
OnCheckedChanged	Occurs when the value of the Checked property changes.

For Example, place the CheckBox controls on the web forms from the toolbox as shown in following Fig. 13.7.

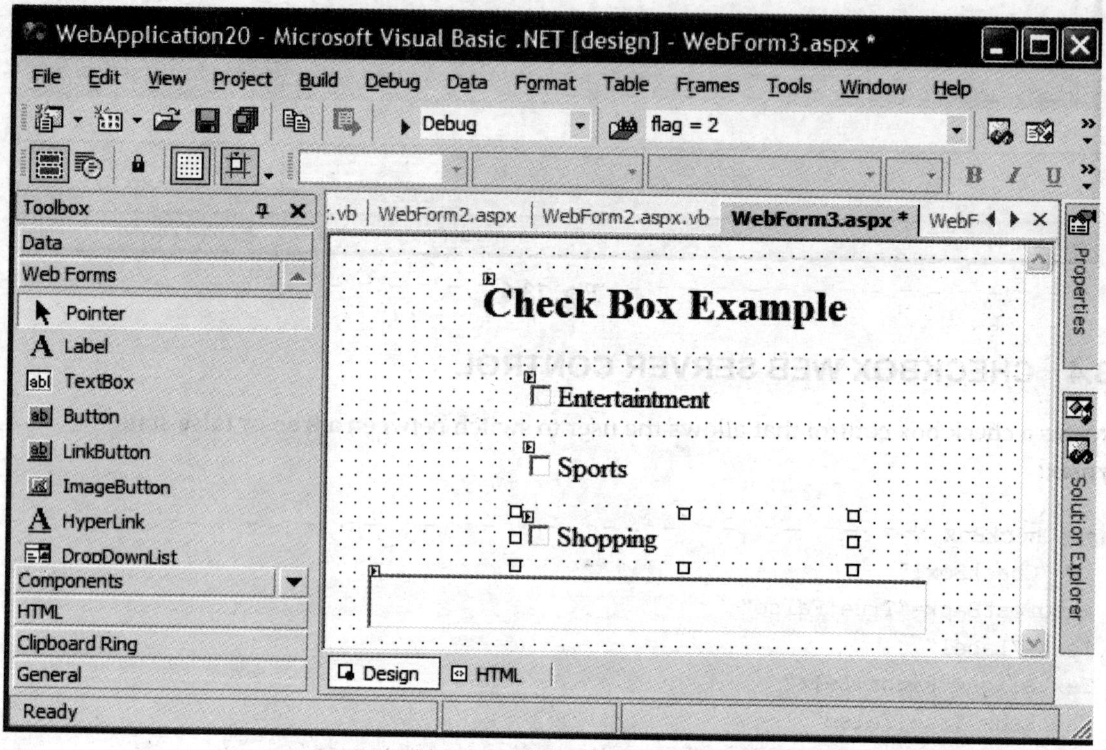

Fig. 13.7 *Placing of the CheckBox on the web form.*

```
<%@ Page Language="vb" AutoEventWireup="false" Codebehind="WebForm3.aspx.vb"
Inherits="WebApplication20.WebForm3"%>
<!DOCTYPE HTML PUBLIC "-//W3C//DTD HTML 4.0 Transitional//EN">
<HTML>
  <HEAD>
    <title>Chech Box Example</title>
    <script language="vb" runat="server">
    Private Sub CheckBox1_CheckedChanged(ByVal sender As System.Object, ByVal e As
    System.EventArgs) Handles CheckBox1.CheckedChanged
```

```
        If CheckBox1.Checked Then
            TextBox1.Text = TextBox1.Text & " " & "Entertainment"
        End If
    End Sub

    Private Sub CheckBox2_CheckedChanged(ByVal sender As System.Object, ByVal e As
    System.EventArgs) Handles CheckBox2.CheckedChanged
        If CheckBox2.Checked Then
            TextBox1.Text = TextBox1.Text & " " & "Spotrs"
        End If
    End Sub

    Private Sub CheckBox3_CheckedChanged(ByVal sender As System.Object, ByVal e As
    System.EventArgs) Handles CheckBox3.CheckedChanged
        If CheckBox3.Checked Then
            TextBox1.Text = TextBox1.Text & " " & "Shopping"
        End If
    End Sub
    </script>
  </HEAD>
  <body MS_POSITIONING="GridLayout">
    <form id="Form1" method="post" runat="server">
      <asp:Label id="Label1" runat="server" Font-Size="Large" Font-
      Bold="True">Check Box Example</asp:Label></TD>
      <asp:CheckBox id="CheckBox1" runat="server" Text="Entertaintment"
      AutoPostBack="True"
      OnCheckedChanged=CheckBox1_CheckedChanged> </asp:CheckBox>
      <asp:CheckBox id="CheckBox2" runat="server" Text="Sports"
      AutoPostBack="True"
      OnCheckedChanged=CheckBox2_CheckedChanged> </asp:CheckBox>
      <asp:CheckBox id="CheckBox3" runat="server" Text="Shopping"
      AutoPostBack="True"
      OnCheckedChanged=CheckBox3_CheckedChanged> </asp:CheckBox>
      <asp:TextBox id="TextBox1" runat="server"></asp:TextBox></TD>
    </form>
  </body>
</HTML>
```

The checkbox controls are displayed in the browser as shown in following Fig. 13.8.

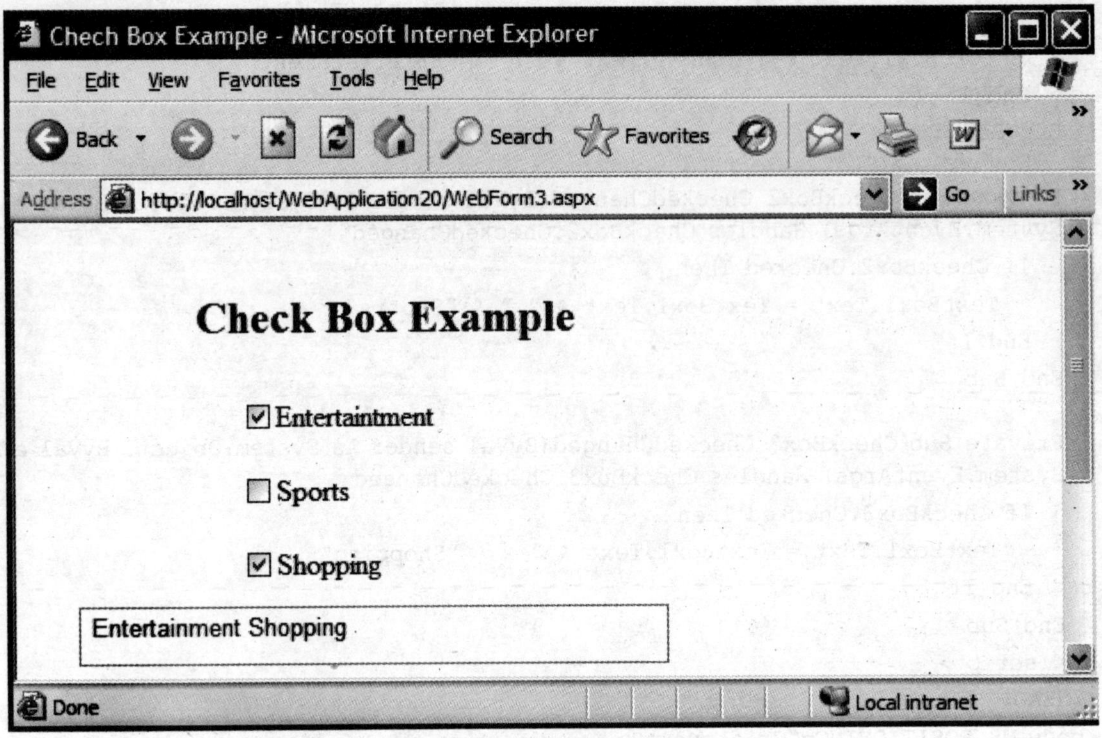

Fig. 13.8

13.5 RADIOBUTTON WEB SERVER CONTROL

Creates an individual radio button on the page. You can group multiple radio buttons together to provide a mutually exclusive set of choices.

Syntax:

```
<asp:RadioButton
  id="RadioButton1"
  AutoPostBack="True|False"
  Checked="True|False"
  GroupName="GroupName"
  Text="label"
  TextAlign="Right|Left"
  OnCheckedChanged="OnCheckedChangedMethod" runat="server"/>
```

The important and widely used properties for the CheckBox control is listed in following table.

Properties	*Use*
id= "..."	Sets identifier to the server control.
Text= "..."	Sets caption in RadioButton control.
AutoPostBack =" TRUE | FALSE "	Sets whether event will be automatically posted back to the server. It accepts TRUE and FALSE values.
Checked="True | False"	Sets whether RadioButton displays a check.
TextAlign="Right | Left"	Sets the alignment of the text caption.
GroupName="..."	Sets the name of the group that the radio button belongs to.

The important and widely events used for the RadioButton control is listed in following table.

Events	*Use*
OnCheckedChanged	Occurs when the Checked property changes.

For Example, place the RadioButton controls on the web form from the toolbox as shown in following Fig. 13.9.

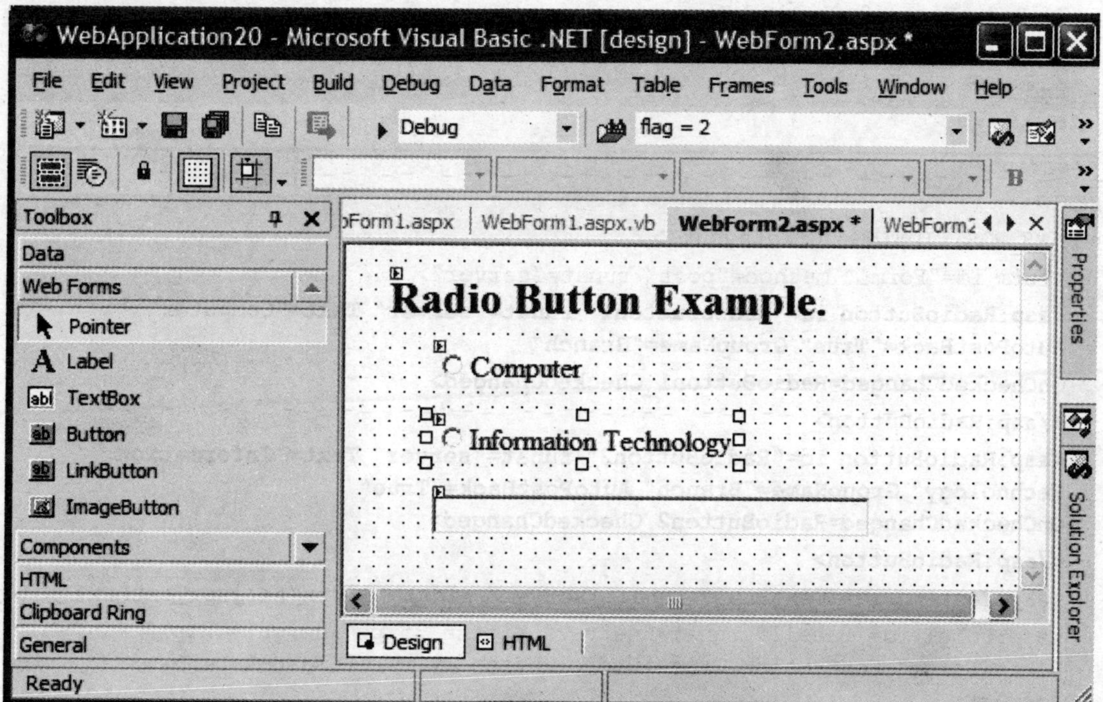

Fig. 13.9 *Placing of the Radio Button control on the web form.*

When you add Hyperlink control on the web, it adds the following code to the ASPX file.

```
<%@ Page Language="vb" AutoEventWireup="false" Codebehind="WebForm2.aspx.vb"
Inherits="WebApplication20.WebForm2"%>
<!DOCTYPE HTML PUBLIC "-//W3C//DTD HTML 4.0 Transitional//EN">
<HTML>
<HEAD>
  <title>Radio Button Example</title>
  <script language="vb" runat="server">
     Private Sub RadioButton1_CheckedChanged(ByVal sender As System.Object, ByVal e
     As System.EventArgs) Handles_RadioButton1.CheckedChanged
     If RadioButton1.Checked Then
       TextBox1.Text = "Computer is selected."
     End If
     End Sub

     Private Sub RadioButton2_CheckedChanged(ByVal sender As System.Object, ByVal e
     As System.EventArgs) Handles_RadioButton1.CheckedChanged
     If RadioButton2.Checked Then
       TextBox1.Text = "Information Technology is selected."
     End If
     End Sub
  </script>
</HEAD>
<body MS_POSITIONING="GridLayout">
     <form id="Form1" method="post" runat="server">
     <asp:RadioButton id="RadioButton1" runat="server" Text="Computer"
     AutoPostBack="True" GroupName="Branch"
     OnCheckedChanged=RadioButton1_CheckedChanged>
     </asp:RadioButton>
     <asp:RadioButton id="RadioButton2" runat="server" Text="Information
     Technology" GroupName="Branch" AutoPostBack="True"
     OnCheckedChanged=RadioButton2_CheckedChanged>
     </asp:RadioButton>
     <asp:TextBox id="TextBox1" runat="server" Width="240px"></asp:TextBox>
     <asp:Label id="Label1" runat="server" Width="352px" Height="24px" Font-
     Size="Large" Font-Bold="True">Radio Button Example.</asp:Label>
     </form>
</body>
</HTML>
```

The Radio Button control is displayed in the browser as shown in following Fig. 13.10.

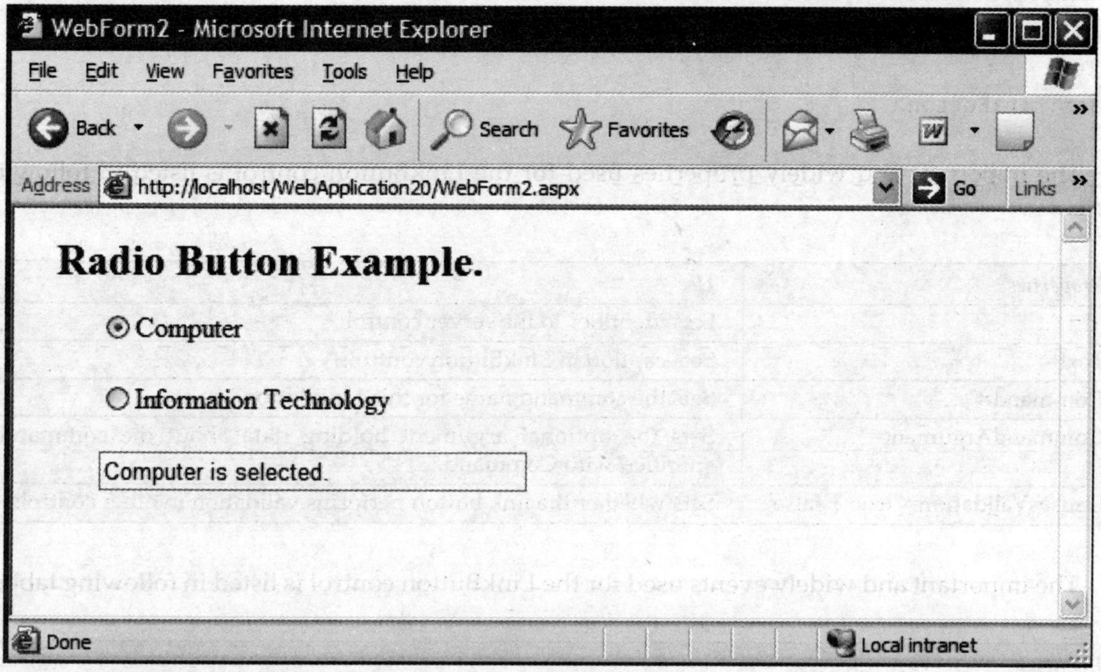

Fig. 13.10

13.6 LINKBUTTON WEB SERVER CONTROL

Creates a hyperlink-style button on a Web Forms page.

Syntax:

```
<asp:LinkButton
   id="LinkButton1"
   Text="label"
   Command="Command"
   CommandArgument="CommandArgument"
   CausesValidation="true | false"
   OnClick="OnClickMethod"
runat="server"/>
         or
<asp:LinkButton
   id="LinkButton1"
   Command="Command"
```

```
  CommandArgument="CommandArgument"
  CausesValidation="true | false"
  OnClick="OnClickMethod" runat="server"/>
  Text
</asp:LinkButton>
```

The important and widely properties used for the LinkButton control is listed in following table.

Properties	*Use*
id= "..."	Sets identifier to the server control.
Text= "..."	Sets caption in LinkButton control.
Command="..."	Sets the command name for this LinkButton.
CommandArgument="..."	Sets the optional argument holding data about the command specified with Command.
CausesValidation="true | false"	Sets whether the link button performs validation in other controls.

The important and widely events used for the LinkButton control is listed in following table.

Events	*Use*
OnClicked	Occurs when the LinkButton was clicked.
OnCommand	Occurs when the LinkButton was clicked.

For Example, place the LinkButton controls on the web form from the toolbox as shown in following Fig. 13.11.

13.7 HYPERLINK WEB SERVER CONTROL

Creates a link on the page that users can click to move to another page.

Syntax:

```
<asp:HyperLink
  id="HyperLink1"
  NavigateUrl="url"
  Text="HyperLinkText"
  ImageUrl="url"
  Target="window" runat="server"/>
    or
<asp:HyperLink
  id="HyperLink1"
```

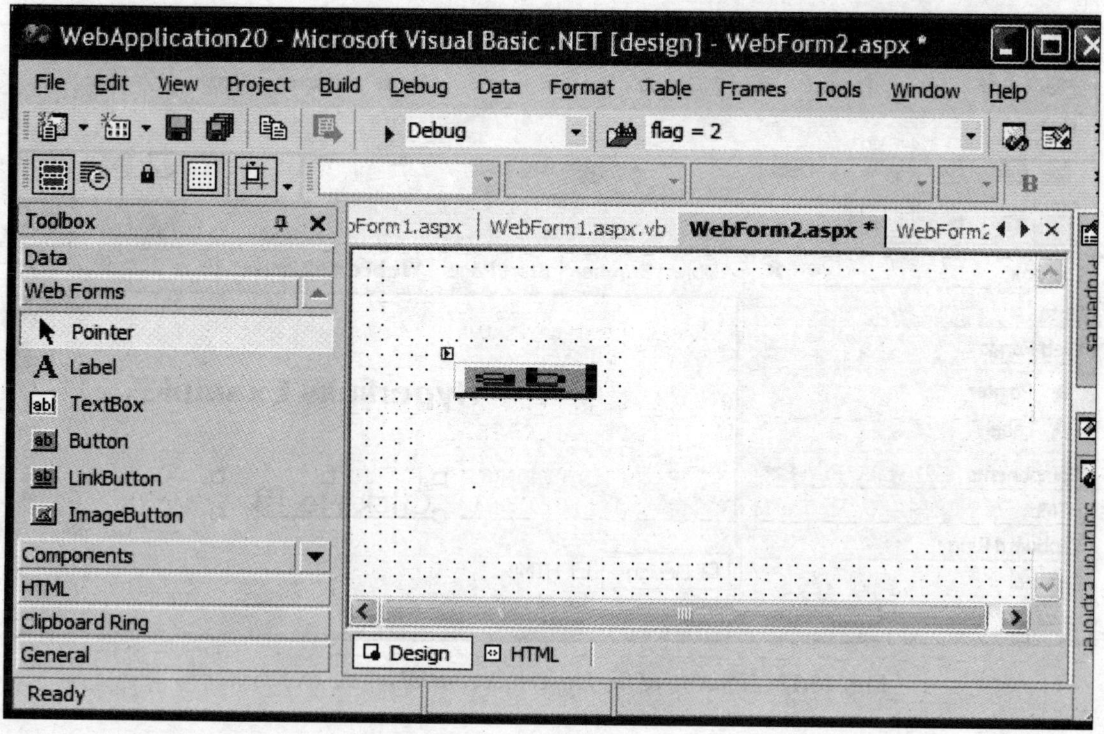

Fig. 13.11 *Placing of the Link Button control on the web form.*

```
    NavigateUrl="url"
    ImageUrl="url"
    Target="window" runat="server">
    Text
</asp:HyperLink>
```

The important and widely used properties for the Hyperlink control is listed in following table.

Properties	*Use*
id= "..."	Sets identifier to the server control.
Text= "..."	Sets the text for the hyperlink.
NavigateUrl="url"	Sets the *url* to navigate to when hyperlink is clicked.
ImageUrl="url"	Sets the *url* of an image you want to use in the hyperlink.
Target="window"	Sets the target window or frame to display the new content in.

For Example, place the HyperLink controls on the web form from the toolbox as shown in following Fig. 13.12.

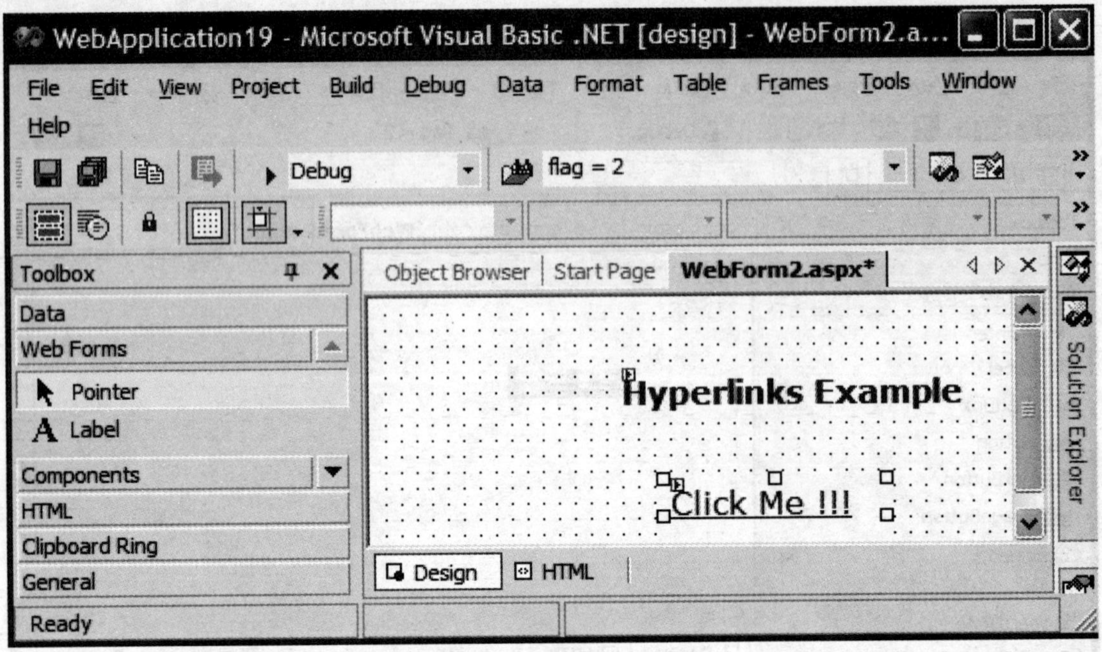

Fig. 13.12 *Placing of the Hyperlink control on the web form.*

When you add Hyperlink control on the web, it adds the following code to the ASPX file.

```
<%@ Page Language="vb" AutoEventWireup="false" Codebehind="WebForm2.aspx.vb"
Inherits="WebApplication19.WebForm2" %>
<!DOCTYPE HTML PUBLIC "-//W3C//DTD HTML 4.0 Transitional//EN">
<HTML>
<HEAD>
     <title>Hyperlinks Example</title>
</HEAD>
  <body MS_POSITIONING="GridLayout">
    <form id="Form1" method="post" runat="server">
      <asp:Label id="Label1" style="Z-INDEX: 102; LEFT: 128px; POSITION:
      absolute; TOP: 40px" runat="server"
      Font-Names="Verdana" Font-Bold="True"> Hyperlink Example</asp:Label>
      <asp:HyperLink id="HyperLink1" style="Z-INDEX: 103; LEFT: 152px; POSITION:
      absolute; TOP: 96px" runat="server" Font-Names="Verdana" Height="32px"
      Width="104px" NavigateUrl="WebForm1.aspx"> Click Me !!!</asp:HyperLink>
    </form>
  </body>
</HTML>
```

The Hyperlink control is displayed in the browser as shown in following Fig. 13.13

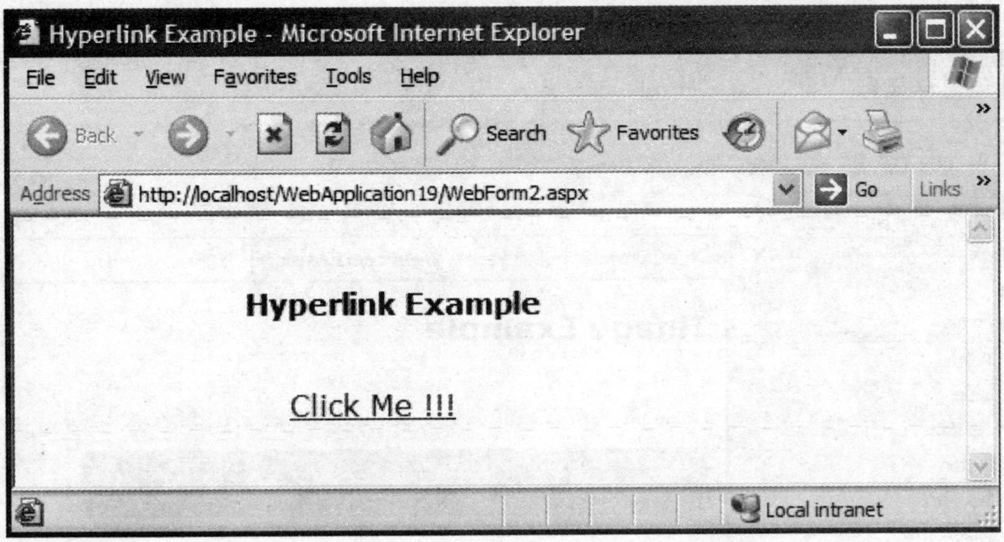

Fig. 13.13

13.8 IMAGE WEB SERVER CONTROL

Displays a Web-compatible image on the Web Forms page.

Syntax:

```
<asp:Image
  id="Image1"
  runat="server"
  ImageUrl="string"
  AlternateText="string"
  ImageAlign="NotSet|AbsBottom|AbsMiddle|BaseLine|
  Bottom|Left|Middle|Right|TextTop|Top"/>
```

The important and widely used properties for the Image control is listed in following table.

Properties	*Use*
id= "…"	Sets identifier to the server control.
ImageUrl="url"	Sets the url of an Image you want to display.
AlternateText="string"	Sets the text to display in an Image control when image is not available. You also use this attribute to display tool tip.
ImageAlign="NotSet | AbsBottom | AbsMiddle | BaseLine | Bottom | Left | Middle | Right | TextTop | Top	Sets the image alignment of the Image control Command.

For Example, place the Image controls on the web form from the toolbox as shown in following Fig. 13.14.

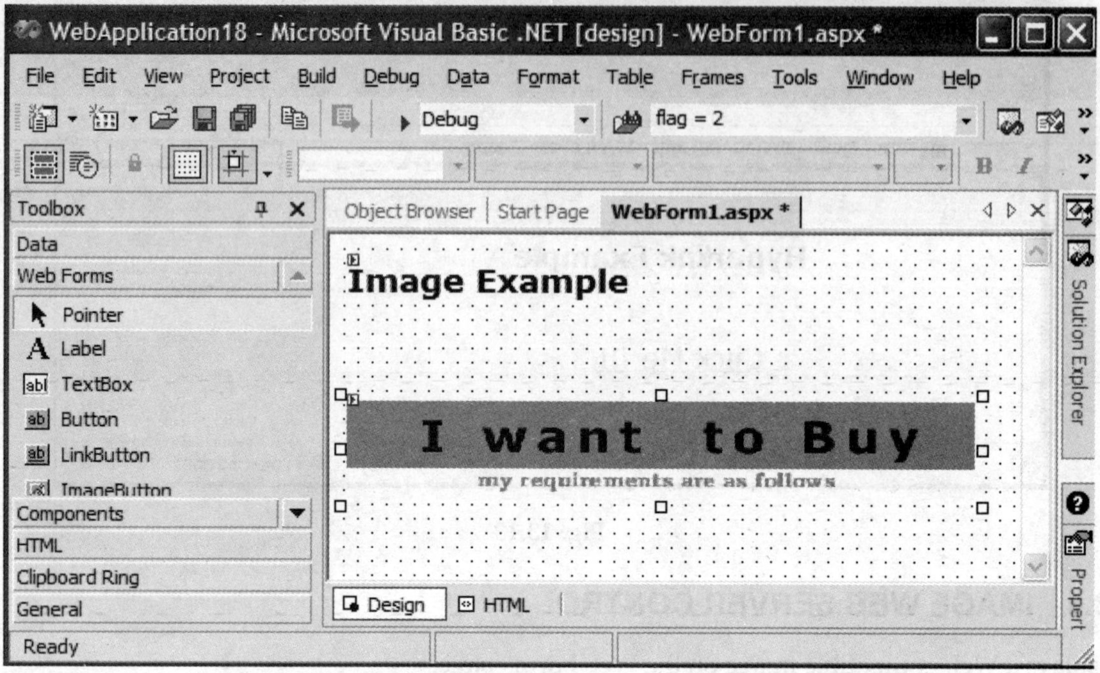

Fig. 13.14 *Placing of the Image control on the web form.*

When you add Image control on the web, it adds the following code to the ASPX file.

```
<%@ Page Language="vb" AutoEventWireup="false" Codebehind="WebForm1.aspx.vb"
Inherits="WebApplication18.WebForm1" %>
<!DOCTYPE HTML PUBLIC "-//W3C//DTD HTML 4.0 Transitional//EN">
<HTML>
  <HEAD>
    <title>Image Example</title>
  </HEAD>
  <body MS_POSITIONING="GridLayout">
  <form id="Form1" method="post" runat="server">
  <asp:Label id="Label1" runat="server" ToolTip="Using Images in Web Forms" Font-
  Bold="True" Font-Size="Medium" Font-Names="Verdana">
  Image Example</asp:Label>
  <asp:Image id="Image1" runat="server" ImageUrl="file:///E:\Web Project\TempKop\
  HomeBazar\Images\Homepur.gif" Height="56px"></asp:Image>
  </form>
  </body>
</HTML>
```

The Image control is displayed in the browser as shown in following Fig. 13.15.

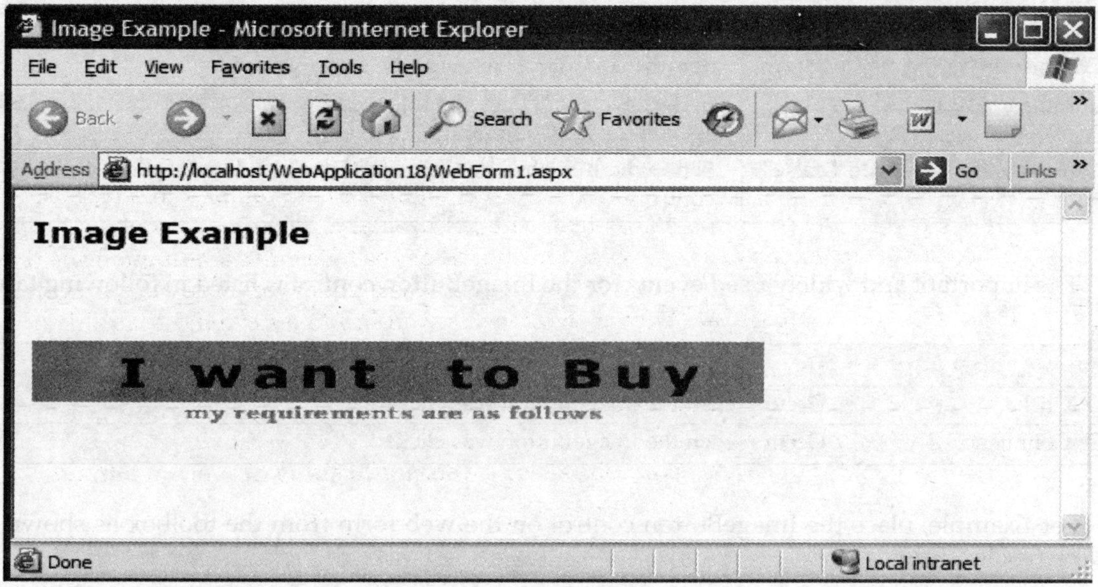

Fig. 13.15

13.9 IMAGEBUTTON WEB SERVER CONTROL

Enables you to handle user clicks in an image, which gives you functionality similar to an image map.

Syntax:

```
<asp:ImageButton
   id="ImageButton1"
   ImageUrl="string"
   Command="Command"
   CommandArgument="CommandArgument"
   CausesValidation="true | false"
   OnClick="OnClickMethod"
runat="server"/>
```

The important and widely used properties for the ImageButton control is listed in following table.

Properties	*Use*
id= "..."	Sets identifier to the server control.
ImageUrl="url"	Sets the url of an image you want to use as a ImageButton.
Command="..."	Sets the command name for the ImageButton.
CommandArgument="..."	Sets the optional argument holding data about the command specified with Command.
CausesValidation="true | false"	Sets whether the ImageButton performs validation in other controls.

The important and widely used events for the ImageButton control is listed in following table.

Events	*Use*
OnClicked	Occurs when the ImageButton was clicked.
OnCommand	Occurs when the ImageButton was clicked.

For Example, place the ImageButton control on the web form from the toolbox as shown in following Fig. 13.16.

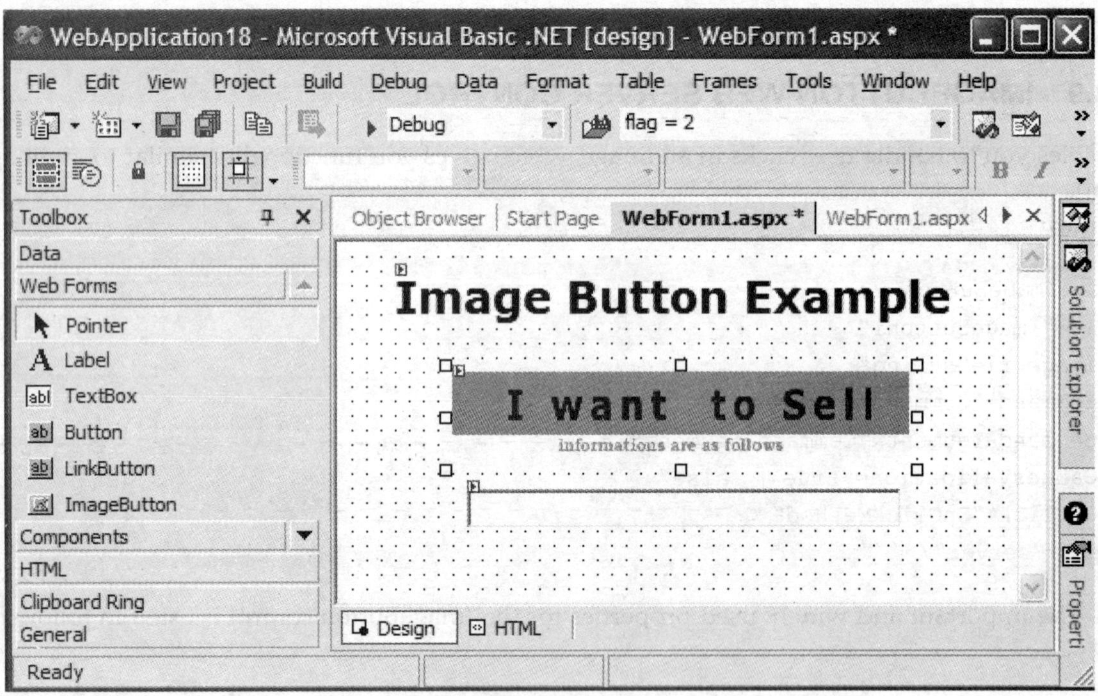

Fig. 13.16 *Placing of the ImageButton control on the web form.*

When you add ImageButton control on the web, it adds the following code to the ASPX file.

```
<%@ Page Language="vb" AutoEventWireup="false" Codebehind="WebForm1.aspx.vb"
Inherits="WebApplication18.WebForm1" %>
<!DOCTYPE HTML PUBLIC "-//W3C//DTD HTML 4.0 Transitional//EN">
<HTML>
<HEAD>
   <title>Image Button Example</title>
</HEAD>
<body MS_POSITIONING="GridLayout">
 <form id="Form1" method="post" runat="server">
    <asp:ImageButton id="ImageButton1" runat="server"
    ImageUrl="file:///E:\Web
    Project\TempKop\HomeBazar\Images\HOMESALE.GIF">
    </asp:ImageButton>
    <asp:Label id="Label1" runat="server">Image Button Example</asp:Label>
    <asp:TextBox id="TextBox1" runat="server"></asp:TextBox>
</form>
</body>
</HTML>
```

The ImageButton control is displayed in the browser as shown in following Fig. 13.17.

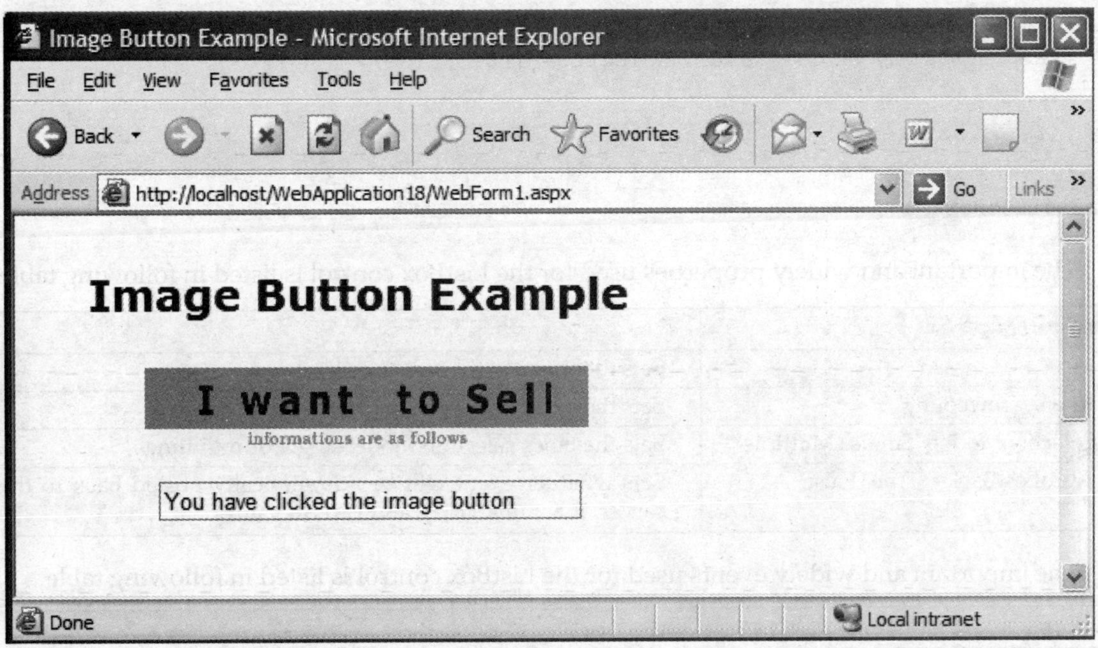

Fig. 13.17

13.10 LITERAL WEB SERVER CONTROL

Displays static contents on the page and allows you to manipulate it programmatically.

```
<asp:Literal
   id="Literal1"
   Text="Text"
runat="server"/>
```

13.11 LISTBOX WEB SERVER CONTROL

It displays the list of choices. It creates a single-selection or multiselection list box.
Syntax:

```
<asp:ListBox
   id="Listbox1"
   DataSource="<%databindingexpression%>"
   DataTextField="DataSourceField"
   DataValueField="DataSourceField"
   AutoPostBack="True|False"
   Rows="rowcount"
   SelectionMode="Single|Multiple"
   OnSelectedIndexChanged="OnSelectedIndexChangedMethod" runat="server">

     <asp:ListItem value="value" selected="True|False">
     Text
     </asp:ListItem>

</asp:ListBox>
```

The important and widely properties used for the ListBox control is listed in following table.

Properties	*Use*
id= "..."	Sets identifier to the server control.
Rows="rowcount"	Sets the number of rows in the ListBox.
SelectionMode="Single | Multiple"	Sets the box's selection mode: single or multiline.
AutoPostBack="True | False"	Sets whether event will be automatically posted back to the server. It accepts TRUE and FALSE values.

The important and widely events used for the ListBox control is listed in following table.

Events	*Use*
OnSelectedIndexChanged="OnSelected IndexChangedMethod"	Occurs when the item in the ListBox was clicked.

For Example, place the ListBox controls on the web forms from the toolbox as shown in following Fig. 13.18.

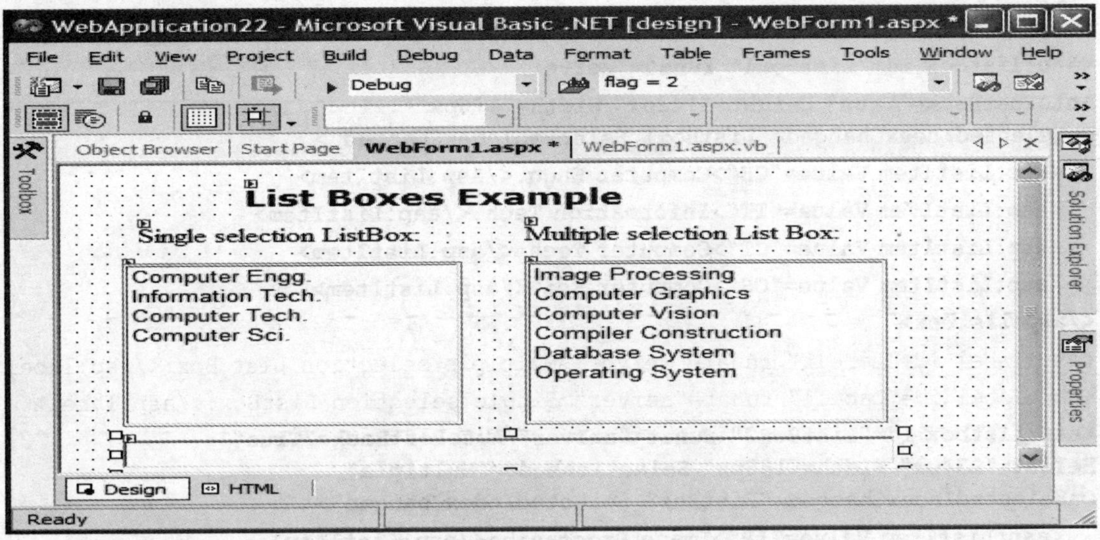

Fig. 13.18 *Placing of the ListBox control on the web form.*

When you add ListBox controls on the web form, it adds the following code to the ASPX file.

```
<HTML>
  <HEAD>
    <title>List Boxes Example</title>
    <script language="vb" runat="server">
    Sub ListBox1_SelectedIndexChanged(ByVal sender As System.Object, ByVal e As
    System.EventArgs) Handles ListBox1.SelectedIndexChanged
      TextBox1.Text = "You selected" & ListBox1.SelectedItem.Text
    End Sub
    Sub ListBox2_SelectedIndexChanged(ByVal sender As System.Object, ByVal e As
    System.EventArgs) Handles ListBox2.SelectedIndexChanged
      Dim loopindex As Integer
      TextBox1.Text = "You selected"
      For loopindex = 0 To ListBox2.Items.Count - 1
      If ListBox2.Items(loopindex).Selected Then
        TextBox1.Text &= ListBox2.Items(loopindex).Text & " "
      End If
      Next
    End Sub
```

```
    </script>
</HEAD>
<body MS_POSITIONING="GridLayout">
   <form id="Form1" method="post" runat="server">
   <asp:listbox id="ListBox1" runat="server"
   AutoPostBack="True" Height="142px" Width="176px"
   OnSelectedIndexChanged="ListBox1_SelectedIndexChanged">
      <asp:ListItem Value="CE">Computer Engg.</asp:ListItem>
      <asp:ListItem Value="IT">Information Tech.</asp:ListItem>
      <asp:ListItem Value="CT">Computer Tech.</asp:ListItem>
      <asp:ListItem Value="CS">Computer Sci.</asp:ListItem>
   </asp:listbox>
   <asp:label id="Label2" runat="server">Multiple selection List Box:</asp:label>
   <asp:label id="Label1" runat="server">Single selection ListBox:</asp:label>
   <asp:listbox id="ListBox2" runat="server" AutoPostBack="True"
   Height="134px" Width="188px" SelectionMode="Multiple"
   OnSelectedIndexChanged="ListBox2_SelectedIndexChanged">
      <asp:ListItem Value="IP">Image Processing</asp:ListItem>
      <asp:ListItem Value="CG">Computer Graphics</asp:ListItem>
      <asp:ListItem Value="CV">Computer Vision</asp:ListItem>
      <asp:ListItem Value="CC">Compiler Construction</asp:ListItem>
      <asp:ListItem Value="DS">Database System</asp:ListItem>
      <asp:ListItem Value="OS">Operating System</asp:ListItem>
   </asp:listbox>
   <asp:textbox id="TextBox1" runat="server" Height="23px"></asp:textbox>
   <asp:label id="Label3 runat="server" Height="32px" Font-Size="Larger" Font-
   Names="Verdana" Font-Bold="True">List Boxes Example</asp:label></form>
</body>
</HTML>
```

The ListBox controls are displayed in the browser as shown in following Fig. 13.19.

13.12 DROPDOWNLIST WEB SERVER CONTROL

Enables users to select from a single-selection drop-down list. The drop-down list can contain any number of items.

Syntax:

```
<asp:DropDownList
   id="DropDownList1"
   runat="server"
```

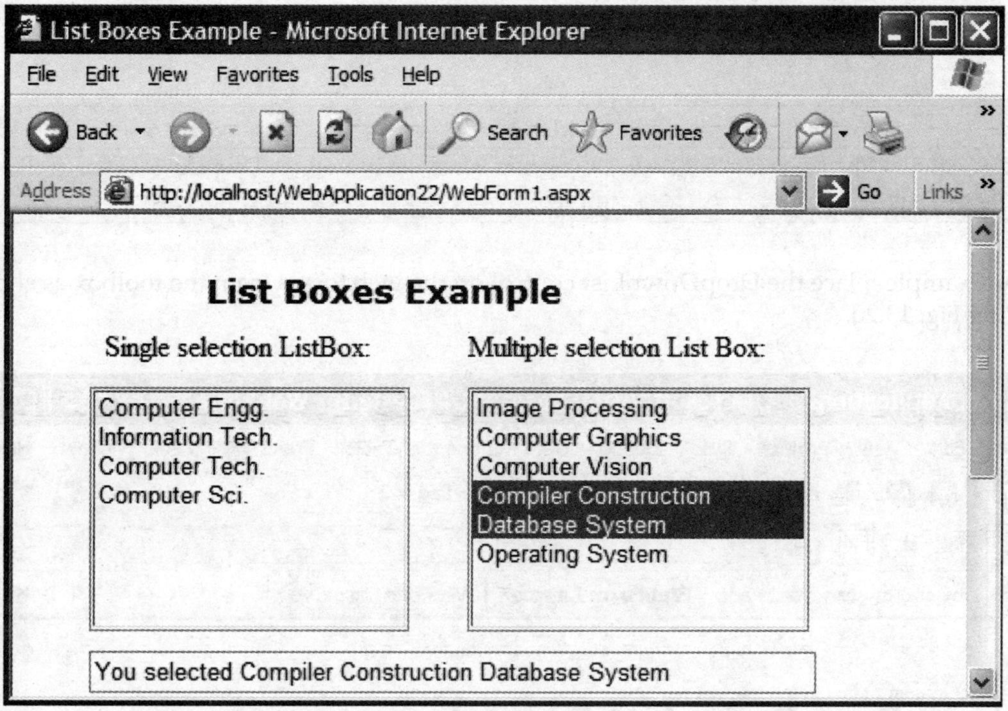

Fig. 13.19

```
DataSource="<% databindingexpression %>"
DataTextField="DataSourceField"
DataValueField="DataSourceField"
AutoPostBack="True|False"
OnSelectedIndexChanged="OnSelectedIndexChangedMethod">

   <asp:ListItem value="value" selected="True|False">
   Text
   </asp:ListItem>

</asp:DropDownList>
```

The important and widely used properties for the DropDownList control is listed in following table.

Properties	*Use*
id= "…"	Sets identifier to the server control.
AutoPostBack="True|False"	Sets whether event will be automatically posted back to the server. It accepts TRUE and FALSE values.
SelectedIndex	Sets selected item's index.

The important and widely used events for the DropDownList control is listed in following table.

Events	*Use*
OnSelectedIndexChanged="OnSelected IndexChangedMethod"	Occurs when the item in the DropDownList was clicked.

For Example, place the DropDownList control on the web forms from the toolbox as shown in following Fig. 13.20.

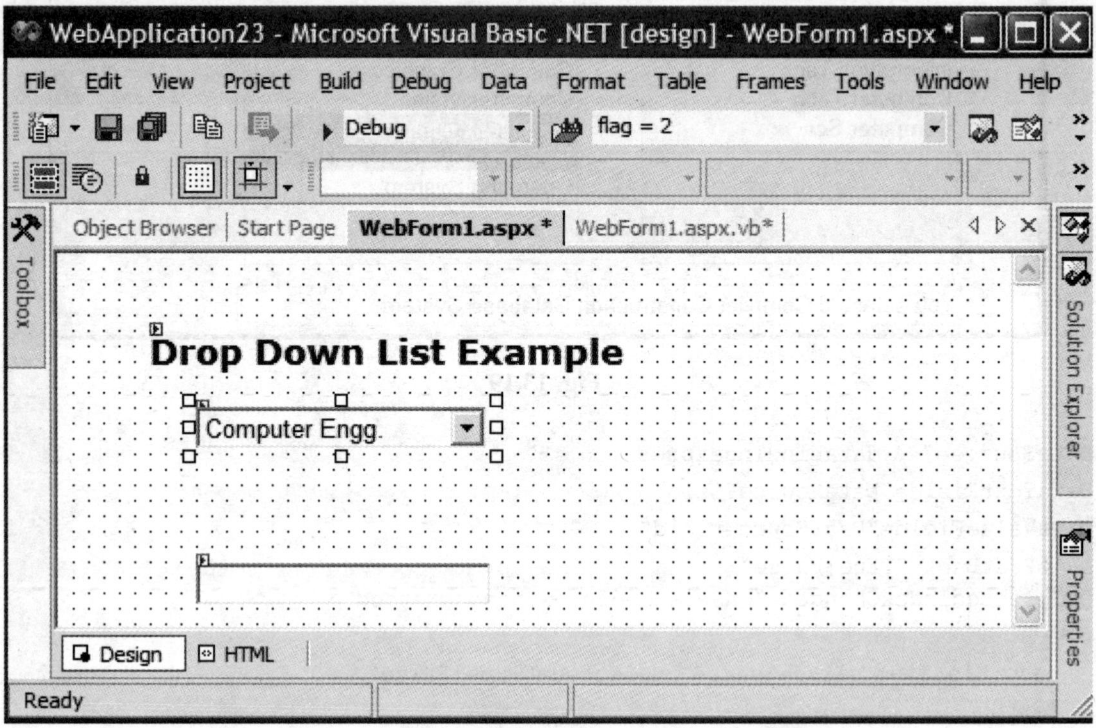

Fig. 13.20 *Placing of the Drop-DownList control on the web form.*

When you add Drop-Down List control on the web form, it adds the following code to the ASPX file.

```
<HTML>
  <HEAD>
    <title>Drop-Down List Example</title>
    <script language="vb" runat="server">
    Sub DropDownList1_SelectedIndexChanged(ByVal sender As System.Object, ByVal e
    As System.EventArgs) Handles DropDownList1.SelectedIndexChanged
```

```
        TextBox1.Text = "You selected " & DropDownList1.SelectedItem.Text
      End Sub
      </script>
   </HEAD>
   <body MS_POSITIONING="GridLayout">
      <form id="Form1" method="post" runat="server">
      <asp:DropDownList id="DropDownList1" runat="server"
      Width="153px" Height="22px" AutoPostBack="True">
         <asp:ListItem Value="CE">Computer Engg.</asp:ListItem>
         <asp:ListItem Value="CT">Computer Tech.</asp:ListItem>
         <asp:ListItem Value="IT">Information Tech.</asp:ListItem>
         <asp:ListItem Value="CS">Computer Eci.</asp:ListItem>
      </asp:DropDownList>
      <asp:TextBox id="TextBox1" runat="server"></asp:TextBox>
      <asp:Label id="Label1" runat="server" Height="24px" Width="248px" Font-
      Bold="True" Font-Names="Verdana" Font-Size="Larger">Drop Down List
      Example</asp:Label>
      </form>
   </body>
</HTML>
```

The Drop-Down List control is displayed in the browser as shown in following Fig. 13.21.

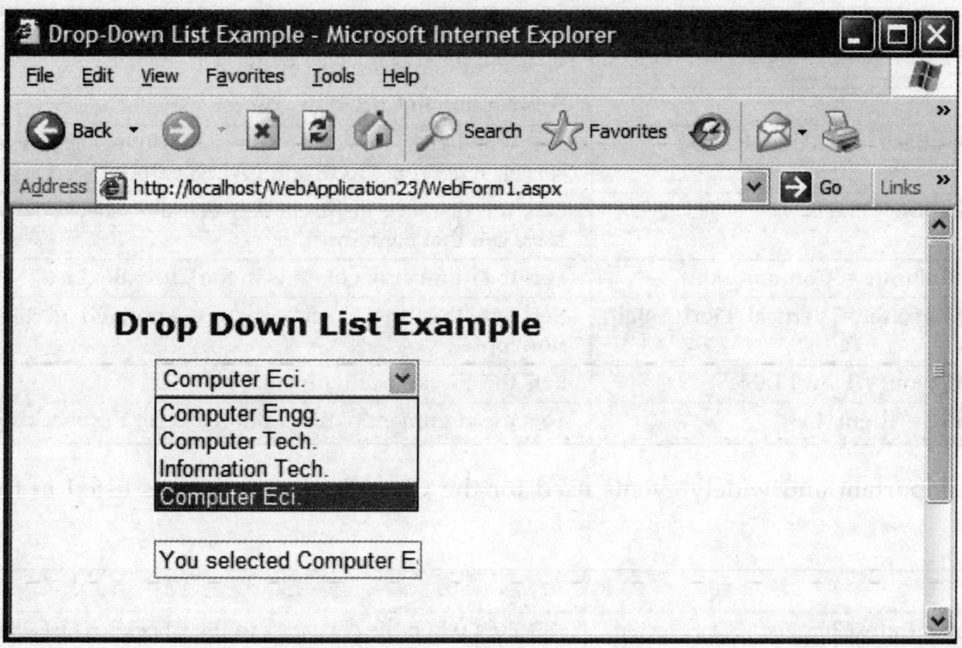

Fig. 13.21

13.13 CHECKBOXLIST WEB SERVER CONTROL

Creates a multiselection check box group. This control supports binding to a data source.

Syntax:

```
<asp:CheckBoxList
  id="CheckBoxList1"
  AutoPostBack="True|False"
  CellPadding="Pixels"
  DataSource='<%databindingexpression %>'
  DataTextField="DataSourceField"
  DataValueField="DataSourceField"
  RepeatColumns="ColumnCount"
  RepeatDirection="Vertical|Horizontal"
  RepeatLayout="Flow|Table"
  TextAlign="Right|Left"
  OnSelectedIndexChanged="OnSelectedIndexChangedMethod"      runat="server">

    <asp:ListItem value="value" selected="True|False"> Text</asp:ListItem>
</asp:CheckBoxList>
```

The important and widely properties used for the CheckBoxList control is listed in following table.

Properties	*Use*
id= "…"	Sets identifier to the server control.
Text= "…"	Sets caption in CheckBox control.
AutoPostBack =" TRUE | FALSE "	Sets whether event will be automatically posted back to the server. It accepts TRUE and FALSE values.
CellPadding="Pixels"	Sets the distance in pixels between the checkbox and the table cell that contains it.
RepeatColumns="ColumnCount"	Sets the number of columns in the CheckBoxList.
RepeatDirection="Vertical|Horizontal"	Sets whether the checkboxes are arranged vertically or horizontally.
RepeatLayout="Flow|Table"	Sets the checkbox alignment.
TextAlign="Right|Left"	Sets the alignment of the caption text for the checkboxes.

The important and widely events used for the CheckBoxList control is listed in following table.

Events	*Use*
OnSelectedIndexChanged="OnSelected IndexChangedMethod"	Occurs when the checkbox in the CheckBoxList was checked.

For Example, place the CheckBoxList control on the web forms from the toolbox as shown in following Fig. 13.22.

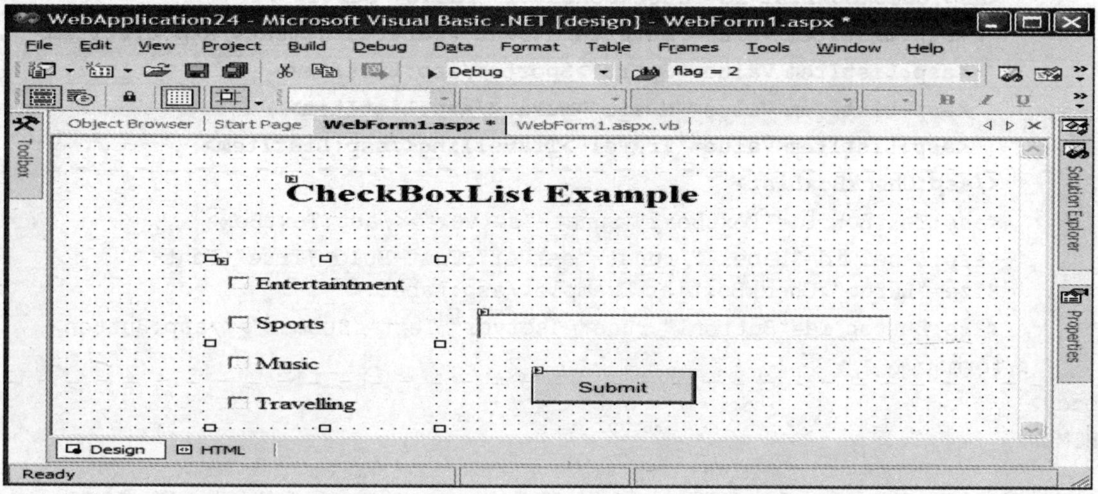

Fig. 13.22 *Placing of the CheckBox List control on the web form.*

When you add CheckBoxList control on the web form, it adds the following code to the ASPX file.

```
<HTML>
  <HEAD>
      <title>CheckBoxList Example</title>
      <script language="vb" runat="server">
      Sub CheckBoxList1_SelectedIndexChanged(ByVal sender _
      As System.Object, ByVal e As System.EventArgs) Handles _
      CheckBoxList1.SelectedIndexChanged
         Dim LoopIndex As Integer
         TextBox2.Text = "You have Selected: "
         For LoopIndex = 0 To 3
            If CheckBoxList1.Items(LoopIndex).Selected Then
               TextBox2.Text &= _
                  CheckBoxList1.Items(LoopIndex).Value & " "
            End If
         Next
      End Sub
      </script>
</HEAD>
```

```
<body MS_POSITIONING="GridLayout">
     <form id="Form1" method="post" runat="server">
        <asp:CheckBoxList id="CheckBoxList1" runat="server">
          <asp:ListItem Value="Entertaintment">Entertaintment</asp:ListItem>
          <asp:ListItem Value="Sport">Sports</asp:ListItem>
          <asp:ListItem Value="Music">Music</asp:ListItem>
          <asp:ListItem Value="Travel">Travelling</asp:ListItem>
        </asp:CheckBoxList>
        <asp:TextBox id="TextBox2" runat="server"></asp:TextBox>
        <asp:Label id="Label1" runat="server" Font-Bold="True" Font-
        Size="Large">CheckBoxList Example</asp:Label>
        <asp:Button id="Button1" runat="server" Text="Submit"></asp:Button>
      </form>
</body>
</HTML>
```

The CheckBoxList control is displayed in the browser as shown in following Fig. 13.23.

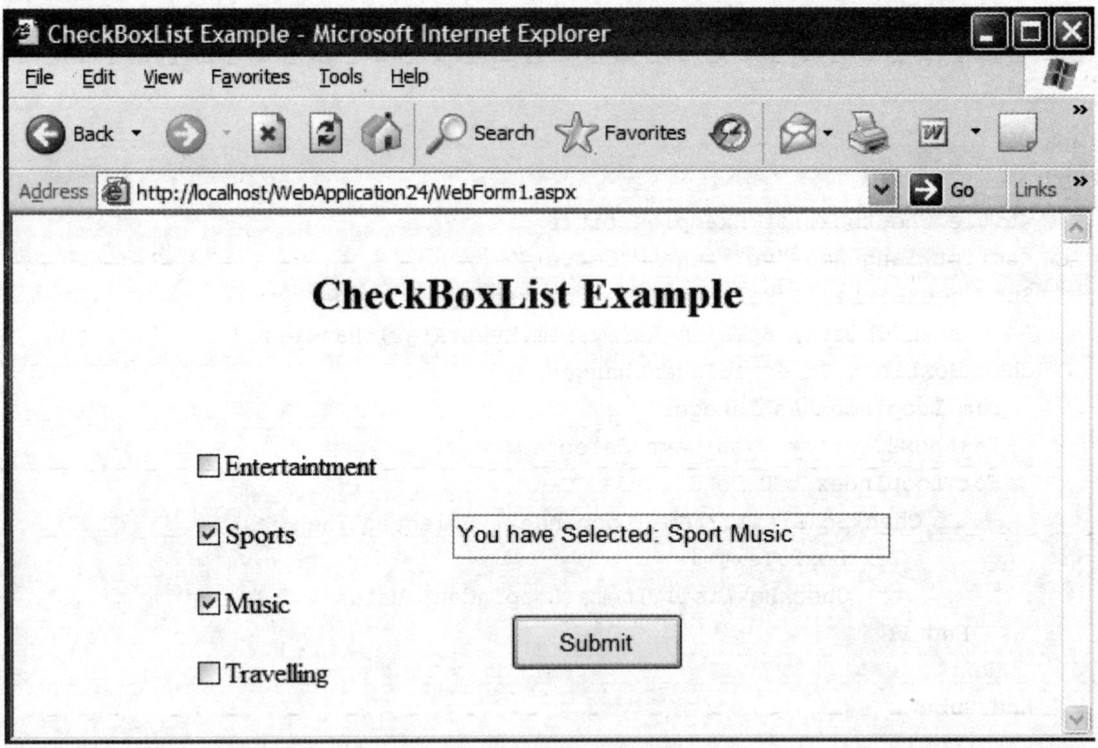

Fig. 13.23

13.14 RADIO BUTTON LIST WEB SERVER CONTROL

Creates a group of radio buttons. This control supports binding to a data source.

Syntax:

```
<asp:RadioButtonList
   id="CheckBoxList1"
   AutoPostBack="True|False"
   CellPadding="Pixels"
   DataSource='<%databindingexpression %>'
   DataTextField="DataSourceField"
   DataValueField="DataSourceField"
   RepeatColumns="ColumnCount"
   RepeatDirection="Vertical|Horizontal"
   RepeatLayout="Flow|Table"
   TextAlign="Right|Left"
   OnSelectedIndexChanged="OnSelectedIndexChangedMethod" runat="server">
      <asp:ListItem Text="label" Value="value" Selected="True|False" />
</asp:RadioButtonList>
```

The important and widely properties used for the RadioButtonList control is listed in following table.

Properties	*Use*
id= "..."	Sets identifier to the server control.
AutoPostBack =" TRUE | FALSE "	Sets whether event will be automatically posted back to the server. It accepts TRUE and FALSE values.
CellPadding="Pixels"	Sets the distance in pixels between the RadioButtonList and the table cell that contains it.
RepeatColumns="ColumnCount"	Sets the number of columns in the RadioButtonList.
RepeatDirection="Vertical | Horizontal"	Sets whether the Radio buttons are arranged vertically or horizontally.
RepeatLayout="Flow | Table"	Sets the RadioButton alignment.
TextAlign="Right | Left"	Sets the alignment of the caption text for the Radio Button.

The important and widely events used for the RadioButtonList control is listed in following table.

Events	*Use*
On Selected Index Changed="On Selected Index Changed Method"	Occurs when the RadioButton in the RadioButtonList was checked.

For Example, place the RadioButtonList control on the web forms from the toolbox as shown in following Fig. 13.24.

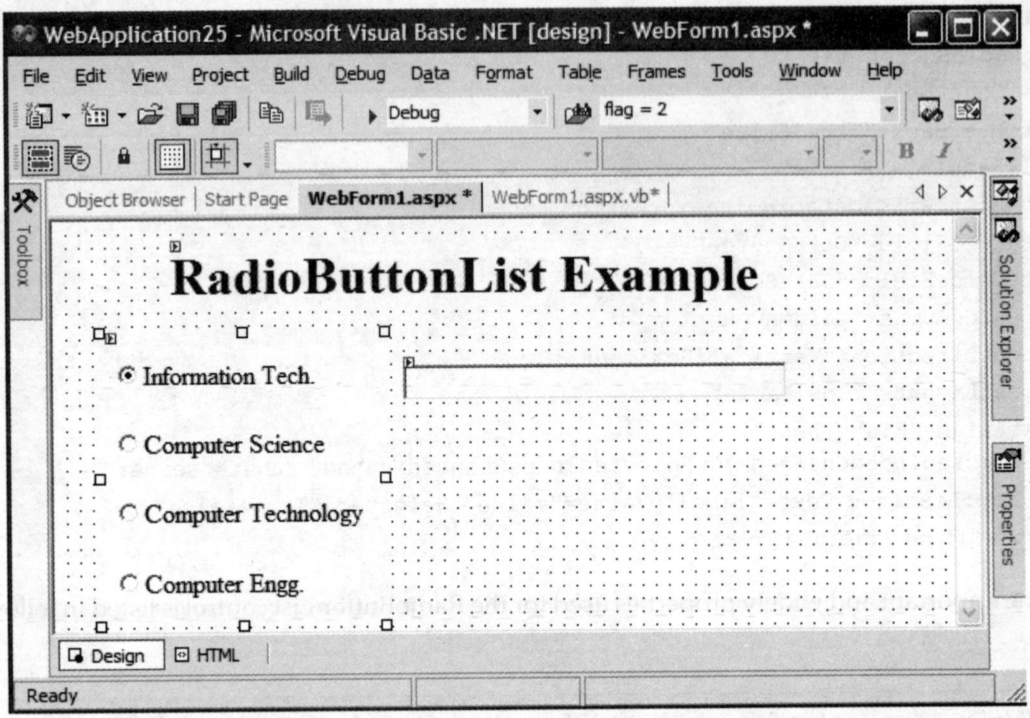

Fig. 13.24 *Placing of the RadioButton List control on the web form.*

When you add Radio Button List control on the web form, it adds the following code to the ASPX file.

```
<HTML>
  <HEAD>
    <title>RadioButtonList Example</title>
    <script language="vb" runat="server">
    Sub RadioButtonList1_SelectedIndexChanged(ByVal sender _
    As System.Object, ByVal e As System.EventArgs) Handles _
    RadioButtonList1.SelectedIndexChanged
      TextBox2.Text = "Your Branch is: "
      TextBox2.Text &= RadioButtonList1.SelectedItem.Value
    End Sub
    </script>
  </HEAD>
```

```
  <body MS_POSITIONING="GridLayout">
    <form id="Form1" method="post" runat="server">
    <asp:radiobuttonlist id="RadioButtonList1" runat="server"
    AutoPostBack="True" Height="172px" Width="116px">
      <asp:ListItem Value="Information Tech."
      Selected="True">Information Tech.</asp:ListItem>
      <asp:ListItem Value="Computer Sci.">Computer Science</asp:ListItem>
      <asp:ListItem Value="Computer Tech.">Computer Technology</asp:ListItem>
      <asp:ListItem Value="Computer Engg.">Computer Engg.</asp:ListItem>
    </asp:radiobuttonlist>
    <asp:textbox id="TextBox2" style="Z-INDEX: 105; LEFT: 240px; POSITION:
    absolute; TOP: 168px" runat="server"></asp:textbox>
    <asp:label id="Label3" runat="server" Height="40px" Width="200px" Font-
    Bold="True" Font-Size="X-Large">RadioButtonList
    Example</asp:label></form>
  </body>
</HTML>
```

The RadioButtonList control is displayed in the browser as shown in following Fig. 13.25.

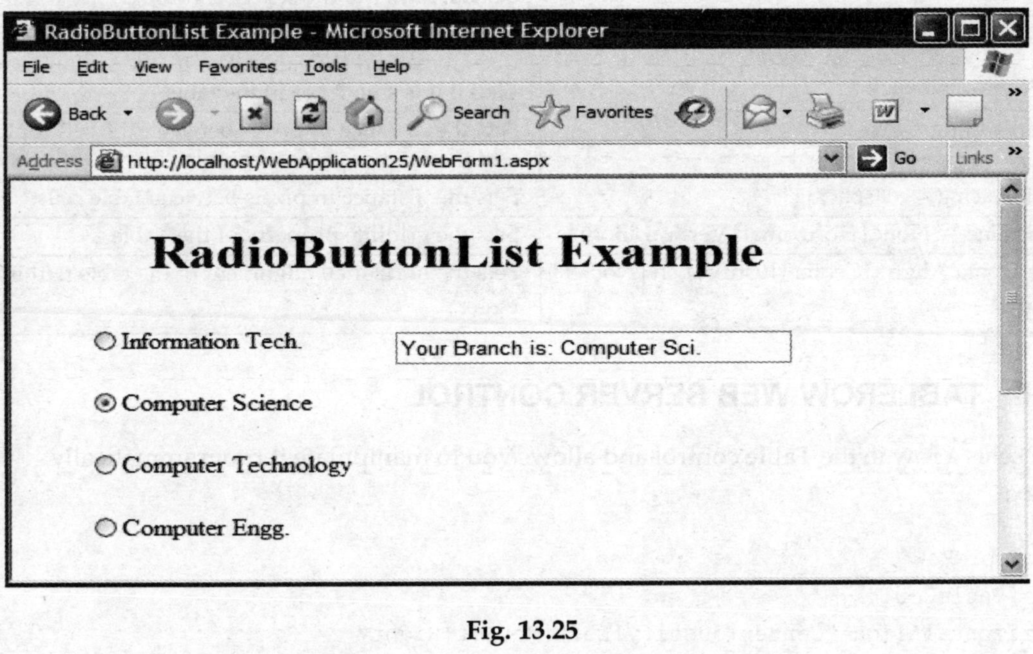

Fig. 13.25

13.15 TABLE WEB SERVER CONTROL

Declares a table and allows you to manipulate it programmatically.

Syntax:

```
<asp:Table
  id="Table1"
  BackImageUrl="url"
  CellSpacing="cellspacing"
  CellPadding="cellpadding"
  GridLines="None|Horizontal|Vertical|Both"
  HorizontalAlign="Center|Justify|Left|NotSet|Right" runat="server">

  <asp:TableRow>
  <asp:TableCell> Cell text </asp:TableCell>
  </asp:TableRow>

</asp:Table>
```

The important and widely properties used for the Table control is listed in following table.

Properties	*Use*
id= "..."	Sets identifier to the server control.
BackImageUrl="url"	Indicates the URL of the background image to display behind the table. The image will appear as tiled if it is smaller than the table.
CellPadding="Pixels"	Sets the distance in pixels between the cell contents and the cell border that contains it.
CellSpacing="cellspacing"	Sets the distance in pixels between table cells.
GridLines="None | Horizontal | Vertical | Both"	Sets the gridline property of the Table.
HorizontalAlign="Center | Justify | Left | NotSet | Right"	Sets the horizontal alignment of the table within the page.

13.16 TABLEROW WEB SERVER CONTROL

Represents a row in the **Table** control and allows you to manipulate it programmatically.

Syntax:

```
<asp:TableRow
  id="TableRow1"
  HorizontalAlign="Center|Justify|Left|NotSet|Right"
  VerticalAlign="Bottom|Middle|NotSet|Top"
  runat="server">
```

```
<asp:TableCell> Cell text </asp:TableCell>

</asp:TableRow>
```

The important and widely properties used for the TableRow control is listed in following table.

Properties	Use
id= "..."	Sets identifier to the server control.
HorizontalAlign="Center | Justify | Left | NotSet | Right"	Sets the horizontal alignment of the row contents.
VerticalAlign="Center | Justify | Left | NotSet | Right"	Sets the vertical alignment of the row contents.

13.17 TABLECELL WEB SERVER CONTROL

Represents a cell in a **Table** control and allows you to manipulate it programmatically.
Syntax:

```
<asp:"TableCell"
  id="TableCell1"
  ColumnSpan="colcount"
  RowSpan="rowcount"
  HorizontalAlign="Center|Justify|Left|NotSet|Right"
  VerticalAlign="Bottom|Middle|NotSet|Top"
  Wrap="True|False"
runat="server">
Cell text
</asp:TableCell>
```

The important and widely properties used for the Table Cell control is listed in following table.

Properties	Use
id= "..."	Sets identifier to the server control.
ColumnSpan="colcount"	Sets the number of columns the cells spans.
RowSpan="rowcount"	Sets the number of rows the cells spans.
Text= "..."	Sets the Text in the cell.
Wrap="True | False"	Sets whether the text content wraps.
HorizontalAlign="Center | Justify | Left | NotSet | Right"	Sets the cell content's horizontal alignment.
VerticalAlign="Center | Justify | Left | NotSet | Right"	Sets the cell content's vertical alignment.

For Example, place the Table control on the web forms from the toolbox as shown in following Fig. 13.26.

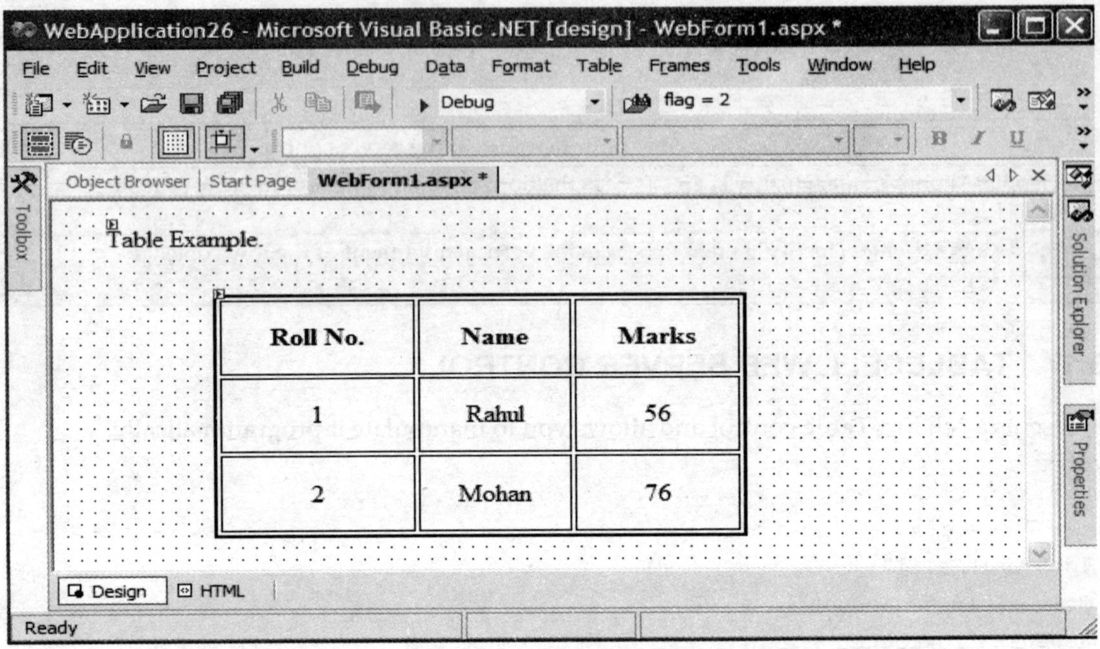

Fig. 13.26 *Placing of the Table control on the web form.*

When you add Table control along with table row and table cell in the web form, it adds the following code to the ASPX file.

```
<HTML>
  <HEAD>
    <title>Table Example.</title>
  </HEAD>
  <body MS_POSITIONING="GridLayout">
    <form id="Form1" method="post" runat="server">
    <asp:Label ID="Label1" Font-Bold=True Font-Size=20>Table
    Example.</asp:Label>
    <asp:Table id="Table1" runat="server" BorderStyle="Solid" Height="163px"
    Width="313px" BorderColor="Black" BorderWidth="2px">
      <asp:TableRow HorizontalAlign="Center">
        <asp:TableCell BorderStyle="Solid" BorderWidth="1px" Font-Bold="True"
        Text="Roll No."></asp:TableCell>
        <asp:TableCell BorderStyle="Solid" BorderWidth="1px" Font-Bold="True"
        Text="Name"></asp:TableCell>
        <asp:TableCell BorderStyle="Solid" BorderWidth="1px" Font-Bold="True"
        Text="Marks"></asp:TableCell>
```

```
      </asp:TableRow>
      <asp:TableRow HorizontalAlign="Center">
        <asp:TableCell BorderStyle="Solid" BorderWidth="1px"
        Text="1"></asp:TableCell>
        <asp:TableCell BorderStyle="Solid" BorderWidth="1px"
        Text="Rahul"></asp:TableCell>
        <asp:TableCell BorderStyle="Solid" BorderWidth="1px"
        Text="56"></asp:TableCell>
     </asp:TableRow>
     <asp:TableRow HorizontalAlign="Center">
        <asp:TableCell BorderStyle="Solid" BorderWidth="1px"
        Text="2"></asp:TableCell>
        <asp:TableCell BorderStyle="Solid" BorderWidth="1px"
        Text="Mohan"></asp:TableCell>
        <asp:TableCell BorderStyle="Solid" BorderWidth="1px"
        Text="76"></asp:TableCell>
     </asp:TableRow>
   </asp:Table>
     </form>
  </body>
</HTML>
```

The Table control along with table rows and cells are displayed in the browser as shown in following Fig. 13.27.

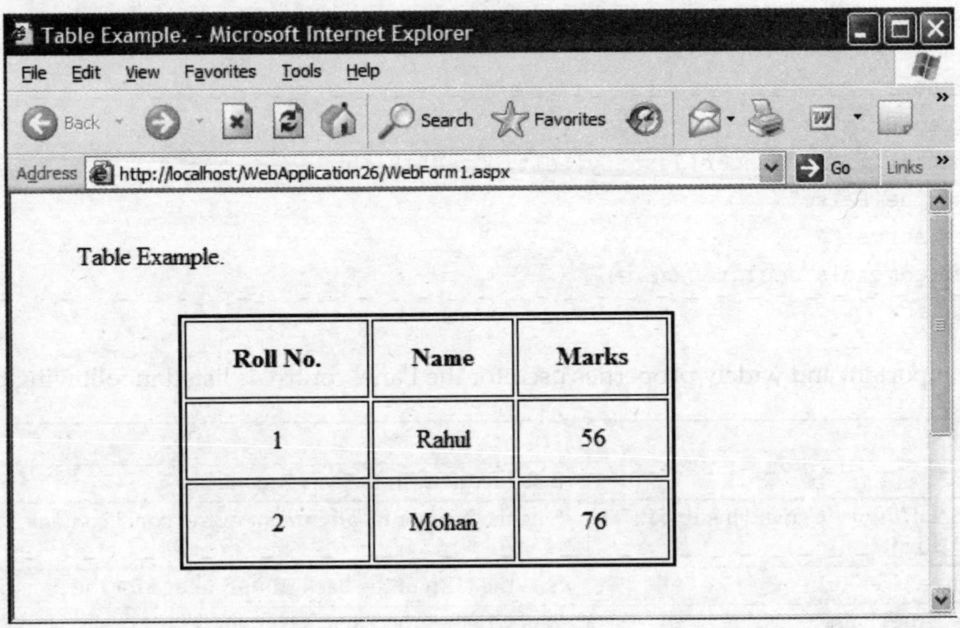

Fig. 13.27

13.18 ADROTATOR WEB SERVER CONTROL

Displays an advertisement banner on a Web Forms page.

```
<asp:AdRotator
   id="Value" AdvertisementFile="AdvertisementFile"
   KeyWordFilter="KeyWord"
   Target="Target"
   OnAdCreated="OnAdCreatedMethod"
runat="server"/>
```

13.19 PLACEHOLDER WEB SERVER CONTROL

Reserves a location in the page control hierarchy for controls that are added programmatically.
Syntax:

```
<asp:PlaceHolder
   id="PlaceHolder1"
runat="server"/>
```

13.20 PANEL WEB SERVER CONTROL

Provides a container for other controls. This control is rendered as an HTML **<div>** element.
Syntax:

```
<asp:Panel
   id="Panel1"
   BackImageUrl="url"
   HorizontalAlign="Center|Justify|Left|NotSet|Right"
   Wrap="True|False"
   runat="server">
   (Other controls declared here)
</asp:Panel>
```

The important and widely properties used for the Panel control is listed in following table.

Properties	*Use*
id= "..."	Sets identifier to the server control.
HorizontalAlign="Center | Justify | Left | NotSet | Right"	Sets the horizontal alignment of the panel contents.
BackImageUrl="url"	Sets the URL of the background image for the panel.
Wrap="True | False"	Sets whether the Panel's content wraps.

For Example, place the Panel control on the web forms from the toolbox as shown in following Fig. 13.28.

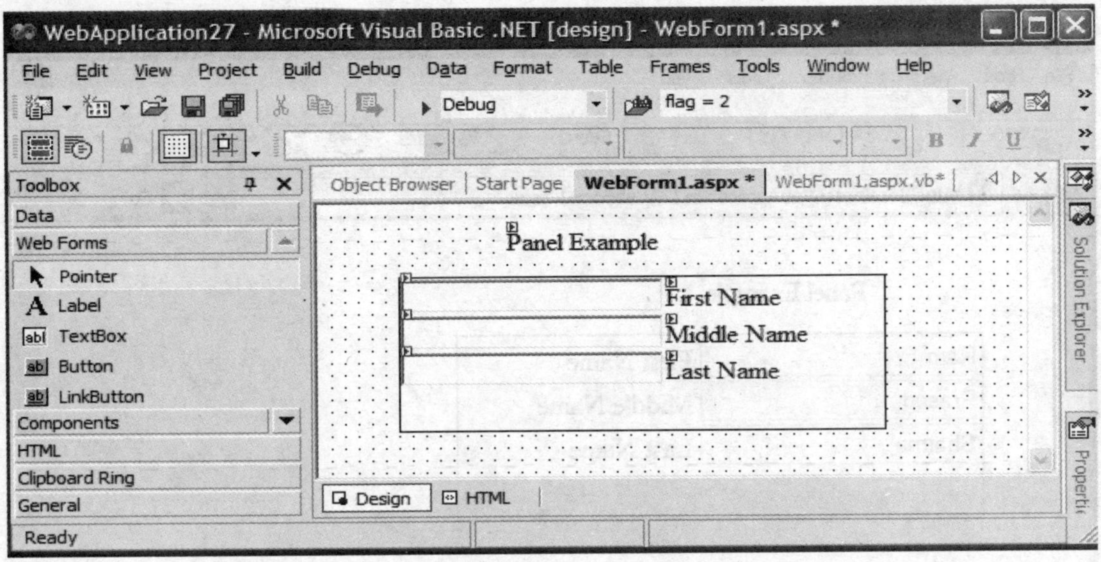

Fig. 13.28 *Placing of the PlaceHolder control on the web form.*

```
<HTML>
  <HEAD>
    <title>Panel Example</title>
  </HEAD>
  <body MS_POSITIONING="GridLayout">
  <form id="Form1" method="post" runat="server">
    <asp:Panel id="Panel2" style="Z-INDEX: 101; LEFT: 48px; POSITION: absolute;
    TOP: 48px" runat="server" Width="288px" Height="102px" BorderWidth="1px"
    BorderStyle="Solid">
      <asp:TextBox id="TextBox1" runat="server"></asp:TextBox>
      <asp:Label id="Label1" runat="server">First Name</asp:Label>
      <asp:TextBox id="TextBox2" runat="server"></asp:TextBox>
      <asp:Label id="Label2" runat="server">Middle Name</asp:Label>
      <asp:TextBox id="TextBox3" runat="server"></asp:TextBox>
      <asp:Label id="Label3" runat="server">Last Name</asp:Label>
    </asp:Panel>
    <asp:Label id="Label4" runat="server" Height="24px" Width="128px">Panel
    Example</asp:Label>
  </form>
  </body>
</HTML>
```

The Panel control along with table rows and cells are displayed in the browser as shown in following Fig. 13.29.

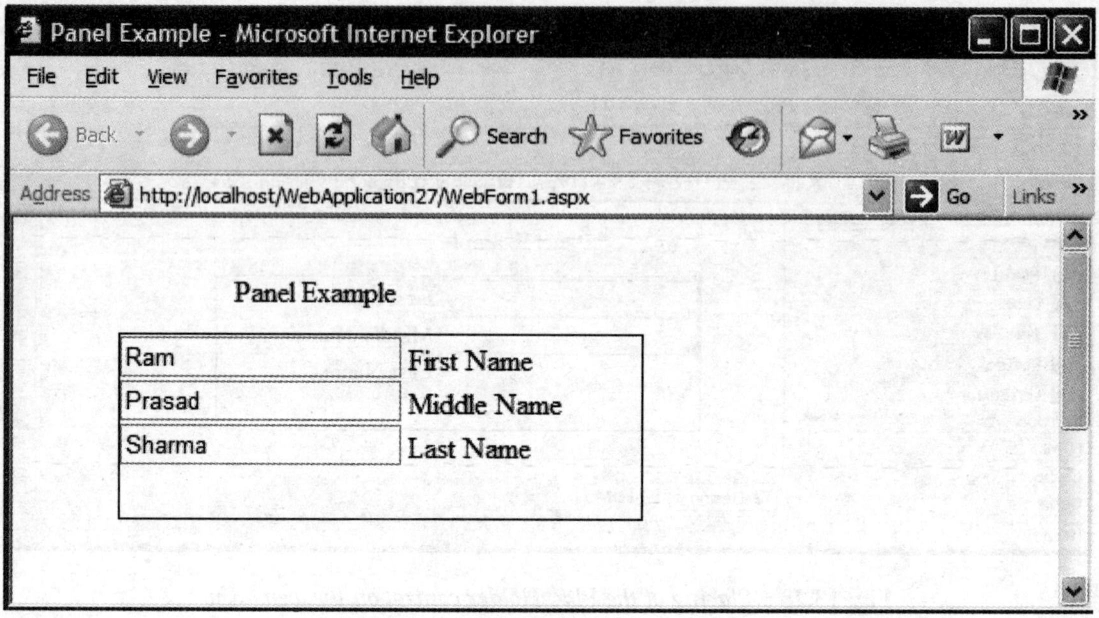

Fig. 13.29

Server Control Events

Server controls, such as a Button, TextBox, and DropDownList, each have their own sets of events that occur in response to user actions. However, not all server control events are created equal. There are three types of server control events:

- Postback events
  These events cause the Web page to be sent back to the server for immediate processing. Postback events affect perceived performance because they trigger a round-trip to the server.
- Cached events
  These events are saved in the page's view state to be processed when a postback event occurs.
- Validation events
  These events are handled on the page without posting back or caching. The validation server controls use these types of events.

The validations controls are evaluated before the page is posted back to the server. When the page is posted back, the Page_Init and Page_Load events are handled, then cached events are handled, and finally the event that caused the postback is processed. Among cached events, the event order is determined by the order of the controls on the Web form.

The Button, Link Button, and Image Button controls all cause postback events. The TextBox, DropDownList, ListBox, RadioButton, and CheckBox controls provide cached events; however, you can override this behavior by setting the AutoPostBack property to True.

QUESTIONS

1. Explain Label Web Server Control in details.
2. Explain TextBox Web Server Control in details.
3. Explain Button Web Server Control in details.
4. Explain CheckBox Web Server Control in details.
5. Explain RadioButton Web Server Control in details.
6. Explain LinkButton Web Server Control in details.
7. Explain HyperLink Web Server Control in details.
8. Explain Image Web Server Control in details.
9. Explain ImageButton Web Server Control in details.
10. Explain Literal Web Server Control in details.
11. Explain ListBox Web Server Control in details.
12. Explain DropDownList Web Server Control in details.
13. Explain CheckBoxList Web Server Control in details.
14. Explain RadioButtonList Web Server Control in details.
15. Explain Table Web Server Control in details.
16. Explain TableRow Web Server Control in details.
17. Explain TableCell Web Server Control in details.
18. Explain AdRotator Web Server Control in details.
19. Explain PlaceHolder Web Server Control in details.
20. Explain Panel Web Server Control in details.

□□□

14

Validation Server Controls

The following are the ASP.NET syntax and description that you use when creating a Validating server control in a text or HTML editor.

14.1 REQUIRED FIELD VALIDATOR CONTROL

Evaluates the value of an input control to ensure that the user enters a value.

Syntax:

```
<asp:RequiredFieldValidator
  id="ProgrammaticID"
  ControlToValidate="ProgrammaticID of control to validate"
  InitialValue="value"
  ErrorMessage="Message to display in ValidationSummary control"
  Text="Message to display in control"
  ForeColor="value"
  BackColor="value" …
runat="server" >
</asp:RequiredFieldValidator>
```

The important and widely used properties for the RequiredFieldValidator control is listed in following table.

Properties	*Use*
ControlToValidate="…"	Sets data entry to validate.
Text="…"	Sets error message to display in control.
InitialValue="value"	Sets initial value in the connected data entry control.

For Example, place the RequiredFieldValidator control on the web forms from the toolbox as shown in following Fig. 14.1.

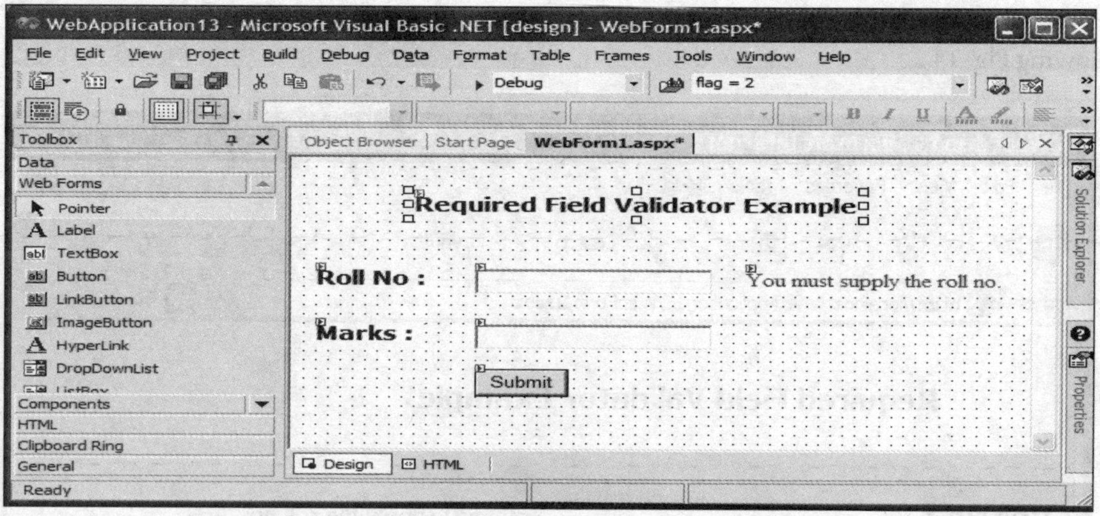

Fig. 14.1 *Placing of the Required Field Validator control on the web form.*

When you add Required Field Validator control on the web, it adds the following code to the ASPX file.

```
<%@ Page Language="vb" Auto Event Wireup="false" Codebehind="Web Form1.aspx.vb"
Inherits="WebApplication13.WebForm1" %>
<!DOCTYPE HTML PUBLIC "-//W3C//DTD HTML 4.0 Transitional//EN">
<HTML>
<HEAD>
<title>WebForm1</title>
</HEAD>
<body MS_POSITIONING="Grid Layout">
<form id="Form1" method="post" runat="server">
  <asp:TextBox id="TextBox1"  runat="server"></asp:TextBox>
  <asp:TextBox id="TextBox2" ="server"></asp:TextBox>
  <asp:Label   id="Label1"   runat="server"   Font-Names="Verdana"   Font-
  Bold="True">Required Field Validator Example</asp:Label>
  <asp:Button id="Button1" runat="server" Text="Submit"></asp:Button>
  <asp:Label id="Label2" runat="server" Font-Names="Verdana">Roll No :</asp:Label>
  <asp:Label id="Label3" runat="server" Font-Names="Verdana"> Marks :</asp:Label>
  <asp:RequiredFieldValidator   id="RequiredFieldValidator1"   runat="server"
  ErrorMessage="You must supply the roll no."
  ControlToValidate="TextBox1"></asp:RequiredFieldValidator>
```

```
</form>
</body>
</HTML>
```

The use of the RequiredFieldValidator control is displayed in the browser as shown in following Fig. 14.2.

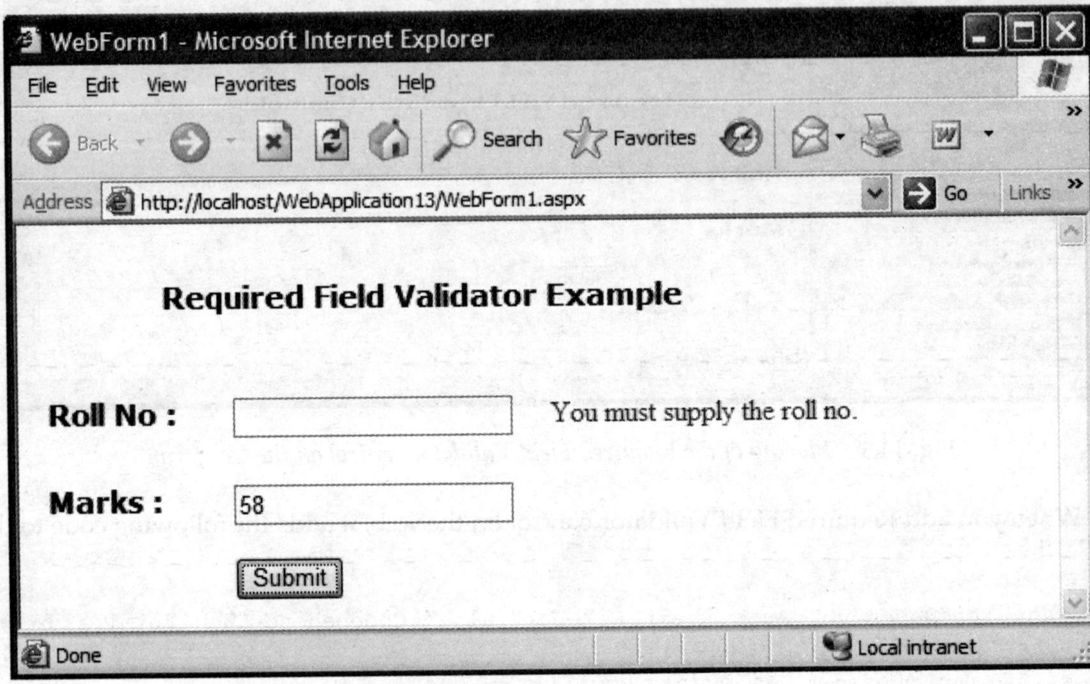

Fig. 14.2

14.2 RANGE VALIDATOR CONTROL

Evaluates the value of an input control to determine whether it is between a specified upper and lower boundary.

Syntax:

```
<asp:RangeValidator
  id="ProgrammaticID"
  ControlToValidate="Programmatic ID of control to validate"
  MinimumValue="value" MaximumValue="value"
  Type="DataType"
  ErrorMessage="Message to display in ValidationSummary control"
  Text="Message to display in control"
  ForeColor="value"
  BackColor="value" …
```

```
runat="server" >
</asp:RangeValidator>
```

The important and widely used properties for the RangeValidator control is listed in following table.

Properties	*Use*
ControlToValidate="..."	Sets data entry to validate.
Text="..."	Sets error message to display in control.
MinimumValue="value"	Sets the minimum value in the range.
MaximumValue="value"	Sets the maximum value in the range.
ErrorMessage="..."	Sets message to display in ValidationSummary control.

For Example, place the RangeValidator control on the web forms from the toolbox as shown in following Fig. 14.3.

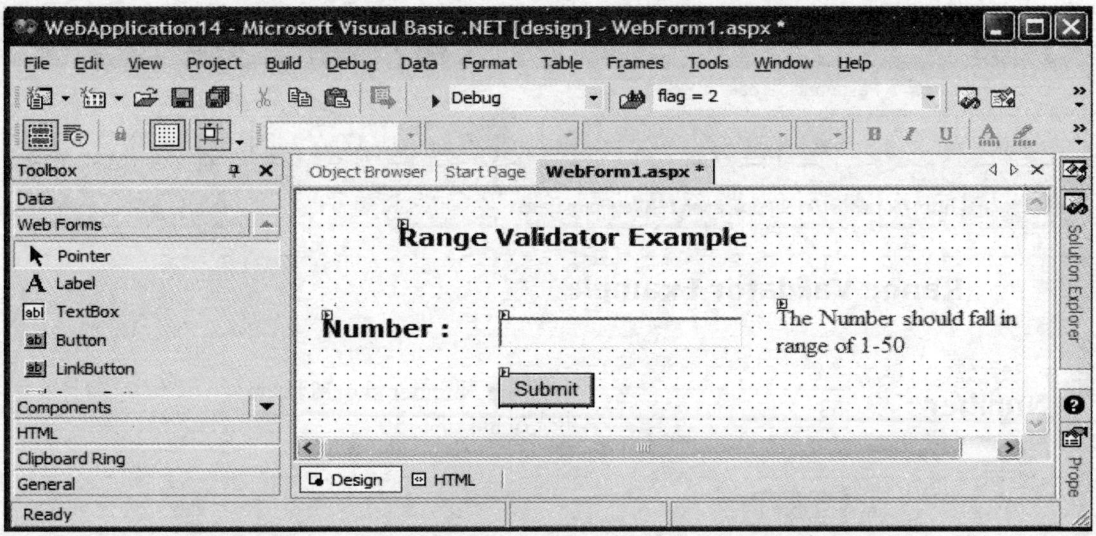

Fig. 14.3 *Placing of the RangeValidator control on the web form.*

When you add RangeValidator control on the web, it adds the following code to the ASPX file.

```
<%@ Page Language="vb" AutoEventWireup="false" Codebehind="WebForm1.aspx.vb"
Inherits="WebApplication14.WebForm1" %>
<!DOCTYPE HTML PUBLIC "-//W3C//DTD HTML 4.0 Transitional//EN">
<HTML>
   <HEAD>
      <title>Range Validator Example</title>
```

```
  </HEAD>
  <body MS_POSITIONING="GridLayout">
  <form id="Form1" method="post" runat="server">
  <asp:Label id="Label1" runat="server">Range Validator Example</asp:Label>
  <asp:Label id="Label2" runat="server">Number :</asp:Label>
  <asp:TextBox id="TextBox1" runat="server"></asp:TextBox>
  <asp:Button id="Button1" runat="server" Text="Submit"></asp:Button>
  <asp:RangeValidator id="RangeValidator1" runat="server" ErrorMessage="The Number
  should fall in range of 1-50" ControlToValidate="TextBox1" MaximumValue="50"
  MinimumValue="1" Width="184px"></asp:RangeValidator>
  </form>
  </body>
</HTML>
```

The use of the RangeValidator control is displayed in the browser as shown in following Fig. 14.4.

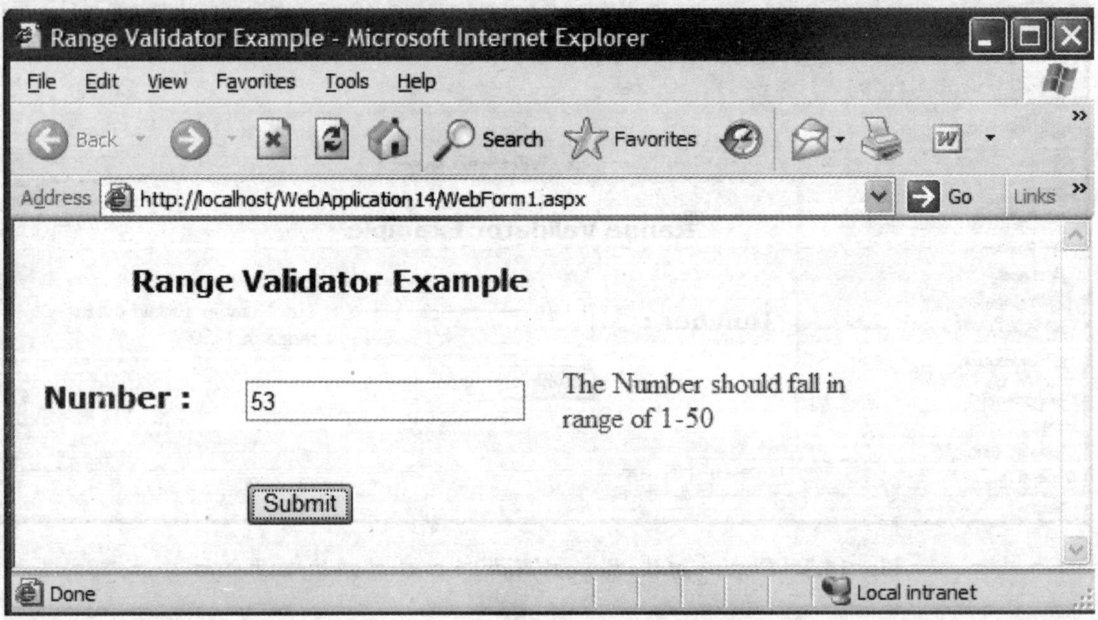

Fig. 14.4

14.3 COMPARE VALIDATOR CONTROL

Evaluates the value of an input control against a constant value or the value of another input control to determine whether the two values match the relationship specified by a comparison operator (less than, equal to, greater than, and so on).

Syntax:

```
<asp:CompareValidator
   id="ProgrammaticID"
   ControlToValidate="Programmatic ID of Server Control to Validate"
   ValueToCompare="value"
   ControlToCompare="value"
   Type="DataType"
   Operator="Operator Value"
   ErrorMessage="Message to display in ValidationSummary control"
   Text="Message to display in control"
   ForeColor="value"
   BackColor="value" …
runat="server" >
</asp:CompareValidator>
```

The important and widely used properties for the CompareValidator control is listed in following table.

Properties	*Use*
ControlToValidate="…"	Sets data entry to validate.
Text="…"	Sets error message to display in control.
ControlToCompare="Value"	Sets the data-entry control you want to compare to the data-entry control you want to validate.
Operator="Operator Value"	Sets the comparison operator you want to use.
ValueToCompare="value"	Sets the constant value you want to compare with the value in the data-entry control you want to validate.
Type="DataType"	Sets the type of the data used in the comparison.
ErrorMessage="…"	Sets message to display in Validation Summary control

For Example, place the CompareValidator control on the web forms from the toolbox as shown in following Fig. 14.5.

When you add CompareValidator control on the web, it adds the following code to the ASPX file.

```
<%@ Page Language="vb" AutoEventWireup="false" Codebehind="WebForm1.aspx.vb"
Inherits="WebApplication15.WebForm1" %>
<!DOCTYPE HTML PUBLIC "-//W3C//DTD HTML 4.0 Transitional//EN">
<HTML>
  <HEAD>
    <title>WebForm1</title>
```

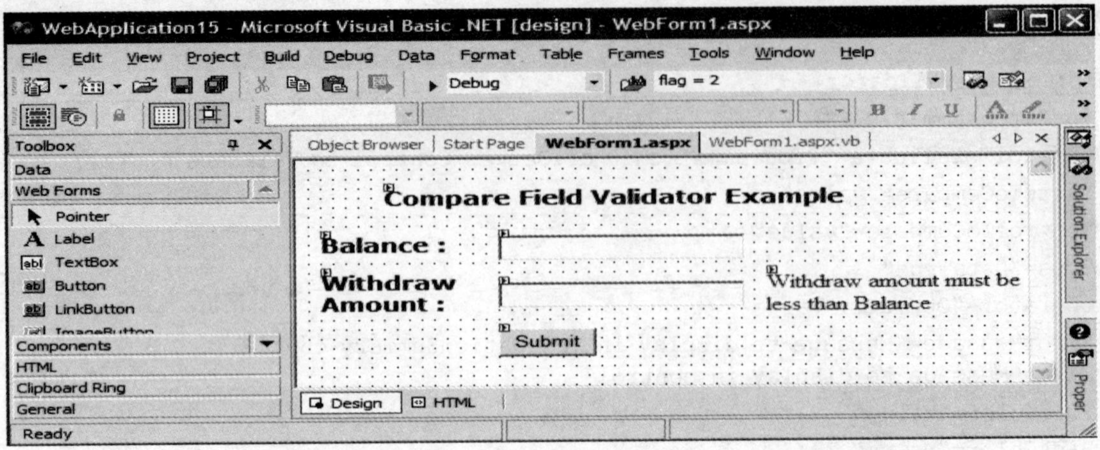

Fig. 14.5 *Placing of the Compare Validator control on the web form.*

```
  </HEAD>
  <body MS_POSITIONING="GridLayout">
  <form id="Form1" method="post" runat="server">
  <asp:Label id="Label1" runat="server">Compare Field Validator
  Example</asp:Label>
  <asp:TextBox id="TextBox1" runat="server"></asp:TextBox>
  <asp:TextBox id="TextBox2" runat="server"></asp:TextBox>
  <asp:Label id="Label3" runat="server">Withdraw Amount :</asp:Label>
  <asp:Label id="Label2" runat="server">Balance :</asp:Label>
  <asp:Button id="Button1" runat="server"  Text="Submit"></asp:Button>
  <asp:CompareValidator id="CompareValidator1" runat="server"
  ErrorMessage="Withdraw amount must be less than Balance"
  ControlToCompare="TextBox1" ControlToValidate="TextBox2"
  Type="Integer" Operator="LessThan"></asp:CompareValidator>
  </form>
  </body>
</HTML>
```

The use of the CompareValidator control is displayed in the browser as shown in following Fig. 14.6.

14.4 REGULAREXPRESSIONVALIDATOR CONTROL

Evaluates the value of an input control to determine whether it matches a pattern defined by a regular expression.

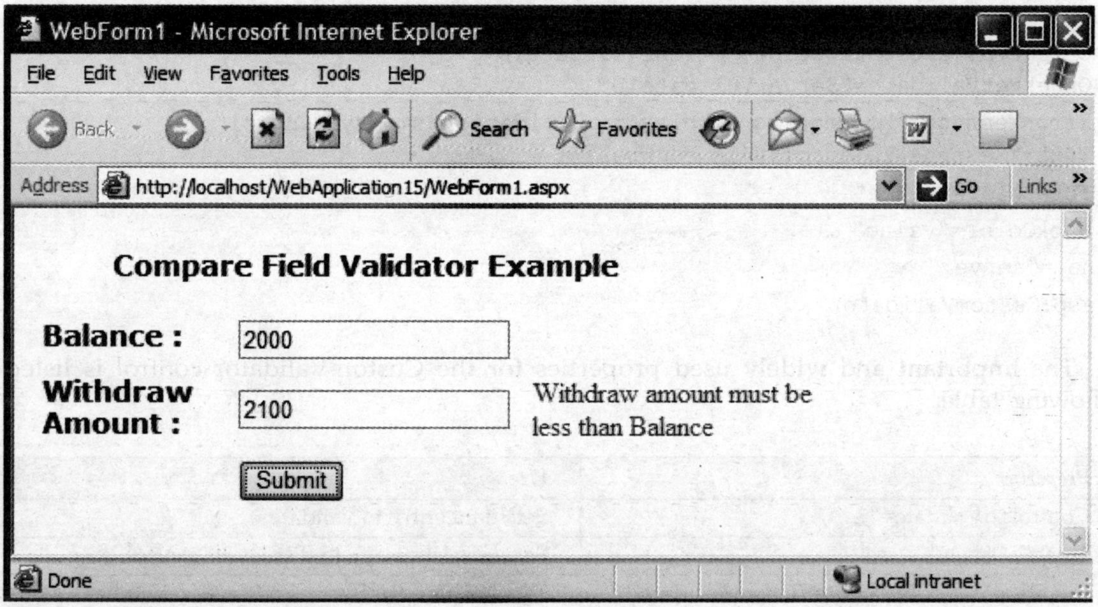

Fig. 14.6

Syntax:

```
<asp:RegularExpressionValidator
   id="ProgrammaticID"
   ControlToValidate="ProgrammaticID of control to validate"
   ValidationExpression="expression"
   ErrorMessage="Message to display in ValidationSummary control"
   Text="Message to display in control"
   ForeColor="value"
   BackColor="value" …
runat="server" >

</asp: RegularExpressionValidator>
```

14.5 CUSTOM VALIDATOR CONTROL

Evaluates the value of an input control to determine whether it passes customized validation logic.

Syntax:

```
<asp:CustomValidator
   id="ProgrammaticID"
```

```
   ControlToValidate="programmatic ID of Server Control to Validate"
   ClientValidationFunction="ClientValidateID"
   OnServerValidate="ServerValidateID"
   ErrorMessage="Message to display in ValidationSummary control"
   Text="Message to display in control"
   ForeColor="value"
   BackColor="value" ...
runat="server" >
</asp:CustomValidator>
```

The important and widely used properties for the CustomValidator control is listed in following table.

Properties	*Use*
ControlToValidate="..."	Sets data entry to validate.
Text="..."	Sets error message to display in control.
ClientValidationFunction="ClientValidateID"	Sets the name of the script function you have placed in the head section of the web page for validation.
ErrorMessage="..."	Sets message to display in Validation Summary control

The important and widely used event for the CustomValidator control is listed in following table.

Events	*Use*
OnServerValidate="ServerValidateID"	Occurs when validation takes place on the server.

For Example, place the CustomValidator control on the web forms from the toolbox as shown in following Fig. 14.7.

When you add CustomValidator control on the web, it adds the following code to the ASPX file.

```
<%@ Page Language="vb" AutoEventWireup="false" Codebehind="WebForm1.aspx.vb"
Inherits="WebApplication17.WebForm1" %>
<!DOCTYPE HTML PUBLIC "-//W3C//DTD HTML 4.0 Transitional//EN">
<HTML>
  <HEAD>
    <title>CustomValidate</title>
    <script language="vbscript">
      Sub Validate(source, arguments)
        If (arguments.Value = "abcd") Then
          arguments.IsValid = True
```

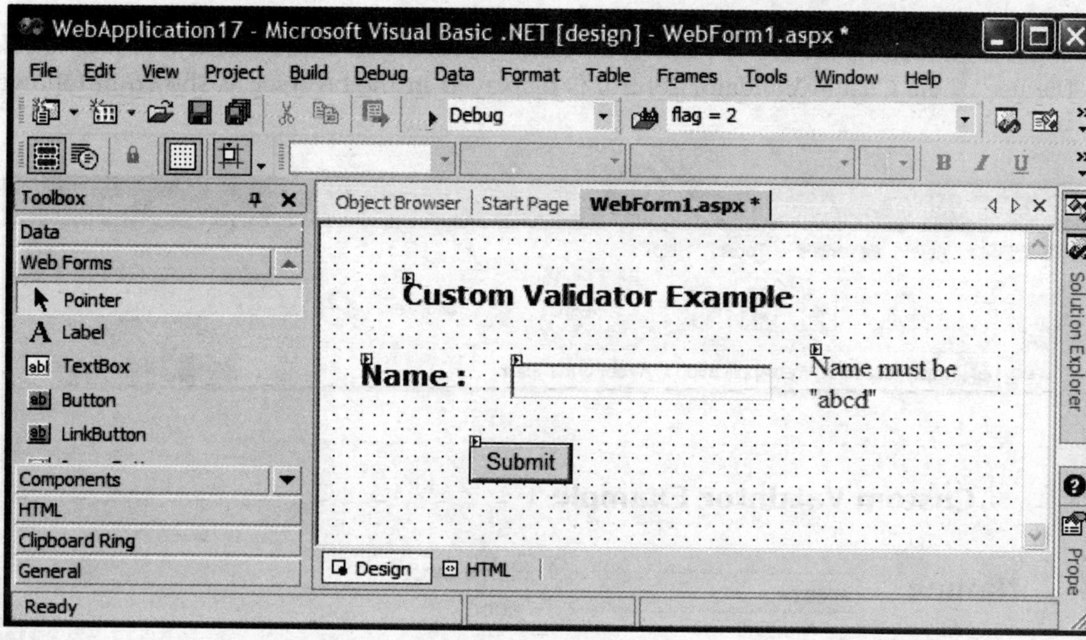

Fig. 14.7 *Placing of the CompareValidator control on the web form.*

```
        Else
          arguments.IsValid = False
        End If
     End Sub
   </script>
 </HEAD>
 <body MS_POSITIONING="GridLayout">
 <form id="Form1" method="post" runat="server">
 <asp:CustomValidator id="CustomValidator1" runat="server"
 ErrorMessage='Name must be "abcd"' ControlToValidate="TextBox1"
 ClientValidationFunction="validate"
 Width="104px"></asp:CustomValidator>
 <asp:Label id="Label2" runat="server">Name :</asp:Label>
 <asp:TextBox id="TextBox1" runat="server"></asp:TextBox>
 <asp:Button id="Button1" runat="server" Text="Submit"></asp:Button>
 <form>
 </body>
</HTML>
```

To use custom validator set ClientValidationFunction property to the name of the script function which is written in the head section of the HTML document. This function will be passed two arguments, **source** giving source control to validate, and **arguments** which holds data to validate as arguments value. If you validate the data, you set arguments, Is Valid to True or to False.

The use of the CustomValidator control is displayed in the browser as shown in following Fig. 14.8.

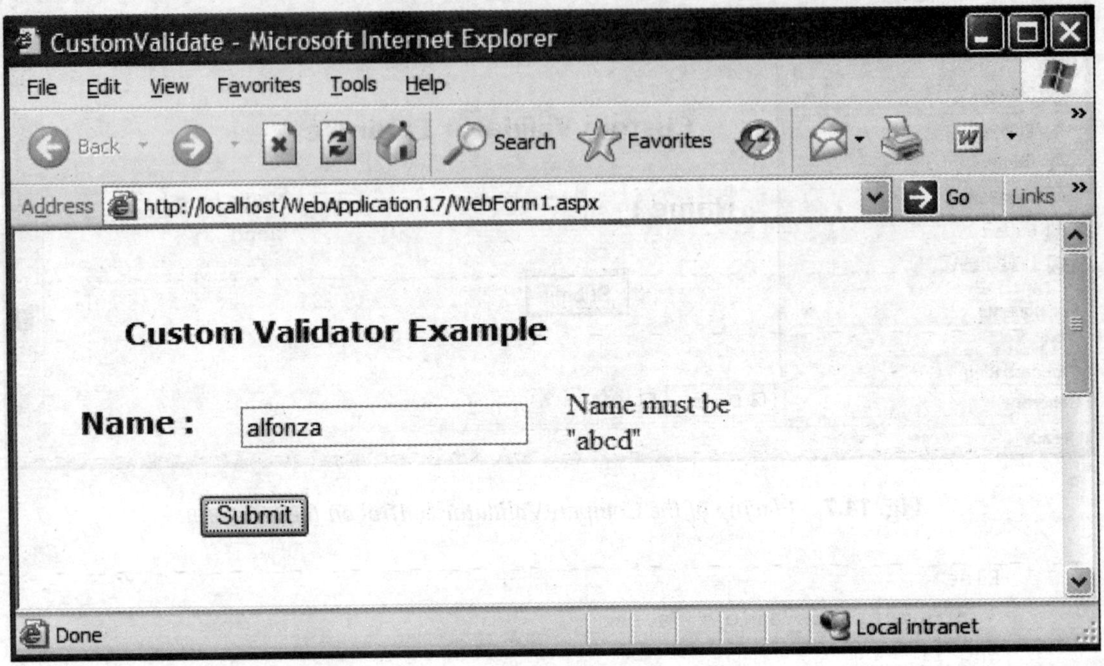

Fig. 14.8

14.6 VALIDATION SUMMARY CONTROL

Displays a list of all validation errors on the Web page.

Syntax:

```
<asp:ValidationSummary
   id="programmaticID"
   DisplayMode="BulletList | List | SingleParagraph"
   EnableClientScript="true | false"
   ShowSummary="true | false"
   ShowMessageBox="true | false"
   HeaderText="TextToDisplayAsSummaryTitle"
runat="server"/>
```

The important and widely used properties for the ValidationSummary control is listed in following table.

Properties	*Use*
ShowSummary="true | false"	Sets whether the summary is displayed in the web page.
ShowMessageBox="true | false"	Sets whether a message box displays the validation summary on the web page.
DisplayMode="BulletList | List | SingleParagraph"	Sets the summary's display mode.
EnableClientScript="true | false"	Sets whether validation should attempted in the browser.
HeaderText="TextToDisplayAsSummaryTitle"	Sets the text displayed at the top of the summary.

For Example, place the Validation Summary control on the web forms from the toolbox as shown in following Fig. 14.9.

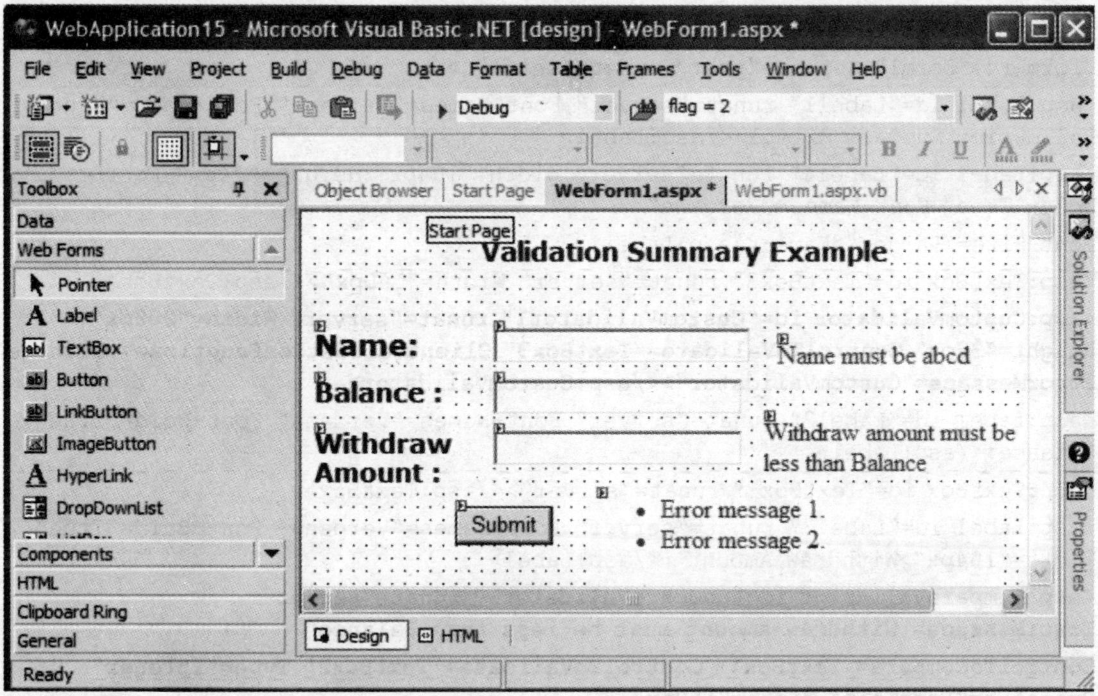

Fig. 14.9 *Placing of the Validation Summary control on the web form.*

For Example, when you add Validation Summary control on the web, it adds the following code to the ASPX file.

```
<%@ Page Language="vb" AutoEventWireup="false" Codebehind="WebForm1.aspx.vb"
Inherits="WebApplication15.WebForm1" %>
<!DOCTYPE HTML PUBLIC "-//W3C//DTD HTML 4.0 Transitional//EN">
```

```
<HTML>
  <HEAD>
    <title>WebForm1</title>
    <script language="vbscript">
      Sub Validate(source, arguments)
        If (arguments.Value = "abcd") Then
          arguments.IsValid = True
        Else
          arguments.IsValid = False
        End If
      End Sub
    </script>
  </HEAD>
  <body MS_POSITIONING="GridLayout">
  <form id="Form1" method="post" runat="server">
  <asp:Label id="Label1" runat="server" Font-Names="Verdana" Font-Bold="True">
  Validation Summary Example</asp:Label>
  <asp:Label id="Label4" runat="server" Width="104px" Height="24px" Font-
  Bold="True" Font-Names="Verdana"
  Font-Size="Larger">Name:</asp:Label>
  <asp:TextBox id="TextBox3" runat="server" Width="160px"></asp:TextBox>
  <asp:CustomValidator id="CustomValidator1" runat="server" Width="208px"
  Height="32px" ControlToValidate="TextBox3" ClientValidationFunction="validate"
  ErrorMessage="CustomValidator"></asp:CustomValidator>
  <asp:Label id="Label2" runat="server" Font-Names="Verdana" Font-Bold="True">
  Balance:</asp:Label>
  <asp:TextBox id="TextBox1" runat="server"></asp:TextBox>
  <asp:Label id="Label3" runat="server" Font-Names="Verdana" Font-Bold="True"
  Width="104px">Withdraw Amount :</asp:Label>
  <asp:CompareValidator id="CompareValidator1" runat="server"
  ErrorMessage="Withdraw amount must be less than Balance"
  ControlToCompare="TextBox1" ControlToValidate="TextBox2" Type="Integer"
  Operator="LessThan" Width="160px"
  Height="40px"></asp:CompareValidator>
  <asp:TextBox id="TextBox2" runat="server"></asp:TextBox>
  <asp:ValidationSummary id="ValidationSummary1"  ShowSummary=True
  DisplayMode=BulletList runat="server" Width="280px" Height="40px">
  </asp:ValidationSummary>
  <asp:Button id="Button1" runat="server" Text="Submit"></asp:Button>
  </form>
  </body>
</HTML>
```

The use of the ValidationSummary control is displayed in the browser as shown in following Fig. 14.10.

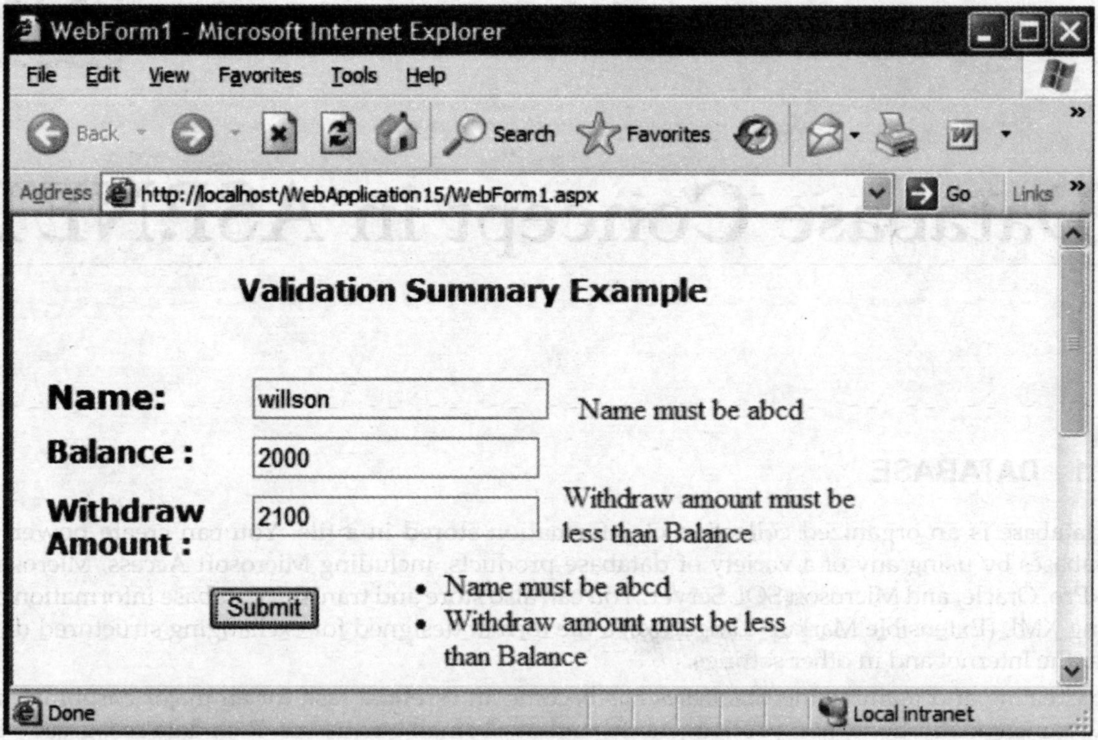

Fig. 14.10

QUESTIONS

1. Explain RequiredFieldValidator Control in details.
2. Explain RangeValidator Control in details.
3. Explain CompareValidator Control in details.
4. Explain RegularExpressionValidator Control in details.
5. Explain CustomValidator Control in details.
6. Explain ValidationSummary Control in details.

15

Database Concept in ASP.NET

15.1 DATABASE

A database is an organized collection of information stored in a file. You can create powerful databases by using any of a variety of database products, including Microsoft Access, Microsoft FoxPro, Oracle, and Microsoft SQL Server. You can also store and transmit database information by using XML (Extensible Markup Language), a file format designed for exchanging structured data over the Internet and in other settings.

Creating and maintaining databases has become an essential task for all major corporations, government institutions, non-profit agencies, and most small businesses. Rich data resources—be they customer addresses, manufacturing inventories, account balances, employee records, donor lists, or order histories—have become the lifeblood of the business world.

Microsoft Visual Basic .NET isn't designed for creating new databases, but rather for displaying, analyzing, and manipulating the information in existing databases. Although previous versions of Visual Basic have also provided this capability, Visual Basic .NET offers a new data model called ADO.NET that provides access to an even greater number of database formats. In particular, ADO.NET has been designed for Internet use, meaning that it uses the same method for accessing local, client-server, and Internet-based data sources. As a testimony to Microsoft's goal of making ADO.NET a great technology for manipulating databases over the Internet, Microsoft has made XML—a standard defined by the World Wide Web Consortium—the internal data format of ADO.NET. Using XML in this way makes ADO.NET easier to utilize with existing Internet data sources, and it makes it easier for software vendors to write data adapters, or "providers," that convert third-party database formats to be compatible with ADO.NET.

Data Controls

Data controls provide a way to connect to, perform commands on, and retrieve data from SQL and OLE databases and XML data files. The data controls appear on the Web form only at design time to provide a visual way for you to set their properties and handle their events. At run-time, data controls do not have a visual representation. For example, following are data controls used to work with the database.

```
SqlConnection, SqlCommand, OleDbConnection, OleDbCommand, DataSet etc..
```

Using the above controls, to access the information in the web form do the following procedure:

First a **connection** is made, which specifies connection information about the database. Next a **data adapter** is created, which manages retrieving data from the database and posting data changes. Then a **dataset** is created, which is a representation of one or more database tables you plan to work with in your program. (You don't manipulate the actual data, but rather a copy of it.) Information in the dataset can then be bound to controls on a form.

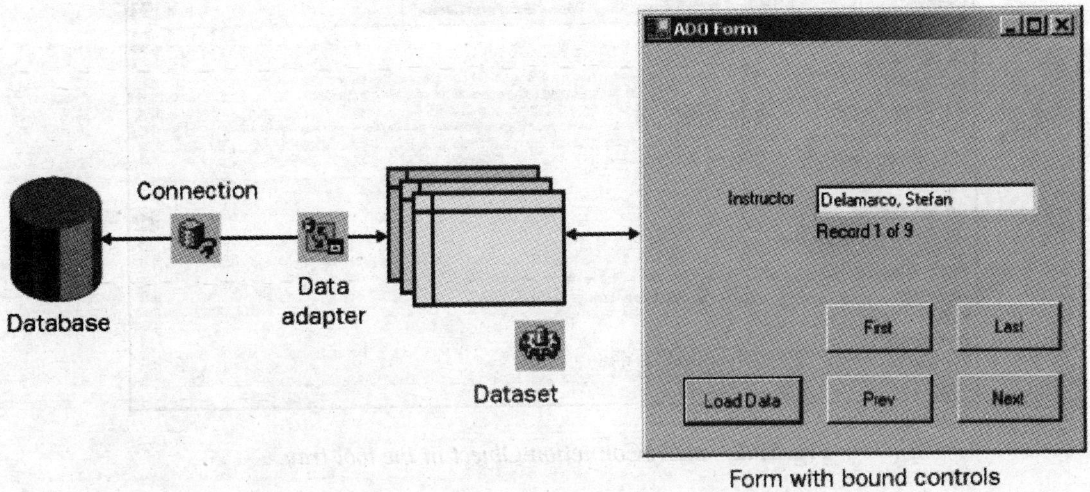

Fig. 15.1 *Accessing data from database through Connection, DataAdapter,DataSet etc.*

Connection: It provides the connection to the data source. It means there is data provider to access the database. The default data provider that the ASP.NET works with is Microsoft SQL server 7.0 or later, ASP.NET can work with any data provider that can support Open Database Connectivity (ODBC).

Data Adapter: After connection to the data source, create the data adapter to work with the data. The data adapter is what actually applies SQL statement to a database and cause the dataset to fill with the data. It is just there to apply the commands to the database. To work with the SQL server data provider use SQLDataAdapter objects, to work with the ORACLE data provider use OracleDataAdapter objects and to work with the ODBC data provider use OdbcDataAdapter objects.

DataSet: Once Data Adapter is created, generate a dataset using that adapter. Datasets are what actually works with the code when you want to use data from the database. The data adapter is what actually applies SQL statement to a database and cause the dataset to fill with the data.

For example:

To access a database and to display its content in the data grid, follow these steps:

1. Create a connection to the database by dragging and dropping the **OleDbConnection1** tool in the tool tray of the page which is at the beneath of the page, as shown in the following Fig. 15.2.

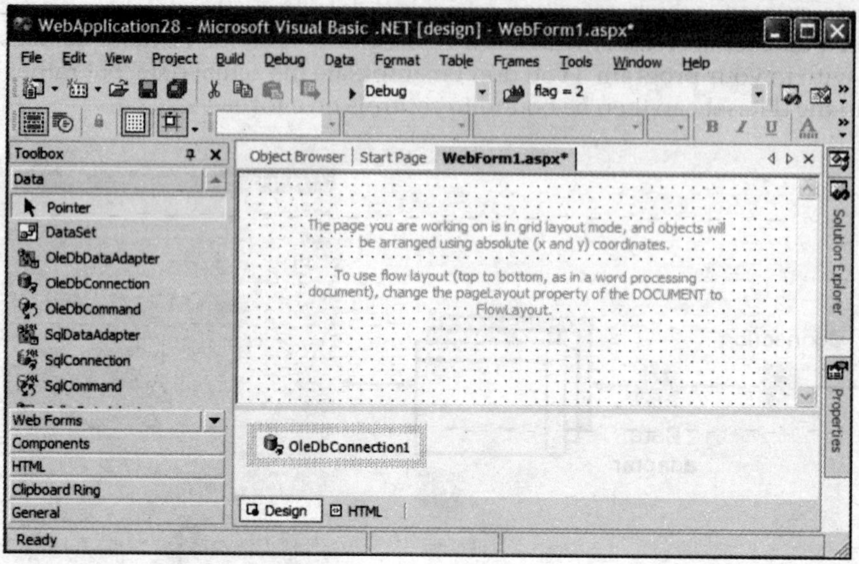

Fig. 15.2 *oleDbConnction Object in the tool tray.*

2. Select **ConnectionString** property of the OleDbConnection in the property window. To this property you can set Provider such as Microsoft.Jet.OLEDB.4.0 for Access, Microsoft OLE DB Provider for SQL server etc., DataSource, persist security info etc. This property is shown in property window as shown in following Fig. 15.3.

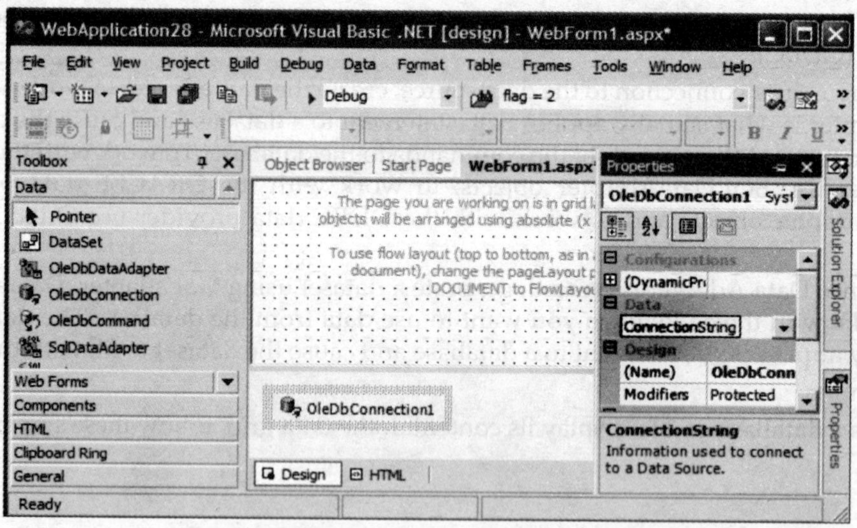

Fig. 15.3 *Setting connection string.*

3. Now click to this ConnectionString property you will get drop-down list as shown on following Fig. 15.4. From this list you select <New Connection…> item to create connection to the database.

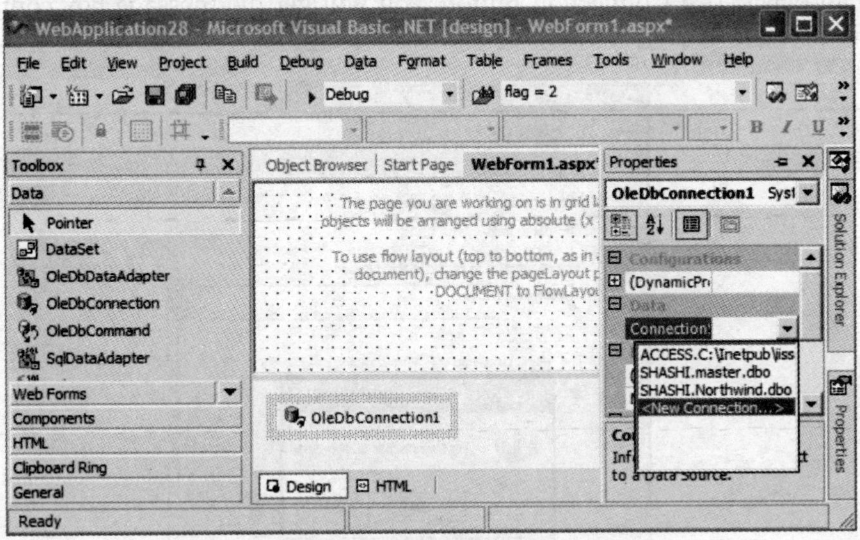

Fig. 15.4

4. After selecting the <New Connection…> item, you will get the dialog box, named Data Link Properties, as shown in following Fig. 15.5. In this dialog box, select Microsoft.Jet.OLEDB.4.0 provider for connection with Access database from Provider Tab.

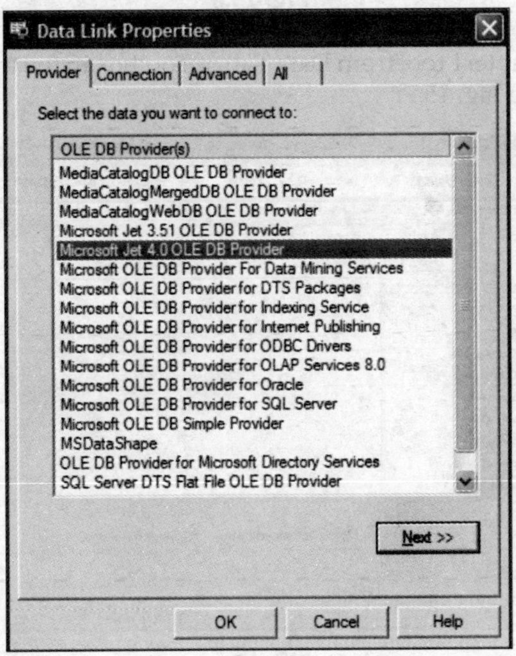

Fig. 15.5

5. After selecting the provider from Data Link Properties dialog box, click next button, you switched in to the Connection Tab of the same dialog box, in which you select or enter the name of the database and click Test Connection Button, you will get the message box containing "Test Connection Succeeded" message as shown in following Fig. 15.6.

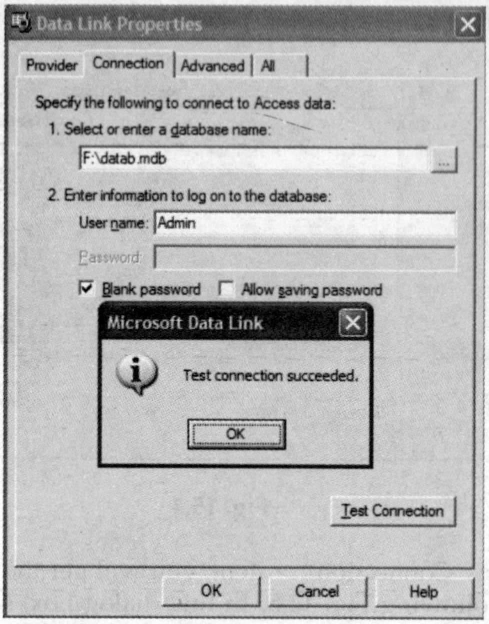

Fig. 15.6

6. Now add oleDbDataAdapter1 tool from Data Tab of Toolbox in the tool tray at the beneath of the page, as shown in following Fig. 15.7.

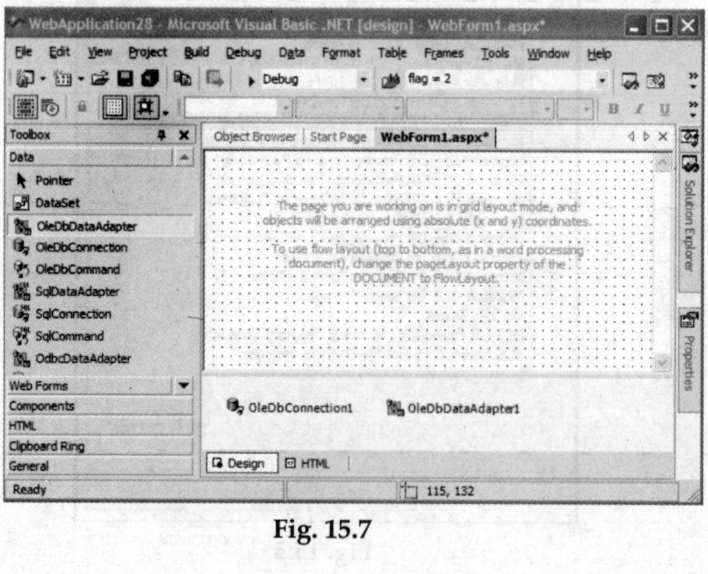

Fig. 15.7

7. Data Adapter Configuration Wizard Starts.

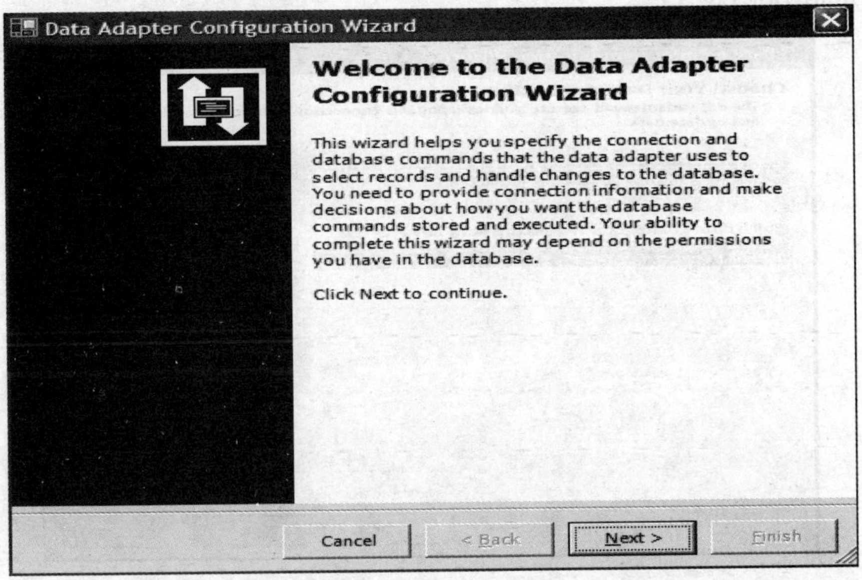

8. In this window of the Data Adapter Configuration Wizard, choose your data connection that you have previously created using OleDbConnection1 from the drop-down list or create a new connection by clicking New Connection button in this window shown in following Fig. 15.8.

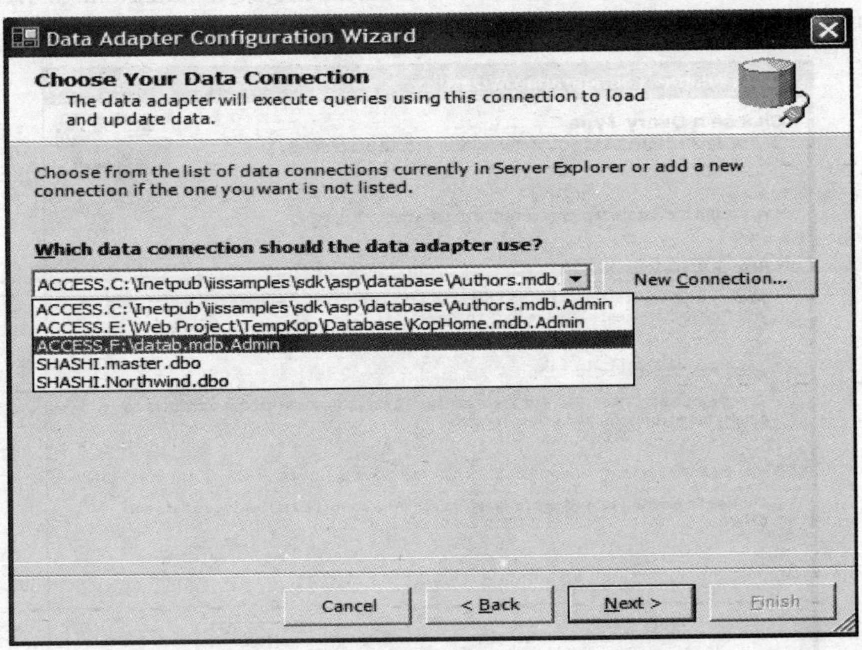

Fig. 15.8

9. After choosing the data connection from the list, the selected data connection comes in the field as shown in following Fig. 15.9.

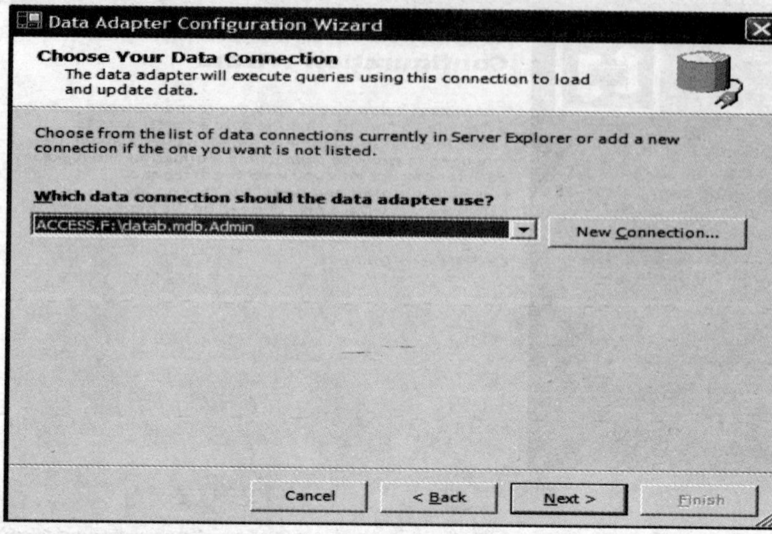

Fig. 15.9

10. Click Next button, to view the next window as shown in following Fig. 15.10, to select the SQL query or Stored Procedure. In this window, you select the SQL statement to write query for accessing data from the table in the database.

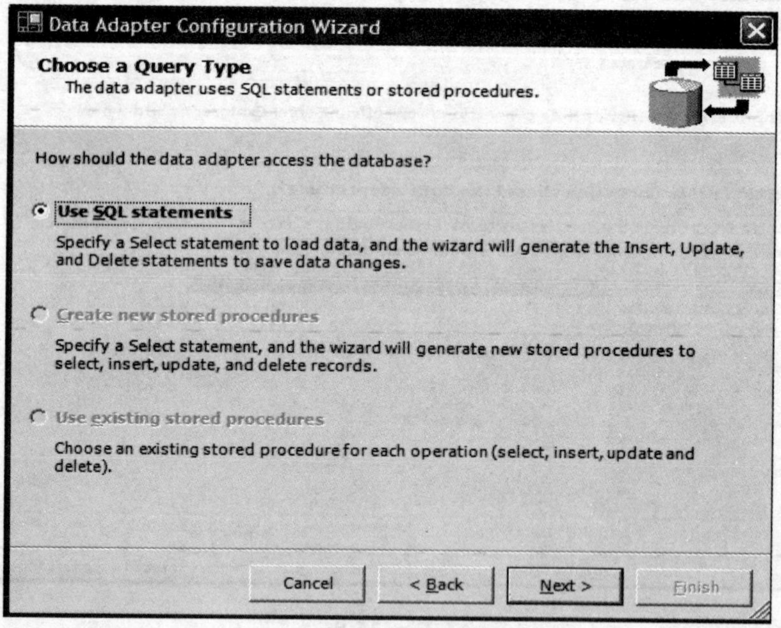

Fig. 15.10

11. After clicking the Next button, you will view the next window as shown in following Fig. 15.11, in which you write the query statements *e.g.* to create, insert, or update the table.

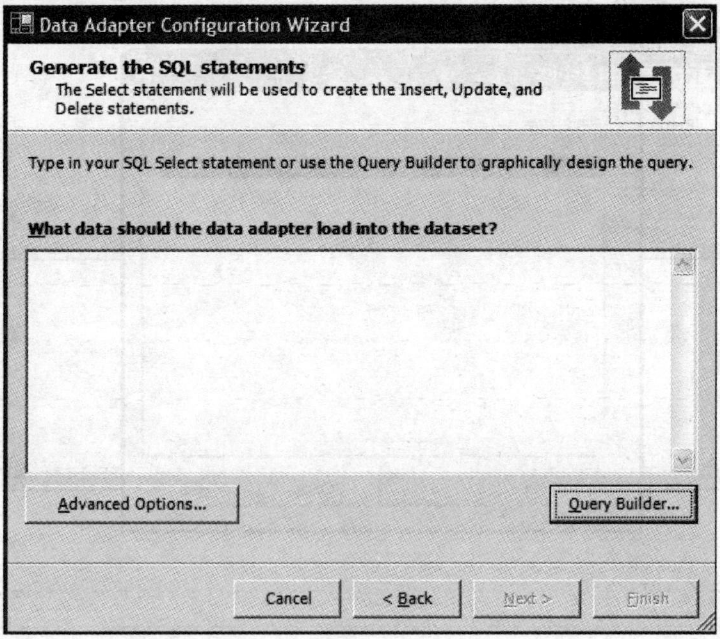

Fig. 15.11

12. Now click the Query Builder... button to generate query for the viewed table as shown in following Fig. 15.12.

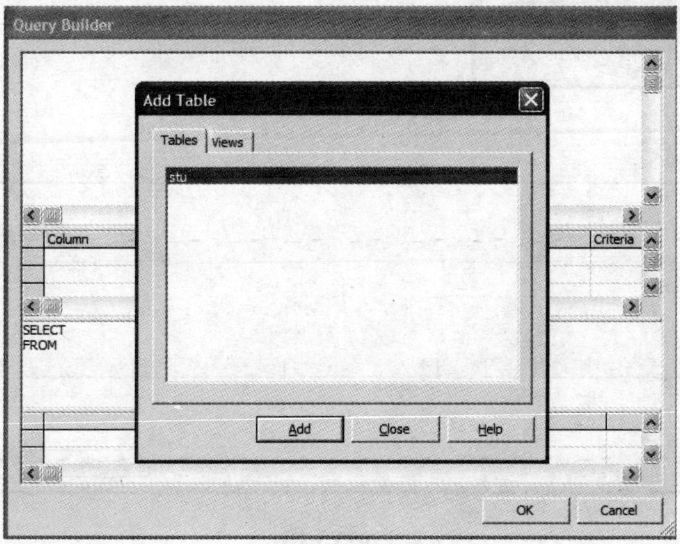

Fig. 15.12

13. Click Add button to add the table in the Query Builder.

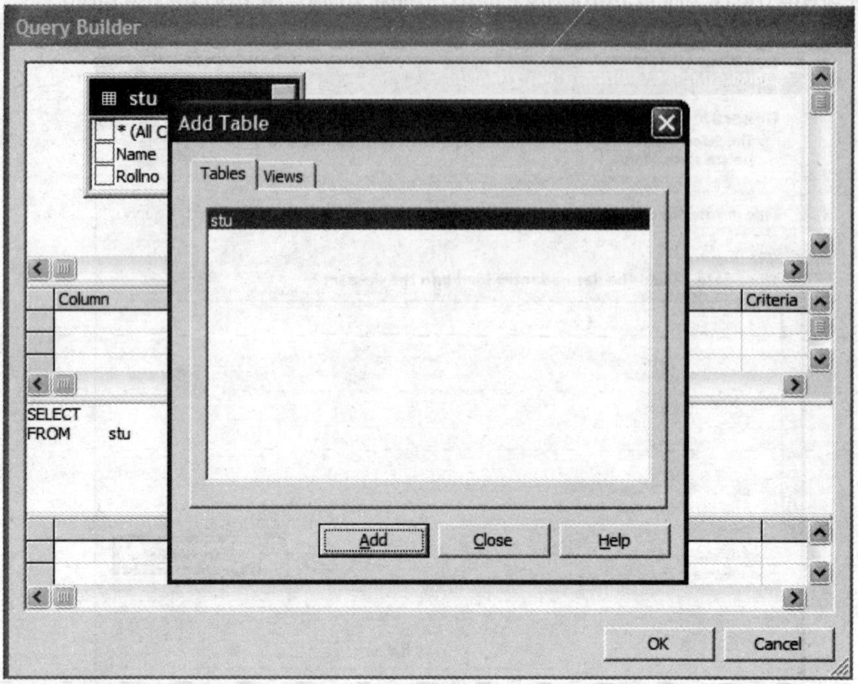

14. Write the query statement for the Added table as shown in following Fig. 15.13.

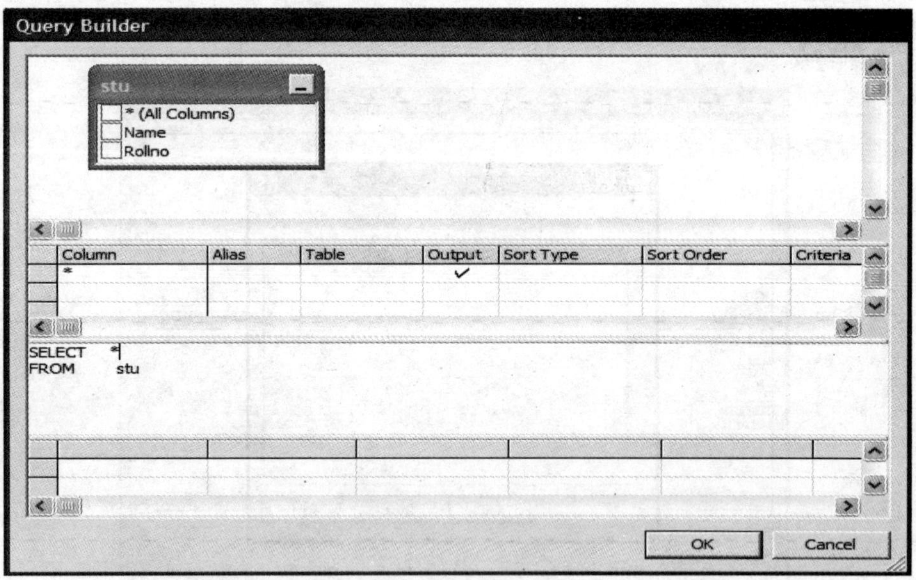

Fig. 15.13

15. Click OK button, the generated SQL statement is shown in following window.

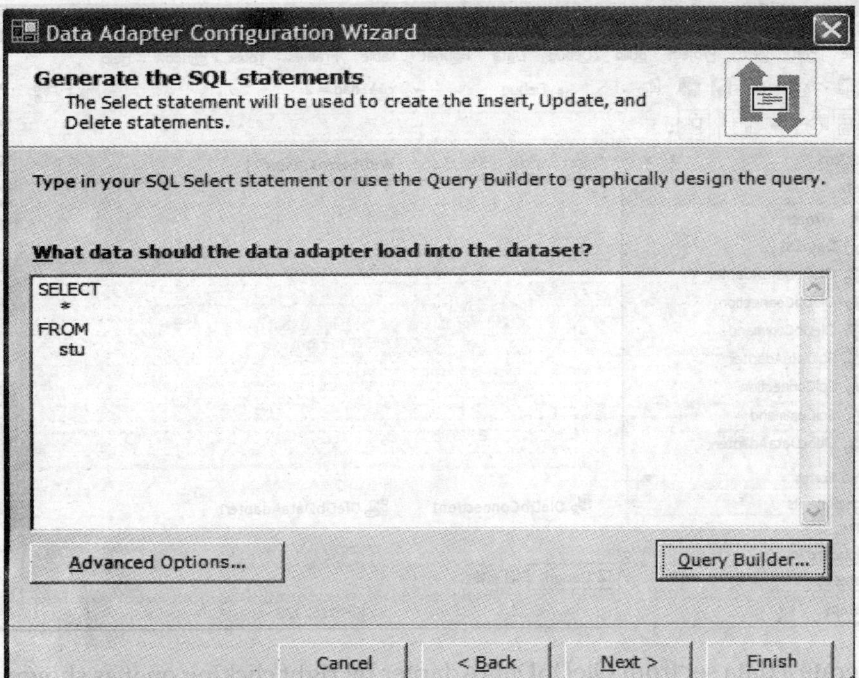

16. Now the data adapter "OleDbDataAdapter1" is configured successfully.

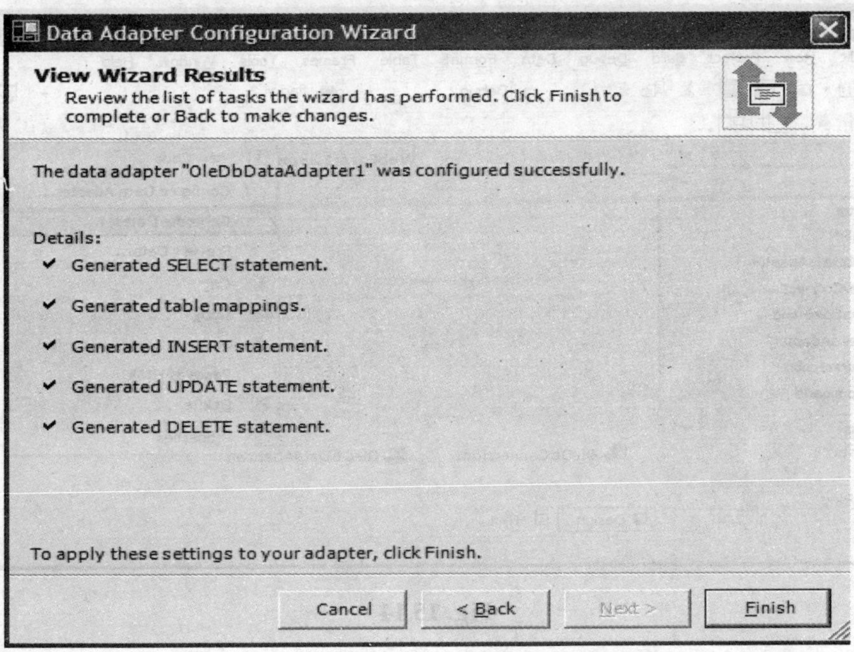

17. Click on the Finish button to end the wizard.

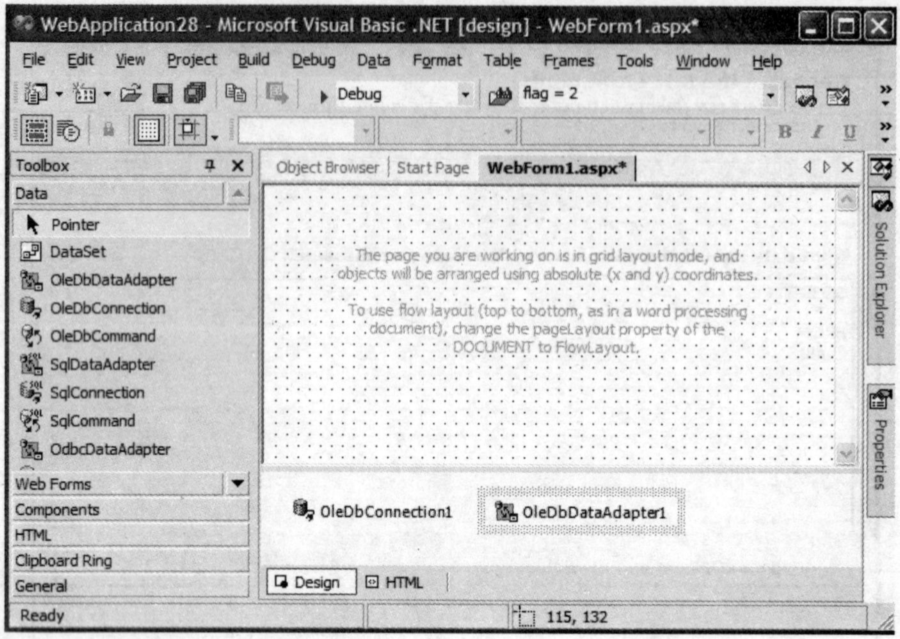

18. Now generate a data set from OleDbDataAdapter by right clicking on it as shown in following Fig. 15.14. A short-cut menu appears from which you select a '*Generate Dataset...*' item to create a dataset as a data source.

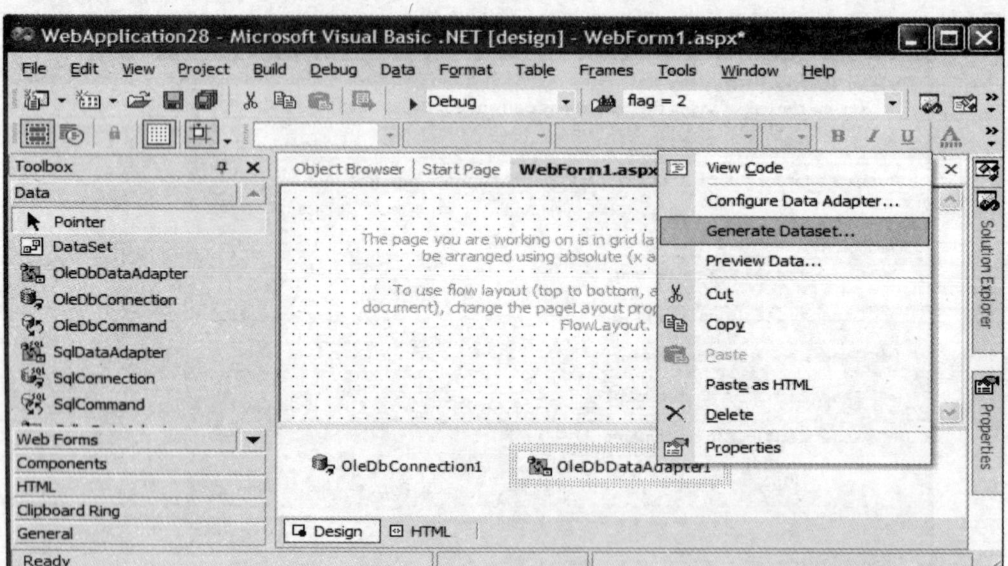

Fig. 15.14

19. After selecting a *'Generate Dataset...'* item following windows appears.

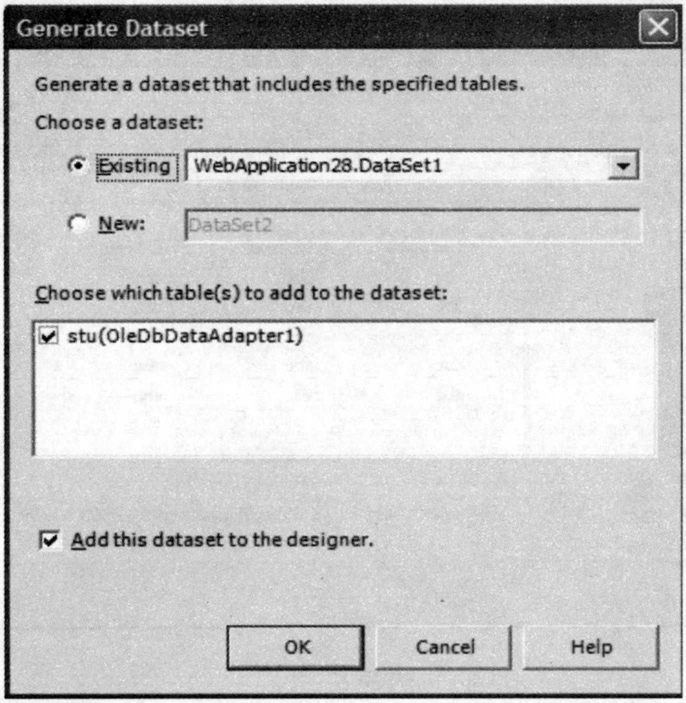

20. Now the dataset "DataSet11" appears as shown in following Fig. 15.15.

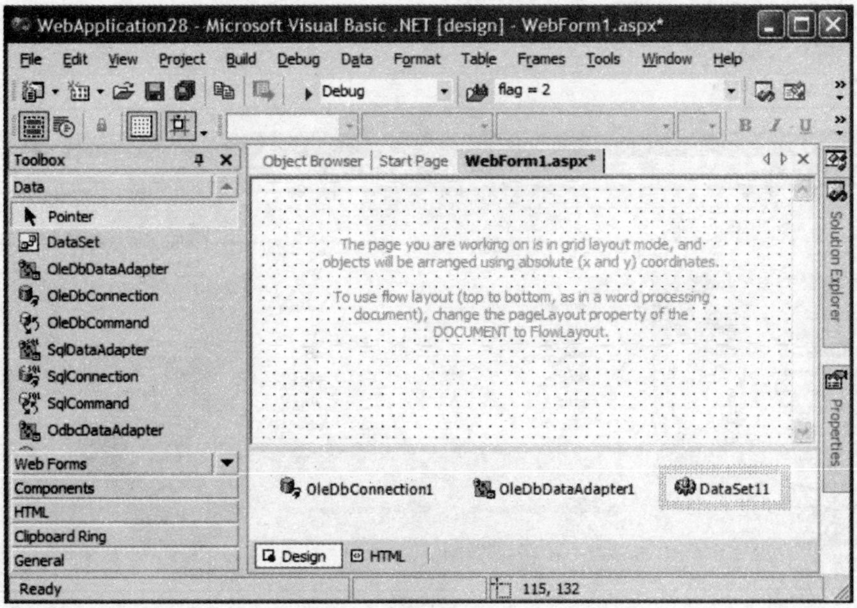

Fig. 15.15

21. Now place a data grid in the page to display records from the table as well as a push button as shown in following Fig. 15.16.

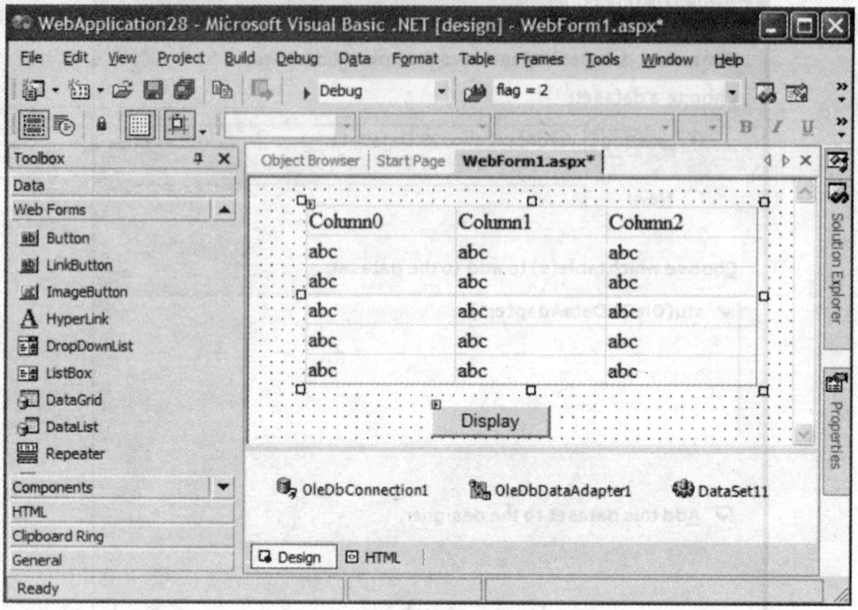

Fig. 15.16

22. Now set DataSource property of the datagrid as the "DataSet11" and DataMember property to the table "stu" as shown in following Fig. 15.17. And write a code behind the button as follows:

```
OleDbDataAdapter1.Fill(DataSet11)
DataGrid1.DataBind( )
```

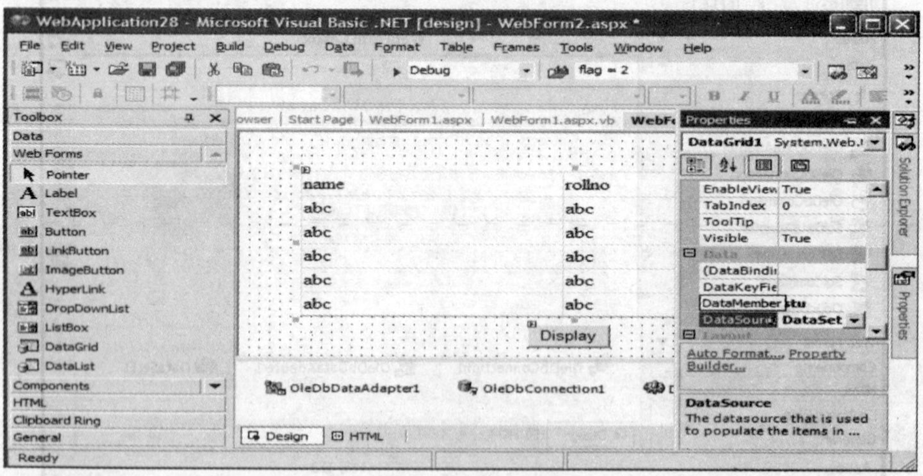

Fig. 15.17

23. Finally after running the above web form the output is shown in browser as shown in following Fig. 15.18 after clicking the button on the form.

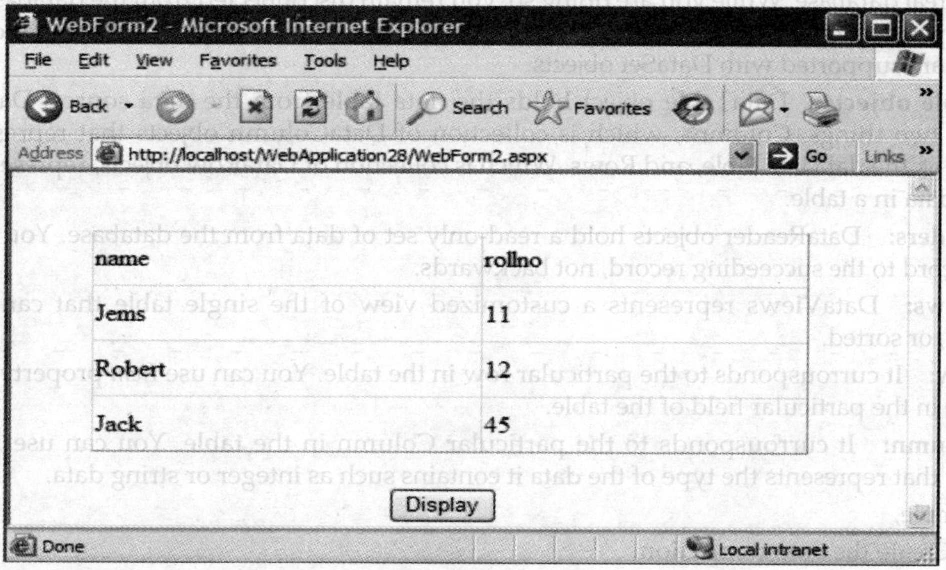

Fig. 15.18

Working with ADO.NET

ADO.NET uses disconnected architecture. It works with a copy of data from the actual database. This copy of data is stored in the dataset, which represent a sort of the data cache of records. It is usually much reduced version data in the database. However, you can work with it in mush same way as with the real database. While you are doing so, you remain disconnected from the database, which lets it to perform other tasks. The structure of the dataset is similar to that of relational database. When you need to update the data in the database, using the data adapters you can update it. The dataset used here container; it is filled by using SQL commands or stored procedures executed from a data adapter. If you want to the latest changes made by the other users, you can refresh dataset by calling the Fill method.

Data Connection Objects: To start working with a database, you must have a data connection. A data adapter needs a connection to a data source to read and write data. It uses OleDbConnection, OdbcConnection, OracleConnection, or SqlConnection objects to communicate with a data source.

Data Adapter: You use Data Adapter to communicate between a data source and a database. The data adapter is what you actually apply SQL statement to a database and cause the dataset to fill with the data. It uses OleDbDataAdapter, OdbcDataAdapter, OracleDataAdapter, and AqlDataAdapter objects to communicate between a data source and a database.

Command Objects: Data adapters can read, write, update and delete records in a data source. To allow you to specify how each of these operation works, data adapter contains command objects for each of them. Data adapters has four properties that give you access to these command objects: SelectCommand, InsertCommand, UpdateCommand, DeleteCommand.

Datesets: Data sets contain a copy of data in the actual database. The data in the dataset is usually much reduced version data in thė database. However, you can work with it in mush same way as with the real database. While you are doing so, you remain disconnected from the database, which lets it to perform other tasks. The structure of the dataset is similar to that of relational database. Datasets are supported with DataSet objects.

DataTable objects: DataTable object holds the data table from the data source. Data tables contains two things: Columns, which is collection of DataColumn objects that represents the columns of the data in a table, and Rows. Which is collection of DataRow objects, representing the rows of data in a table.

DataReaders: DataReader objects hold a read-only set of data from the database. You can only move record to the succeeding record, not backwards.

DataViews: DataViews represents a customized view of the single table that can filtered, searched, or sorted.

DataRow: It currousponds to the particular row in the table. You can use *Item* property to get or set value in the particular field of the table.

DataColumn: It currousponds to the particular Column in the table. You can use *DataType* property that represents the type of the data it contains such as integer or string data.

For Example,

1. Create the data connection.

   To connect with the datasource Data.mdb, use OleDbConnection object as follows:

```
Public con As String =
"Provider=Microsoft.Jet.OLEDB.4.0;DataSource=..\Database\Data.mdb;Persist
Security Info=False;"
Public oledbcon As New OleDbConnection(con)
```

2. Create a data adapter.

   To make communication between datasource and the dataset, declare OleDbDataAdapter object as follows:

```
Public da As OleDbDataAdapter
Public ds As DataSet
Public dt As DataTable
Public dv As DataView
```

3. Create a data set.

   To read data from the table "Company" contained in the datasource "Data.mdb", you specify the command object contained in the data adapter. The command object actually applies SQL statement to a database.

```
strsql = "SELECT DISTINCT Company FROM Company"
Dim cmd As New OleDbCommand(strsql, oledbcon)
```

```
da = New OleDbDataAdapter(cmd)
ds = New DataSet
```

4. Fill the data set.
   And to fill/read the data, declare and use dataset object as follows:

```
da.Fill(ds, "Company")
```

5. To fill the values from number of records of the particular field (*e.g.* Company field) in the table (*e.g.* Company table), in a particular input field (*e.g.* Combobox), you use datareader object, as follows:

```
oledbcon.Open()
Dim objreader As OleDbDataReader = cmd.ExecuteReader()
Do While objreader.Read()
ComboBox1.Items.Add(objreader("Company"))
Loop
oledbcon.Close()
```

QUESTIONS

1. What is DataAdapter?
2. What is dataset?
3. What is Datareader?
4. What is the use of the fill() method?
5. What is DataView?
6. What is DataTable?
7. How to create data connection?

□□□